HRF Keating:
A Life of Crime

HRF KEATING: A LIFE OF CRIME

by Sheila Mitchell

LEVEL
BEST BOOKS

For Harry's and my four children; Simon, Bryony, Piers and Hugo;
And nine grandchildren; Zoe, Charlie, Hannah, Phoebe, Rosie, Ed,
Lydia, Jay and Jo and one great-grandson, Douglas Fitz

Contents

Introduction by Len Deighton

Harry Keating was, in many ways, the most distinguished writer of his time. Like most other writers, I believe that writing fiction is to invent a convincing world that exists only on the pages of the book. Stories and novels that depend heavily upon reportage and journalism, even memoirs, produce only second-rate fiction. Harry, more than any of his contemporaries, and most of his predecessors, created a world, an intriguing and believable world; and made it his own unique one.

In the jealous, myopic world of publishers and writers, Harry Keating stood apart. He was a gentle man, unfailingly supportive of his fellow writers. He searched for, and found, only the good in the world about him. Or perhaps he chose to overlook the bad. Harry knew what he liked, and endured what he didn't like. When I heard of a fine new restaurant in Queensway that served the most delicious Indian dishes to be found anywhere in London, my wife and I knew it was the place to take Harry and Sheila Keating. All four of us went there. My knowledge of Indian cooking being patchy, I accepted the advice of our enthusiastic Indian waiter. I remember that array of dishes: delicate vegetable preparations and skewered lamb kebabs and kormas, crisp papadums and steamy chapati, together with the sealed-lid biryani, fragrant dahl and fresh mustard pickles. We talked about everything from the chaos of Bombay street life to the wonders of word processors. It was long afterwards that Harry confided to me that he did not like Indian food. It was just another example of Harry's good manners and wonderful equanimity that he had given no hint of this, and had calmly and politely worked his way through creamy kormas, fierce vindaloos and garlicky aubergine puree as Inspector Ghote would have done. (I was later to discover that Harry did not share my enthusiasm for modern technology, and was never dazzled by the glitter of the Internet.)

I should have remembered that Inspector Ghote had shown little interest in food of any kind over the years. One would have to go back to the remarkable kidnapping case recorded in *Inspector Ghote Trusts the Heart* to find a reference to food. The almond-favoured gulab jamun floating in scented sirup is a tempting delicacy but the devoted Inspector Ghote leaves this sweetmeat for the wealthy Mr Desai rather than be deflected from his duty.

In this fine and most accomplished biographical study,—a labour of love without doubt—his wife Sheila has given full measure to Harry's writing. That is illuminating, and it is as Harry would have wanted. And Sheila's biography gives proper emphasis to the enjoyable and successful books that Harry published both before and after Ghote. He was a devoted and happy family man and, as you will see, Harry had a talent and determination that withstood the ups and downs that all dedicated writers suffer.

Harry wrote more than fifty books and only twenty-five of these were his Ghote stories. We all have our favourites, but for most of his fans he will always be remembered as the creator of the immortal Inspector Ghote, the Bombay detective. This decision to write about a fictional professional man, a government employee, doing his complicated job on a continent that Harry had never visited, was an astounding decision. How many other writers have risked such an endeavor? I can't think of any. But we were not surprised that Harry succeeded. His many friends and admirers shared his pleasure when his highly original creation brought cheers from the literary critics, awards and a very large devoted readership. *More Ghote! More Ghote!* came the cries, and Harry obliged with books that, despite having the same rather eccentric but scrupulously honest hero were delightfully varied in both texture and style. And the plots were magnificent, with twists and turns that kept us guessing right up to the final page. But Harry did not write 'detective stories.' Despite his modesty, Harry wrote insightful stories which delved into the minds and motives of his characters. And while his fame mostly rests upon the Ghote mysteries, Harry demonstrated his writing talent in many other quite different works.

But why India? Harry explained that when his American publishers complained that his stories were too British he decided to set his next book outside England. This also explains why Harry was not tempted to write about British India and the people of the Raj, as so many other British writers had done. 'Very well,' said Harry. 'A murder mystery. To be set in India. Within the background well hidden, hidden even from the conscious minds of most readers, the theme of perfection and imperfection.' The diffident Inspector Ghote also provided Harry with the subtle thread of comedy that is so cleverly woven into all his stories.

Harry's talent was recognized by his fans and by his peers. The Crime Writers' Association, in a most unusual gesture, have, over the years awarded him more than one of their coveted Gold Daggers and the Diamond Dagger too! Recognition came to him from the USA where the Mystery Writers of America gave him a special award of the Edgar Allan Poe Prize. As well as novels and short stories, Harry produced meticulous non-fiction works. A particular favourite of mine is *Sherlock Holmes: The Man and His World*. I have read it at least half a dozen times and each time I marvel at Harry's dissection of Conan Doyle's writings. Equally I admire the way that Harry leads us through Britain's colourful social history; the Victorian seventies and eighties, and that revolutionary belle époque that so influenced Doyle and his anarchic alter ego.

Harry's talents include his skill as an editor, perceptive critic and expert reviewer. *Whodunit? A Guide to Crime, Suspense and Spy Fiction* is an unsurpassed work of research, writing and compilation to which I frequently resort and then settle down to read afresh.

Harry was a scholar in every sense of that word. He was a linguist with all the extra sensitivity that comes from the mastery of foreign languages, and the literary foundation that such study provides. To have a second language is to acquire a second soul, it is said. Harry's inspired choice of Dublin University—and thus residence in the most literary town in the world—not only set him mercifully apart from the pernicious Oxbridge literary mafia but gave him an eye view of England from a foreign shore. But that would have counted for nothing had he not had that magical and elusive ability to hold his readers, and keep the pages turning. It is this rare and very enviable gift that defines him. Lurking within his seemingly straightforward narrative are the consummate skills and intellectual abandon that surprises and delights us all. We miss him of course but his books remain and provide us with the opportunity to visit this remarkable man and his remarkable creative imagination.

Len Deighton

Chapter 1

L uck, as H.R.F. Keating many times remarked, is a fundamental element of success and what greater stroke of luck could there be for his biographer than to find, after his death, a printed biographical article by the man himself. It could almost be called an article of instruction so clear are the guidelines. When he was sixty-two and already an author of some thirty books, an American multi-volume publication 'Contemporary Authors' ran a series in which they asked authors to indicate how they would approach writing their autobiography. His contribution appeared in 1989 in Volume 8 and in a typically forthright yet modest manner he began his article, *'In a way I have been ready and waiting these many years to give the world my autobiography.'* He goes on to say that his preferred title would have been 'Ancestors and Influences', while at the same time acknowledging that he did not believe anyone would ever ask him to undertake such a venture, he then says that he secretly hoped his life might ultimately count for something. He also states, *'my putative title also says that I am, indelibly, a viewer from a distance'.*

Of course, he expands on this view of himself during the article, but in the preface he adds a further generality, *'My life in terms of the events that have occurred has been no different from thousands, from millions, of others. It is worth no particular record. But the books that it has come to me to write are, perhaps perhaps, worth considering.'.* The repeated word *'perhaps'* demonstrates his almost trademark modesty, while his secret ambition ultimately *'to count',* reveals a trait that could be said to verge on hubris. Did he have each quality in equal measure? Maybe by considering the books themselves, as

1

he suggests, it will be possible to find out. But was he, as he claimed, actually influenced by his ancestry?

That there was an awareness of it is indisputable because the children and I remember him speculating, from time to time, how much he had inherited of the tenacity of spider-watching Robert the Bruce. The Bruce descendants were pillars of the Church of Scotland, one of whom eventually sired a daughter, Harry's grandmother, whose marriage made the link with the Scottish Keatings. Then there were the Irish Keatings who could trace their ancestry back to the Dukes of Tuscany and the days of King Alfred the Great and about whom there is written evidence in a bound tract entitled:

A Memorial
On the origin of the
Family of Keating, etc
of the
Kingdom of Ireland

This is a splendid historical record put together by the Garter King of Arms (Dublin) in 1760 and might well account for the patrician side to Harry's personality, occasionally to be glimpsed just beneath the surface, as well as an equally buried romantic streak. After all, who could not fail to be affected by the knowledge of the blood running in his veins chronicled in this paragraph in that eighteenth century document, *'JOHN the fourth son of MAURICE the eldest son of GERALD FITZ WALTER FITZ OTHO from whom the family of CUTH-TINE KETYNGE or KEATING in Ireland derives its origin passed into the Kingdom along with his brother REYMOND le GROSSE under the command of their father.'* The original spelling of the name, *CUTH-TINE* (the 'c' being pronounced 'k', which letter did not exist in the Irish language of that time) apparently meant 'Shower of Fire', deriving from, *'the great flashes of fire which emitted from the clashing of Arms against those of the enemy.,'* which graphic phrase was surely enough to have set his pulse racing with the romance of the days of chivalry.

But these influences were buried deep and were seldom mentioned even among the close family. They might or might not have become apparent had he written that autobiography, but who is now to say how consciously they played a part in forming his character? What is beyond doubt is that had he written the autobiography he would have analysed the books he wrote and almost certainly found, buried within them, aspects of his own character. From the very start of his life, at his christening, it would seem he was destined to write. Those initials hide the formidable array of names, Henry Reymond Fitzwalter, but his father, when asked why he had misspelt Reymond, did not reply because of his ancestors, choosing instead to say, 'Because it will look good on the spines of his books.' What, of course, ultimately appeared on those spines were initials rather than any of those ancestral names and this might have been a disappointment to Mr. Keating senior but sadly he did not live long enough to know that his son had fulfilled his prediction.

Names were a problem that dogged him throughout his boyhood and, indeed, it was still with him in his teens. At the insistence of his mother's sister, a dominant lady, he was always known as Pip. This arose from her exclamation on first seeing the quite small infant lying in the cradle, '*What a little pip-squeak*.' Pip he remained until around fifteen or so when he was helping a local farmer with the war-time harvest and his fellow workers—Italian prisoners-of-war—asked him his name. Seeking release from the hated pet name, and absolutely not seeing himself as a Henry, he hit on the more familiar form of Harry. He then went on to create further trouble for himself when he chose to publish as H.R.F. Keating because no-one except family and friends knew what to call him. The initials did, however, not only look good on the spines of the books but also appear to have been quite memorable, even if sometimes in correspondence, he was mistakenly elevated to HRH.

From that earliest of anecdotes told in the autobiographical article there are glimpses of Harry's formative years to fill in the gaps that personal memory of survivors cannot provide. From the time he becomes a published author the books will, to some extent, as he suggests, take over the narrative. However that illuminating article, less than 10,000 words long, only covers just over half his writing life being published in 1989 with his copy having been delivered in 1987, but there is, fortunately, a wealth of critical material on the books themselves, as well as many articles about the man himself, to take the story beyond that time. Between 1959, when he was thirty-two and 2009 when he was eighty-two, two years before he died, there were sixty-one books published with his name on the title page. Fifty-four of these were fiction, the rest were 'non-fiction'. That is to say books examining the skills and lives of other writers or exploring crime fiction as a genre, a subject about which he held strong opinions, and about which he was very knowledgeable, having not only been the crime critic for The Times newspaper for fifteen years but also having read extensively from the earliest days of the genre. Added to these there are more than a hundred published short stories and countless articles on a variety of subjects, some of which explore his own life.

There is a very small archive of unpublished work some dating back to his late teens, although sadly little juvenilia have survived. One of the exceptions is a story, just twenty lines long, 'Jim's Adventure', hammered out on his father's exceptionally old typewriter when he was eight years old. The following short extract shows a desire, sometimes misplaced, to punctuate—something that later, it could be said, he found not quite so important. It is also a reminder, in those pre-computer days, of the difficulties facing the writer should there be a need to make corrections like the positioning of commas, the running together of words, to say nothing of the spelling.

'The captain looked at them all; and as he turned to ask the mate something ,a weak looking youngster who was crying , told the captain that he was his nephew ,& wanted toget aboard ,the captain immeaditly gave him the poslace.'

From later diaries, which he kept over four years, we know that as a child and particularly as a late teenager there was always at least one writing project on the go, these included a play—written sometimes in verse and sometimes in prose—set in the court of William the Conqueror. It seems to have occupied him, quite seriously, on and off, for some years during his late teens but, sadly, has vanished without trace. The diaries also tell us the title of a novel. *Pride Comes....* And a subsequent entry talks of 40,000 words having been written, but, again, it has vanished. Although there are later records of the writing of these and many short stories, there is silence about submitting anything for publication—apart from unsuccessfully entering an occasional newspaper competition.

His father, almost certainly continuing to offer encouragement, must have felt that he had been overly optimistic at the christening. Certainly, and this is something all those who knew him as a boy would confirm, he was, by nature, solitary. This undoubtedly resulted in his living more in his imagination than in reality. What is also certain is that, in those formative years, he can never have been the easiest person to live with. He was, for one thing, quick to lose his temper and, equally, did not suffer fools gladly. Some of the blame for this must be attributed to his education. This was partly conditioned by the fact that his father, after a year up at Cambridge, had then joined the army and spent some years in the First World War trenches. On being demobbed he did not return to Cambridge because a grateful University was apparently able to give him his degree without any further study. Instead he joined the burgeoning firm of ICI out in Japan. When commerce ceased to satisfy him, he returned to this country to take up a new career as a school master and he and his wife settled in St Leonards-on-Sea, where in due course Harry was born. By the time he was old enough to start school his father's career had expanded into owning his own preparatory school. It was apparently felt that it was not desirable for a boy to attend the school of which the father was the headmaster and at the tender age of six Harry was sent away to a boarding prep school.

Sport, even for one so young, played a large part in any boy's life in those days, especially at a boarding school where free time was organised by the school rather than under the gentler care of a mother at home. Unfortunately, this was something at which Harry did not shine, especially anything involving chasing after and catching a ball. Apart from a basic lack of co-ordination, he had inherited his mother's asthma which rendered him breathless very quickly and made running a labour—something that, even after growing out of the asthma, stayed with him all his life. An anecdote from those days paints a vivid picture of early morning football practice.

Shoes had to be exchanged for football boots in the changing room, which of course demanded an ability to tie up laces. Harry remembered struggling with this task long after all the other boys were out on the playing field, noisily kicking the ball about. He recalled that he only achieved the desired result when the practice was over, and his fellow pupils were streaming back to the changing room. It is difficult to believe that a six-year-old would have worked out that he could save himself the anguish of breathlessly chasing a ball by such a subterfuge, but it is always possible.

His inclination to solitariness was not helped by remaining an only child until he was nine. And even after his brother Jeremy (as he was then called) arrived, the gap in age between them was not conducive to many shared interests. There could have been a solution if things had worked out differently. The same Aunt Wendy who had so blighted Harry's life by calling him Pip, herself had a son, Rob Fitzherbert, of almost exactly the same age and the cousins developed a great liking for each other. Rob's father worked abroad in India for much of Rob's young life, but the custom was for children from families domiciled abroad to return for their education to Britain. Rob actually attended Harry's father's prep school for a short while and after moving on suggested to his parents that he should continue to spend the holidays at the Keating's home, but his mother had grown apart from her sister and had some idea that this would have had a bad influence on her son. Wendy and her sister were as different from each other as it was possible to imagine, with Mugie (Harry's mother), being the kindest and most giving person imaginable, hard to see her being a bad influence. But it was not to be. Rob had to be content with brief visits, thus denying the boys the opportunity of a closer relationship. However, when they were together, they would go on long cycle rides, a pastime he always enjoyed. Then there was swimming—there was a pool attached to the school—which was something else he was always prepared to do, perfecting a steady and efficient crawl. On the other hand, Rob recalls that he would always choose to read a book rather than kick a football around. The childhood bond remained and grew into a lifelong friendship even if contact was often possible only through letters as Rob made his life abroad and finally settled in Kenya.

The Second World War was declared shortly before Harry's thirteenth birthday the year he was due to leave his prep school. State schools both elementary and secondary were, of course, available at that time but it had not yet become the custom for the middle and upper classes to think them suitable for their children so he was sent, as a day boy, to an acceptable, nearby Public School, Merchant Taylors. Some four years later, aged sixteen and having acquired his School Certificate, the decision was taken to truncate his formal education.

On the face of it a strange thing to do considering that his father was a school master, especially one having hopes of a literary career for his son. But there were perhaps extenuating circumstances. A school master's earnings were not great and by now he had given up running his own school and was employed by someone else as a geography teacher. Fees at public schools, although not comparable with present day levels, were not inconsiderable and Sandy—Harry's father—was about to start paying for younger brother Jeremy's education as well. And to be absolutely fair, Harry was not proving brilliant, and although well above average, once winning the essay prize, he would not have been described as particularly academic. Sandy, so-called because of his hair colouring and not as a derivative of his actual name which was John, had a tendency to flights of fancy and in this instance he had convinced himself that something he termed 'The University of Life', would be an excellent alternative to two years in the sixth form. A career in the Army would, he thought, fit the bill. It was indeed fortunate that Harry failed the medical because of his asthma—anyone less suited to soldiering it would be hard to imagine.

But the BBC—Radio only at that time—came to the rescue with a training scheme. This time fitness did not come into it. Mugging up such things as Ohms Law, Harry sat the entrance tests successfully and became a youth-in-training leading to work as a sound engineer. He joined the World Service which at that time occupied buildings at 200 Oxford Street in the West End of London. It was 1942 and the country had been at war for three years. It was a time of great uncertainty with the outcome far from certain. Air-raids were a constant hazard and you carried a gas mask wherever you went.

Harry seems to have moved from country to urban living, from the protection of family life to living in digs, with comparative ease. His landlady was kind and he seems to have made friends in her house and at work as well. Later diaries mention, over a period of years, quite frequent letters exchanged with three or four girls who were his colleagues at the BBC. Undoubtedly for much of the time he continued to live in the world of the imagination, reading voraciously and continuing to write, particularly when he was at home and had access to his father's typewriter. What is more he definitely enjoyed working for the BBC and, contrary to what might have been expected, became rather good at the job.

The war eventually came to its end and, ironically, he was called up on VJ Day, the day the fighting stopped. The medical was no obstacle this time presumably because it was no longer a question of a career option but one of fulfilling your obligation to do National Service. It must have seemed natural to those who decided these things to assign him to REME, after all the BBC could more or less be said to have given him the basis of Electrical and Mechanical Engineering. In point of fact it was a total mismatch and Harry would be the first person to acknowledge that throughout his life practical things like DIY were a burden. Hammers and nails were not natural partners in his hands.

At this point he decided to write a diary and the first volume is headed 'Diary of my Nineteenth Year' and states on the cover **No. 140642-31 PTE KEATING H.R.F.** The **PTE** is later scored through and in a different ink replaced by **L/CPL**. There are twenty-five, closely-written, small black notebooks, spanning the years 1945 to 1950, they cover two and a half years in the army and the first two years at University.

That they survive at all is largely due to his brother—by now having decided to replace Jeremy by his second name—Noël, who, towards the end of the last century, while clearing out the family home after Mugie, their mother, had died, had to sort through the family papers before going to live abroad. He handed over a rather ill-made small wooden box—thought to be Harry's own construction—with the diaries inside. Harry must at least have glanced at them because when they were later found, after he had died, they were in a stout cardboard box, so it must be assumed that the only reason for their survival must have been his own forgetfulness. They were buried deep amongst a multitude of manuscripts that filled a cupboard in his study, from floor to ceiling. As they had never been mentioned to the family, it is a fair assumption that they were never intended to be seen by eyes other than his own, and that the most personal of the thoughts recorded were written as a catharsis, arising as they did from what had always been fundamental to his way of life, his religion. His mother, though not his father, was Roman Catholic and at that time he was still accepting sincerely and, above all, unquestioningly, the teachings of the Church. These entries reveal the guilt he felt at his inability to conform to all the Church's more rigid principles and read like a private confessional. It must surely be fair to assume that he would not have wanted to share some of these entries with others and that he only initially preserved the diaries on the off-chance that he might want to refer to them in his own life-time. Given his near obsession with throwing away anything that seemed to have lost its usefulness, it has to be assumed that, in the long term, he had forgotten their existence.

Apart from the 'Dear Diary' element there are entries about the day-to-day life of an ordinary soldier in a peace-time army, but they are frustratingly short on detail. What comes over quite clearly is that it is a chronicle of a fish very much out-of-water. The actual words 'I hate the army' only appear occasionally but the references to things connected to the parade ground, the kitchen duties (he wasn't at all good at removing the 'eyes' when peeling potatoes), the 'blancoing' (applying of a white paste to objects made of webbing) and polishing of pieces of the uniform and, above all, many references to his fear of failing in the tasks expected of him, paint a picture of a young man who is not at peace with himself.

A lot of the time, from just before his 19th birthday until six months after he was 21, he does seem to have been anxious and miserable. But perhaps, as well as causing him grief, his Catholicism did also help him because often when having struggled and finally completed some technical job or successfully passed a qualifying exam, he would note this and add at the end

'Thanks be to God' or 'By the Grace of God'.

He must have done some things right because he did reach the dizzy height of lance corporal, but it was only 'acting' and 'unpaid'. He tells us that there was thought of his being included on the OCT (officer's training course), but this in fact never materialised. Furthermore, he was under absolutely no illusion about his own abilities and he recognised that he was not officer material. Undoubtedly life would have been more comfortable with a commission, but it does not seem to have worried him unduly and he found friends among those he worked with. When assigned to clerical duties his intelligence and 'way with words' was not only much appreciated by those he worked for, but he himself felt he could make a contribution and so was able to enjoy the work.

But the diaries are by no means all doom and gloom and are a wonderful record of his self-education. A lot of pages are devoted to what seem to have been very generous leisure hours and these he spent going to concerts and cinemas, the theatre and opera, art galleries, and above all reading. All these activities were subjected to rigorous and reasoned criticism, a talent that stayed with him and of which he was able to take advantage later on as a well respected book critic. Part of his ability to assess what he heard and saw went back to his younger days when the family, in the days before TV, did a lot of serious listening to the radio. Apart from classical music—the Home Service—covering the ground of what has now become Radio 3 and Radio 4—broadcast a lot of talks on what could be called intellectual matters and a lot of time was devoted to Drama and dramatised documentaries. No question of the BBC planners scheduling material to suit the lowest common denominator and not a great deal of attention given to how many listeners tuned in to any one given programme as happens nowadays. The founder of the BBC, Lord Reith, famously declared, 'That the public should be given something that they do not know they want', and this uncompromising principle dominated the choice of programme. For the most part the Keatings were happy to be entertained both by adaptations of the classics or more controversial new material and having listened there would be discussion.

The habit of analysis remained with Harry so that when he was listening on his own, he quite naturally used his diary for a written appraisal and he was a hard task master, no-one got away with a performance that was sub-standard. For instance, after listening to what he felt was an indifferent installment of Galsworthy's 'Man of Property', he commented, *'which demonstrated the use of music at its worst.'* Sometimes the entry was more a dialogue with himself, *'...reading Yeats, which I like, though many of them are difficult to understand, partly due, I think, to grammar.'* Followed by a question, *'Does this account for the 'Lake Isle of Innisfree'?'* In this case he went on to resolve his worries by extensive reading of this poet who certainly became one of the literary influences in his life.

The Public Library was his main source of reading material and conditioned to some extent what he would read next. At one point the diary records his frustration when the next volume of Proust was not available when he returned the one he had finished and on another occasion he had to take back a volume unfinished because he had been posted elsewhere and the worry was that the next Public Library might not have it in stock and he would not be able to carry on where he had left off. One way and another it took him almost the whole of his two-and-a-half years in the army to complete the 12 Volumes. Later he managed to buy a set which remained on the bookshelves throughout his life and although certain passages were indelibly impressed in his memory and he did occasionally refer to the books he would only re-read the entire oeuvre once more. He was never without a book, even being allowed to read during a lull in work if he was on office duties. But whether it was politics, history, fiction or literary criticism, Harry, with his fortunate ability to retain what he read, was probably building up a far wider knowledge of books than any sixth form education would have provided.

He was helped in his choice of books to read when his father introduced him to an academic friend from his own earlier time at Cambridge. The friend offered to provide reading lists and general encouragement with a view to Harry doing a degree in History after his military service was over. But although this guidance was appreciated and certainly opened up whole new areas for study, there is no doubt that he would have done it anyway, for Harry reading was a fundamental necessity, both fact and fiction.

His choices were wide, ranging from James Joyce, although he always found 'Ulysses' tough going, through Bernard Shaw, DH Lawrence—in this case declaring about his 'Essay on Poe', *'very provocative and bitter attack, but some very interesting philosophy. Must read it again.'* The November diaries of that first year tell us that apart from those authors he also read with much appreciation GK Chesterton's letters quoting a Chesterton aphorism, *'Never seem wiser or more learned than the people you are with.';* Dostoyevsky, at this stage, was only represented by what Harry considered one of his lesser novels; there was Damon Runyon; Jules Verne's 'Adrift in the Pacific'; Chesterfield's letters. Later he was tackling more DH Lawrence and Conrad from whom Harry made this deduction, *'I eventually gained a not-at-all-modest notion of what a writer of fiction should aim for.'* With a direct quotation from Conrad himself, *'You must squeeze out of yourself every sensation, every thought, every image—mercilessly, without remorse.'* This youthful diary entry was to play a major part in the way Harry thought and felt when tackling each new type of book he subsequently wrote. EM Forster was another whose publication 'Aspects of the Novel', particularly struck him; Yeats was joined by TS Eliot, Shakespeare, and the essays of De Quincey.

For light relief he continued to read detective novels—a taste for which came from his mother. She was an avid reader of the genre, borrowing her books from the Boots circulating library and not Public Libraries which in those days were thought by the middle classes to be, that class-dividing thing, 'common', not to mention unhygienic, convinced that the books harboured germs. Later Harry would take that risk, but in the mean-time he was able genteelly to acquire an extensive knowledge of crime fiction.

Plainly the Arts offered him a relief from the misery of the life of an acting lance corporal (unpaid). With the one stripe in place he had to take charge of groups of soldiers from time to time. One entry records, *'Did a terrible thing: was taking Guard down to rehearsal this morning and nearly marched them right into the rest of the parade and had to start again.'* But most of the time things went according to plan and under his brief command they all survived.

12

Finally, after more than two years, on the first of April 1948 his demob papers came through. He records the lengthy process moving from one building to another to sign innumerable forms and then, finally, receiving his demob suit and mackintosh enabling him to shake off the dust of a life in army barracks and hopefully being able to resume a prematurely truncated education. He had managed to spend his final month on an educational course which made the last few weeks pass quite quickly, and his intention was to go to University in the autumn. First, he had to make sure he would have the money to live on while he was there. He had to fill in yet more endless forms and make many telephone calls to secure his ex-service government grant. Perseverance paid off and finally he knew that he would receive the standard £4 a week maintenance grant, which, in those days, meant that financially the way was clear.

What was an even greater hurdle to be cleared was the question of Latin. The requirement for University entrance was matriculation and you could not matriculate without Latin. Had he done it for School Certificate that would have sufficed, but he had not. It turned out that Cambridge would require him to study Latin for a year before taking the exam and, already twenty-one, he was not prepared to wait. Fortunately, there were family links to Trinity College, Dublin because an uncle and, more illustriously, a grandfather who had been a scholar, had gone there, and Harry's father had made enquiries and tried to pull strings. In the event, the college turned out to be much more relaxed than Cambridge. Yes, he would need to matriculate but he could go over to Dublin at the beginning of the academic year, sit the Latin exam on the 19th of October and if he passed would be accepted and be able to enroll for lectures on the 21st.

Something that is not explained in the diaries is the switch that was made from the initial idea of doing a history degree to what he was seeking to do at Trinity, Modern Languages. Apparently, a combination of any two was permissible and, what is more, being Ireland, English was acceptable as one of them. Harry's choices were English and French. His wide reading programme made sense of the first and, having acquired a basic knowledge of the second through school, augmented by visits to France with his father, he had the ability to speak with a convincing accent.

The diaries are quite expansive on the Latin front with frequent mentions of Virgil not to mention North and Hilliard's 'Latin Prose Composition for the Middle Forms of Schools'. To begin with he was living at home, where he divided his time between study, often spending hours in the Public Library, and typing out and revising William the Conqueror, his epic Drama. There are also references to his relationship with his younger brother. At one point he frankly reflects that he thinks he must be jealous of Jeremy, citing as the reason that he fears his brother is more intelligent than he is. Playing catch-up with his own education which had been truncated, among other reasons, to free up money for his brother's schooling, might be considered a slight justification for these mean thoughts. But whatever the ups and downs of a life at home, Harry was highly motivated towards achieving the next step, a University degree.

But he had to support himself for the intervening six months and so he wrote to his old department at the BBC asking if there were any vacancies. He was delighted to be offered the same job back at £6 and 10 shillings a week. Surprisingly he records that he was also interviewed for a job as an announcer which he had not applied for. The audition did not go well. He was told he sounded too young and anyway his voice was too harsh. A strange judgement given that later it was universally acknowledged that he possessed a very pleasing voice, one he used to much advantage when broadcasting or lecturing, but, as he had never contemplated becoming an announcer, he was not too devastated. He also heard from his old landlady in Highbury that she had a vacant room.

The diaries, that only started from the day he joined up, do, to some extent, make up for the lack of a written record of his youth-in-training days by giving us the names of people he had known then, occasionally giving us a glimpse of his social life when he was aged 16 to 19, but they are tantalisingly sketchy. Ricks and Theresas, Jacks and Sarahs and Sues, flick in and out but there are no references to any special relationships. We learn for the first time the name of his landlady, Mrs. Brown, who always made him feel welcome as well as sometimes joining in outings such as that to the Harringay Arena to hear Kirsten Flagstad sing Beethoven and Wagner—whether Mrs. Brown was motherly or winsome, old or young, we will never know. They also record that, from time to time, he would spend a day at Lords by courtesy of friends and relations who were members there. Watching cricket seems an unlikely occupation for him but the entries sound quite enthusiastic with casual references to such greats as Compton and Edrich. But this must have been one of the aspects of his life he chose not to retain because, in later life, when his daughter Bryony's husband Rupert, talked about their visits to Lords, Harry gave the impression that he was totally ignorant of the game.

The references to things that happened in the months from August 1945 to September 1948 when he was in the army are, for someone who later had a conspicuously ordered mind, quite disjointed, with a chance statement after he was demobbed that he had had a good mark for his first essay just back from Ruskin College and on the next day telling us that he was working on his Philosophy Course, which makes sense of references to reading Kant and Professor Joad but only by inference telling us that he was actually formally studying this subject by correspondence with Ruskin College. Throughout this period the Aeneid constantly crops up. Although he never actually says that this is going to be the set text for his examination it plainly was so. Sometimes he would admit failure to come to grips with it on a specific day. but he would nevertheless battle on. Obviously not without success because there is one entry that admits he is beginning to grasp 'the *principles of inflected language.*'

Working again for the BBC involved being part of the technical team recording the commentary on rowing events at Henley-on-Thames during the 1948 Olympics. Apart from the experience having been very pleasurable, it was also the place where he acquired a highly significant piece of equipment. He saw a typewriter in a second-hand shop and bought it. He later referred to this, with little justification, as 'liberating' because it was a German model, umlauts and all. But, however mundane the purchase, it became his most treasured possession. Many of his subsequent publications originated on that typewriter and the family remember that if you were on the floor below the study where he worked, you were subjected to rhythmic thudding as he pounded the keys with two fingers of each hand. Unfortunately, he seemed unable to abandon this technique and still thumped away when he eventually moved to the more sensitive keyboard of a computer after the old portable packed up. But the machine had a small extended life when it was shipped to Japan to take its place in an exhibition of crime writing which his Japanese publishers used to market the translations of his books. Later still it had another outing when it was hired as a period 'prop' in a TV show. Most of the time it gathered dust in the junk room but, sad to say, it was recently, and without my prior knowledge, thrown away in a black bin.

Returning from Henley to the BBC he continued in employment until nearly the end of September when he would take the holidays owing to him, returning home for three weeks of intensive Latin study. In the event his mother was quite ill with bronchitis and he had to look after the house and do the cooking for about a week. But he did do some Virgil and even records that he was beginning to enjoy it although he seems to have fluctuated in his belief of his ability to pass the exam. He left for Dublin on the 16th October and somehow managed to mislay his luggage on the boat but fortunately, although we get no details in the diary, he appears to have known a kind family, the Longfords, who lent him pyjamas and shaving things. The luggage was retrieved the next day during which he also met and got on with the man, simply called Quin in the diary, who was to be his tutor so that he was ready to sit the exam the following day. Twenty-four hours later he learnt that he had scraped a pass and on the 21st October he enrolled as a student—an undergraduate at last.

Chapter 2

The first lecture turned out to be no more than a form to be filled in but the second flung him in at the deep end. It was conducted in French which Harry describes as a bit of a strain but fortunately when the class was divided, he found himself in the half being addressed in English and had an illuminating talk about XVIIth century France. The diary entry for that first day, October 21st, ends, '*The evening I spent looking warily at 'L'Avare'. 'So, so.'* Whether this comment referred to his own inability to absorb the finer points of the French language or to Molière's skill as a dramatist he did not enlighten us.

He became a bit impatient with the pace of lectures, finding it irritating still to be on L'Avare in the second week, fearing there would be too much to do later on. Otherwise he found that he was pretty much up-to-date with the theory of grammar but frustrated when asked to address the class and found that he did not fully understand the lecturer's questions and so was unable to '*air my accent*' and could only mutter his replies. But he was pleased that he would be giving an '*exposé sur le film Hamlet Mardi prochain*'.

His lodgings were not very conducive to quiet reading and he realised he needed to explore what library facilities were available to him. But these difficulties did not faze him for too long and he also found time to attend an audition for the University players—he does not tell us what play he auditioned for—but, laughing at himself, he says, '*I read in my beautiful resonant tones a passage*' but when asked to act a further piece, '*I simply read it in tones more resonant and more beautiful*'. After some banter, which centred on American accents, he left—it seems partless—but with an exhortation to come again.

He had been writing a poem called 'The Beggarman' during his last few days in England and having revised it he submitted it to the college magazine, TCD, who, to his amazement, published it at the end of the first month. They did not subsequently accept everything he submitted but on that first occasion he was pleased to be able to describe himself as '*a published author*'. Around this time he admits, in the privacy of the diary pages, though not publicly, that his ambition is to be a writer.

He was finding time for some other leisure activities as well which included going to Rugger matches which he went to with a couple of new acquaintances admitting that, '*I wasn't bored, though I wasn't thrilled.*' The same entry continues more seriously, '*I am reading G.B. Harrison's Penguin* 'Introducing Shakespear' *and find it very good, he gives a useful bibliography and groundwork for Shakespear study.*' It must have been from some esoteric conviction—surely not ignorance—that Harry opts to spell Shakespeare without the final 'e' throughout the diaries. Other light entertainment was found playing Bridge, although he had reservations about his abilities in this direction, but he seems to have found indulgent friends and enjoyed long evenings in this manner.

In those early days, after managing to acquire a gown, a necessity for undergraduates attending lectures, he records his initiation into the studies he will be doing. An essay on 'Romeo and Juliet'; phonetics, which contrary to received opinion he found not too bad; French grammar exercises and a lecture from the renowned Dr Skeffington entitled, '*Good advice given to young students*', in which he stated that, '*the main purpose of coming to the University is to meet people, work is for the holidays.*'

He seems to have filled his days with mostly exceedingly pleasurable experiences though he finds time to record that he listened to a performance of Trollope's 'The Warden' on the radio which he found poor. He also says that he finds one lecturer properly eccentric but sane about Shakespear and interesting about Mediaeval drama, '*though he got his voices mixed up when he read to us.*' He refers to the legendary Professor White as '*A charming old man, who lectures in a sort of rhythmic cadence and read us a letter about the OTC two days too late. I think it may have been deliberately. He gave us good advice to "Look over the wall".* And, taking advantage of everything on offer, he makes full use of the library as well as going to the open meeting of 'The English group' (a literary society) which would later occupy a great deal of his time and energy. In short Harry was beginning to be at peace with himself and blossom in a world he was meant to inhabit.

Later in life he admitted that when it came to studying 'Middle English' he found it so boring he nearly gave up, but for the most part he was highly motivated and tackled whatever was flung at him. He assiduously attended the various recondite literary and debating opportunities, the Historical Society, shortened to The Hist, the Modern Languages Society, Mod Lang, and as time went on he became deeply involved with them, being elected to join the committees that ran these organisations and eventually serving as an officer.

He also made some very good friends some of whom lasted up to the time of his death. One of these was the highly intelligent, iconoclastic Cecil Jenkins, an undergraduate from Northern Ireland who was two years ahead of him but younger because he had come to Trinity straight from school. He, too, was doing a degree in Modern languages—French and German. Cecil went on to be Reader in French at Sussex University and then Dean of the School of European Studies as well as publishing fact and fiction books and writing many plays. But before all this, in his final undergraduate year and very much involving Harry, he founded a literary magazine called 'Icarus'. Cecil was nothing if not a firebrand and wanted to create something new which would 'clear the air', or, as someone put it, writing much later in the college magazine, TCD, to 'épater les bourgeois' This same article recalled that that first edition aroused some fury and a certain reputation for decadence, although other sources say that it received favourable reviews. It certainly continued to be published three times a year so that when Harry graduated it was well established and indeed still exists today with a claim to be Ireland's longest running literary magazine.

From the beginning Cecil wanted an editorial team drawn from those in the years below him so that the magazine would have a future and as Harry was part of that team he was deeply involved in such things as fund-raising, a nightmare which he freely admitted he did not do very well. But he was rather better at the strictly editorial part and also became secretary to the committee eventually formed to run the magazine. All this was of course against the background of his academic work. During his first year he had established quite a reputation for writing and debating skills and now he was nearing the end of his second year with a daunting revision schedule in preparation for a scholarship exam. But Icarus remained a very important part of his life and once whatever storm that was caused by the first issue had blown over the venture never looked back. Cecil graduated in a blaze of glory and left Harry and the others to carry on the good work.

Another lifelong friend was someone mentioned in the very first entries of the College pages of the diary, a rugger enthusiast, Frank Davies. Like Cecil, Frank was younger than Harry but senior, so graduated a year before him. The fact that Frank was doing a Science degree as well as going into industry when he left does not seem to have been a problem and the friendship endured for 60 years. There seemed to have been plenty of shared interests like theatre and concerts even if Harry did not enjoy the rugger as much as Frank and perhaps Frank did not find the debating quite as absorbing as Harry. Frank was also a Roman Catholic and one whose faith was built on sturdy foundations; he was educated by the Jesuits whereas Harry did not even go to Catholic schools. Frank seemed to have absorbed the Jesuit's famous knack of reasoned and placid acceptance. In 1957, some years after Trinity, Harry had no hesitation in asking him to be godfather to his daughter Bryony something Frank reciprocated by asking Harry to be godfather to his first daughter, Clare. It says much for Frank's loyalty that even after this when he knew that Harry was no longer a practising Catholic he remained a friend. When they were both Scholars of the House they shared rooms. The tradition was to call your roommate your 'wife' so for Frank's last and Harry's penultimate year they were each other's wife.

There were countless others whose names—mostly just a forename—peppered the pages of the diary. What emerges is a man transformed, a man in his element living a life among friends with whom he endlessly debated and enjoyed a friendly, for the most part, rivalry, as well as going to theatres, art galleries and concerts while all the time reading and reading and reading and still writing. There was time for a splendid balance of recreation which included plenty of Guinness—quaintly during Lent the Catholic authorities judged this to be a food so had to be foresworn, although strangely whisky was allowed. But there was also a great deal of hard work. His own words from that article on writing an autobiography say it all.

'Trinity at that time was a good place for one of my innate modesty. No high-flying intellectual whizz kids were there greatly to overshadow me. There was time enough, too. Time to send a poem or two to the college magazine and see them printed. Time to debate. Time to act. Time to write short stories...........Time to found a college literary magazine. Time to gain a scholarship and be entitled to wear an extra-voluminous gown. Time, above all, to talk. Talk is the great Irish virtue, and vice. I blossomed swinging from talk's benign branches.

'I wrote, I edited, and I was beyond doubt one of Trinity's literary set, as well as gulping up such of the great masters of literature I had not yet devoured. Proust and Joyce's Ulysses had already capitulated in front of my relentless intellectual snobbery. Dickens I had delighted in from boyhood. I recall, indeed, myself sitting quietly reading 'The Pickwick Papers', aged eleven or even less, with my father absorbed in the newspaper opposite, and in my intense pleasure voicing just aloud the exclamation 'Pickwick!' My father thought I had uttered the then rudest word. Happily he accepted my explanation. But the Dickensian vividness has set me a tremendous target, little though I knew it then'.

But back in that first year at the end of the first month, on the eve of his 22nd birthday, October 30th , the diary tells us *'This is the day that I have annual reflections: how different, praise be to God, is my situation now from what it was a year ago, then I was in the Army, tormented by Regimental Training, discipline, and a thousand other ills; now, I am free, I have achieved an immediate ambition by getting to the university, and it cannot help but widen my outlook, even at the cost of convincing me that I am not a genius.*

There is no question that he set himself the highest standards and inwardly was very competitive. His entries in the diary are very honest not only stating at one point that as far as he is concerned fame is the ultimate name of the game but also and, more mundanely admitting that his understanding of say French grammar is less than it should be or that he finds some set text obscure. The wonder is that he was as high up the pecking order as he was considering that he had been deprived of those vital sixth form years which can teach you how to study and organise the way you work.

He did not entirely take Dr. Skeffington's advice about the time to work because he fitted in a great deal of work into his term time but then he was conscious that he would be required to sit exams at the beginning of the second term. He did, however, go home for the Christmas break armed with all his revision. His journey took him via Cheshire, where his paternal grandmother and maiden Aunt Joan lived. There he was introduced to the French au pair, Micheline, who then became his pen friend, the closer relationship perhaps intended by his relatives not having developed. He does seem to have found her attractive, he tells his diary so, but he did not manage to carry through any slight plans he made, from time to time, to further the relationship. He then arrived home and by his own admission was very snappy with everyone. Unfortunately, he was particularly irritated by his father who was undoubtedly upset by this. The irritations were for the most part petty, such as a disagreement about what programme they should listen to on the radio. But Harry himself admits that he was not an easy person to live with. His solution was to keep to his room a great deal and tackle the revision. A tense time.

It is very noticeable that when he goes back to Trinity he once more relaxes, and the work goes much better. With about a fortnight to go before the exams he set himself a ferocious programme. But he had not quite caught up with himself and although getting creditable marks in both English and French he did not achieve his hoped for top grades and others did better than he did. However, such was his pleasure at being back in college that he was not too cast down. Indeed, he appears more cast down should his speech-making during debates be not entirely successful. His ambition to succeed as a figure in that world, to be witty and be well thought of, was almost as great as his determination to shine academically.

By May of his first year there begin to be references to being put up for the committee of the 'Hist' and before the end of the academic year in June this has been achieved as well as becoming secretary of the 'English Group'

Throughout this time there was a novel being written. It was a long time in the writing but was apparently completed and much of it was typed up on his portable typewriter. However, by the time anyone else had sight of it in 2011, only 27,000 long-hand words remain in an exceedingly fat Irish exercise book. The title is 'The Deep Depression of Oliver Mudd' and although in 1949 Harry had hopes for its future, he must have realised that there would be obstacles to finding a publisher. His very invention of the hero's name almost inevitably would have doomed it to failure because apparently the sole purpose was to have him reply to the question, *'What is your name?'* : *'My name is Mud.'*

The extant manuscript does depict a very deep depression in poor Oliver and perhaps he was drawing on personal experience because Harry himself suffered from the same tendency from time to time, assuredly not as profound as his fictional character but nevertheless very real. His congenial surroundings made life infinitely more tolerable, but he was still some way off feeling at peace with himself all the time. It was fortunate that life at Trinity was so full and presented such a variety of occupation that the depressions seem to have been quite short-lived. He had begun the novel when he was in the army where his own gloom was never far from the surface but fortunately for his sanity he had a more robust side and by the time he was at Trinity the parallels between Oliver and himself were beginning to be contained within the pages of fiction. In hindsight it offers an interesting reflection on how his style changes after he becomes a professional writer and particularly after he creates Inspector Ghote, who, on his own admission, was himself, although at the same time thousands of miles from the personality Harry presented to the world. This endorses his autobiographical assertion that, *'I am indelibly a viewer from afar'*

Another of his contemporaries, Mark Samuels, who somehow managed to compress his four year course into three, had left before Harry graduated and so had lost touch with him, but later read the published books and recently remarked to me that he was astounded at the transformation in the writing from University days. He was not, of course, talking about 'Oliver Mudd', which he could not have read, but about the articles, poems and short stories that appeared both in Icarus and TCD the official college magazine. To Mark the earlier offerings were a mite pedestrian in sharp contrast to the vibrancy and sparkle of the professional publications. Unfortunately, Harry must have been of the same mind given that he destroyed so many manuscripts that are known to have been written before his first published book in 1959. He was as forthright in criticism of his own work as he was when writing about others and a devastating diary entry from December 1949 mentally consigns his drama about William the Conqueror to the bin, *'...hopeless in dialogue. Quite impossible, a mixture of modern idiom and contorted prose.'*

But even if so much never saw the light of day these lost works must be regarded as a series of nursery slopes where he practised and could take a tumble or two before tackling more ambitious heights. Then there were all the debates he attended and spoke at where his burgeoning love of words and his cherished exercise of wit must have contributed to his facility later on when he would retreat behind the shut door of his study and produce up to 3,000 words a day. Equally astonishing is his chameleon ability to change the style of his writing. There are books set in Victorian times that are as historically convincing and authentic as are the sights, smells and language he creates in his Indian novels but the difference is that they are written with a directness that would have been quite out of place in the, in many ways, gentler world of Inspector Ghote. There was even a period when he would alternate between India and a set of books exploring the problems faced by very British detectives culminating in a seven book series with a female detective, Harriet Martens, as the protagonist. Once again these could easily have been written by a completely different author in that the problems do not lie buried under the narrative but are addressed head on, problems like facing death and terrorism. Harry would probably have legitimately claimed that he was still writing 'at a distance' because he was seeing everything through the eyes of a woman. Something he would do again in the short stories featuring a charlady, Mrs. Craggs—originally created as the sleuth in the novel 'Death of a Fat God'—these are a tongue-in-cheek, light-hearted collection yet manage to read like small dramas. She was created with broad humour in mind in sharp contrast to the ironic humour of the Ghote books.

The diaries also confess that it was important to him to make people laugh. Almost as important as it was to be making an impression as a writer or an orator or, once again quoting himself, '..that I counted or would one day count.' It all boiled down to his use of words, as his daughter, Bryony, percipiently said at his funeral, words were of paramount importance to him. They were his very life's blood. If he knowingly fell below his own standards he would, in his own mind, have failed and be ruthlessly critical of himself.

His first partially successful academic year came to an end and the long vacation began. Once again, he visited Cheshire on his way home where he re-encountered Micheline. He seems to have had notions of advancing the relationship but according to the diaries he was a bit lacking in the technique and once again failed to do so. Soon after returning home he goes to visit someone who had been a lifelong childhood friend, Christopher O'Brien, at his rooms in Cambridge. It is typical of the diaries that this is the first mention of someone who was a family friend and someone he had seen with reasonable frequency and with whom he must have maintained contact. They plainly got along very well and indeed four years later he was best man at Harry's wedding. However, after that first mention, another year goes by without Christopher's name coming up. Christopher makes a return visit to Trinity as Harry is frenziedly revising for the Scholarship exam. This is the point at which the chronological diaries stop. There is, however, a separate one-topic diary written during a month-long pilgrimage he and Christopher took to France and Italy during Holy Year in the summer of 1950, undertaken to fulfill their joint Catholic obligations. But this is a factual account and does not talk about personal relationships.

The diaries for the earlier 1949 summer holidays are more personal and they make for uneasy reading, chronicling, as they do, time at a French sea-side resort shared with quite a close college friend. The relationship was sorely tested during their time in a tiny village pension having to share a bed. The friendship was only narrowly salvaged later through a tactful exchange of letters. Harry tells us that it was he who left first to continue his holiday at Micheline's parent's house in Paris. These next entries draw a picture of a somewhat taciturn and sulky young man where it is also quite evident that there is no question of the relationship with Micheline developing. However, his Art education galloped apace with hardly a gallery unvisited, an occupation he infinitely preferred to those being pursued by the rest of the party in their more robust outdoor activities.

But his reading was progressing well and his French speaking, one of the reasons for the visit, was improving, if not quite at the pace he would have liked. He only has a short time after his travels before the start of the new academic year at Trinity. This he spent at home and the diary entries seem to focus more on the programmes they listened to on the radio than anything more personal. It is astonishing how many hours the BBC was prepared, in those days, to devote to culture. Shakespeare and other classics were constantly being produced, as well as contemporary drama, in marked contrast to the ever increasing paucity and quality once TV started to absorb the funding that came from the license fee. A major building block in Harry's early education was provided by BBC radio.

Diary no. 21, October 1949, comes to an abrupt stop in mid-sentence apparently before he gets back to Dublin and it is at the beginning of volume 23 that we are told that he had lost, or someone had stolen, volume 22. This caused him more than a little anguish and he seriously thought of abandoning writing them altogether. Ultimately, he decided to continue although he vows to be more circumspect when recording his innermost thoughts. These comments confirm that he was writing more for himself than for posterity and would have been mortified to think that some of the entries—the ones he intended to be more circumspect about—would ever be read by all and sundry. His comments at this time are amplified later on when he is writing the article about autobiography where he says that he writes best when he is writing at 'arm's length'.

That gap of just over a month when he arrived back in Dublin for the start of his second year means that there is no way of knowing what problems he had had to solve regarding where he would be living among other things.

But when volume 23 resumes in November 1949 it is apparent that he has achieved his desire to find rooms in college. Apparently, he was sharing with someone called Otway with whom he does not seem to have had more than a workable relationship but at least he no longer had digs at some distance from College. This all made his greater involvement in the Societies much easier and there are references, with absolutely no detail, to late night talks on matters of grave importance such as the difficulty they all seem to be having with sex.

But this is a period of progress. Crucially Cecil Jenkins' new magazine, 'Icarus', starts to be mentioned. The academic side is also beginning to look up. And, although there is still a way to go until the essays get the very best ratings, he has arrived in the top third of his year. At the beginning of January 1950 he adds acting to his timetable, appearing with reasonable acclaim and great pleasure in a production of Marlowe's Edward the Second with the College Players.

By March ambitions begin to be achieved. He writes a competition essay on 'Our Indispensable 18th Century' and shares the first prize, and as well as this he shares the prize money in the short story competition run by the 'Mod Lang Society'. And just to make sure there are no spare moments he accepts an invitation to join the group of undergraduates running the college magazine, 'TCD'

At the same time he says that he is going to start work revising for '*the exam*'. Unfortunately diary No 24 comes to an abrupt end in April 1950 in the middle of this revision. He had already confessed that he was getting behind with the diary entries so presumably this, added to the shock of losing volume 22, proved too much and the facts about his last two years at Trinity have to be deduced from archival material and memories of any of his contemporaries who are contactable. We do know, from College records, that from October 1950 when he returned for the start of his third year, he was a Scholar of the House so this must be the exam for which he was revising. Along with quite a few material benefits attached to being a scholar, such as moving into the best rooms in college; free meals and, frivolously, being able to wear a more voluminous gown, it was also pivotal.

Academically he was now acknowledged to be among the high achievers. He had finally caught up with himself.

Chapter 3

During the long vacation there came the opportunity to travel. As has already been fleetingly mentioned he and his old friend Christopher O'Brien, both being Roman Catholics, needed little encouragement to fulfil a duty required of them by the Church, to make a pilgrimage to Rome during 'Holy Year'. Fortunately for Harry, Christopher owned a car, admittedly a small ancient Austin which had a tendency to break down rather a lot, including break failures which was not only alarming but proved expensive to repair. Nevertheless they were able to travel reasonably cheaply through France, Switzerland and on through Italy to Rome. Because Harry did not drive Christopher needed someone to share the task with him from time to time. The diary records that his friend John was that person. Diary No. 25, devoted entirely to that journey, is a little short on personal details so John's surname is never disclosed. But other things like their search for affordable accommodation during the month they were on the road was vividly recounted. The whole journal reads very much like the poor man's version of The Grand Tour as they drove by way of St Quentin, up the Jura and on to Dijon where they were able to stay cheaply at the Cité Universitaire. At this point we are told indirectly that Harry is planning a novel called 'The Tour' and we are given some detail about the characters involved. He always seems to need a piece of writing on the go and the diary not only would serve to remind him of locations but, from time to time gives details of twists and turns in the story as well as sketchy character outlines. Alas that is all we will ever know about the assorted characters he created during that tour because whatever manuscript was subsequently written has once again vanished.

Considering that the itinerary had them crossing into Switzerland to reach Lausanne before continuing along the shores of Lake Geneva and then up the Rhone Valley to Martigny, the lack of time devoted to writing of any sort is scarcely surprising. From there they have to tackle The Alps. This gives him the opportunity for some graphic description of the hazards for the driver of that hairpin bend ascent, *'It was worse really than we expected. The road never more than 20 feet wide and surfaced with some white pebbles and earth, like a good cart track.'* Although he does, elsewhere, acknowledge that Christopher and John were doing the driving, the descriptions read as if he himself was the driver, but even if he was not actually at the wheel he was totally involved and giving spiritual if not physical support.

Having spent the night in a mountain-top hotel they drive on to the heights of the Simplon Pass and so to the frontier, not stopping for lunch until they were in Italy. After that it was Milan and having found a reasonable hotel with some difficulty could not find a restaurant that displayed a menu outside. Not having much of that day's budget left, they settled for cakes which they ate in the street. The next day brought them to Lake Garda where they enjoyed swimming. *'There were quite a lot of people on the strand about equally divided between swimmers and washerwomen, who brought flat wooden barrows which they pushed into the water at the lake's edge, and then battered at the clothes on them.'* Making up for dining on cakes the previous night they pushed the boat out with a meal that consisted of, *'vermicelli soup with powdered cheese, steak with lemon, a fruit and we drank two fiascos of good red wine.'*

Nearly at the end of August they are two weeks into their pilgrimage and heading for Venice. In the pouring rain they take the *'dull autostrada'* where, appropriately, *'half the advertisements are for impermiabili'.* After Verona, where they bought fruit, he continues, *'I planned my novel. I have filled all eighteen places'* Earlier he had seen a tourist coach with room for eighteen passengers which was quite enough information for someone of Harry's fertile imagination to assemble a posse of assorted characters to make a novel. There were apparently to be students in various states of rivalry, two priests likewise, a youngish couple with a small son who develops appendicitis which Harry feels will give him an opportunity for some reflections on death, as well as pairs of characterful middle aged ladies. The stage is set, but alas not for us. Did it ever get written? The secret is up in heaven because not a vestige remains. The only surprise is that he never did produce a novel using the unique experience of the tour. One possible explanation is that writing something with a background that he had personally experienced would run the risk of too much personal exposure. A problem he later solved by being present in a character who was outwardly the antithesis of himself.

But the main purpose of the diary was to record what they saw and there is plenty of assured architectural comment, *'the late 19th Century imitation baroque of the Palais de Justice'* or the off-beat observation about St Mark's Square in Venice, *'Two sailors walking with their arms around each other's waists seemed perfectly in keeping with the bizarre enormity of the Church'*

Many hours were spent searching out Art Galleries or churches with pictures on display. At some stage Harry had taken time to familiarise himself with the facts about the classic painters and, armed with Thomas Bodkin's 1927 book 'An Approach to Painting', he has no hesitation in recording his feelings about the great works of art housed in the locations they were able to visit. From Venice comes this entry, *'Went in the morning to look at Tintorreto's Wedding Feast at Cana in the sacristy of the Church of Santa Maria della Salute. At first rather disappointed with it, as the colour seemed so bad and the whole picture had the air of lurking behind deep layers of varnish. After a while I discovered, having been told by the attendant and disbelieved him, that the light was better when it was seen from the side, and I began to like it.'* He remains studying it for an hour, attempting to build on this liking, but in the end still finds it lacks colour.

From Venice it was on through Padua to their destination for the night, Bologna where, of course they ate Spaghetti Bolognese and had some repairs done to the car in a garage forecourt *'that might have been the setting for some romantic play—pillars, balconies and faded crests painted round the walls.'* After more mountain driving up the Appenines and an encounter with a tarring machine which, when it had finally moved, made it necessary for them to back away down the hill, *'in order to gather enough speed to rush it.'*, they arrived in Florence where they *'suddenly emerged into the Piazza del Duomo and were confronted with it and the baptistery at their iced cakiest.'* The next morning took them, *'to the old monastery of San Marco and there looked, Thomas Bodkin in hand, at Fra Angelico's Annunciation. I took one look at it and tore up my reproduction which entirely misses the delicacy of the colouring.* The stay in Florence which they extended for a further day was filled with a feast of art, their only disappointment being the absence of a particular Botticelli which was being cleaned. However they found solace in, among others, Reubens.

Then the final 176 miles to reach Rome where they spent their first night under canvass in The Campo San Gorgio. Having found the centre for English speaking people Harry has this relatively even-handed comment to make, *'it was really rather horrible, full of our fellow countrymen who always appear so intolerable out of their setting. I can imagine that our disparagement and standoffishness are equally annoying.'*

After getting their breath back they embarked on *'the conditions necessary to fulfil our pilgrimage we took the car to the Vatican having first taken our laundry to the blanchiseuse of the Anglo-American hôtel.'* Priorities having been established they visited St Peters which was not only architecturally overwhelming but teeming with, *'sight-seers, marching, singing pilgrims and people,'* then having made his confession to a priest with an American accent he left, *'feeling rather battered.'* In the afternoon they took a round bus trip to San Paola Without the Walls about which he records nothing except to comment on the heaving mass of people. They visited some rather dull basilicas but put up the necessary pilgrim's prayers and then found comfort in a good meal. After that they were off to the Baths of Caracalla where they were able to see a performance of Madam Butterfly. The rather long diary entry not only gives Harry the opportunity of rudimentary criticism but captures the informality of the event. *'It was even more fantastic than opera generally is.....the short curtain that ran between two of the enormous broken pink columns of the baths, which formed a natural proscenium, was parted to reveal a very Japanesey, and, it must be admitted, a very pretty scene. The orchestra was rather far away from us, although for the price we had good seats, but the singing was generally easily audible. It was difficult in the circumstances to judge of quality but the singing as a whole seemed to be pretty good, and the acting certainly was. The auditorium would have held ten thousand and reminded me vividly of an international at Leeson Park in Dublin. There were cries of 'Gelati' and 'Birra, birra calda'. There were programme touts, and there was shouting to people to sit down. The performance was scheduled for nine and began about twenty-five past, it ended at midnight.* Once again he did not use this setting for a novel directly, although the chaos of the provincial Opera House he used in 'Death of a Fat God'—one of his earliest crime books—might have sprung from this slightly nightmarish experience.

The next morning, having attended Mass and made his communion, he tells us that he has completed his own personal pilgrimage but it seemed that voluntary additions could be added and they set out on a round of saying Masses for the souls in Purgatory. There is no doubt that religion was at this stage still genuinely an important part of his daily life. Returning to central Rome there was a lot more they wanted to see. First, the Vatican museum and then the Sistine Chapel which, although overwhelmingly beautiful, was difficult to appreciate fully, given the heaving mass of people. But the pinnacle of the visits was when they attended a general audience with the Pope. With some difficulty they gained admittance and found places not far from the central aisle, '*A file of Swiss Guards went up the aisle and there was enormous jostling; we were poked in the back, pushed, pulled and almost punched. The minutes went by. Hymn singing was begun over the loud speaker, and various exhortations were given us in various languages. At last shortly after six, all the hundreds of chandeliers, that before had seemed tinsel among the marbles and alabasters of St Peters, suddenly were illuminated and the Pope appeared carried high above our heads in his great chair, dressed all in white. It was a genuinely moving moment.*' The ceremony continues with the Pope addressing them, '*first in Italian, then in French, then a few indistinguishable words in English.*' The heat and press of people began to be intolerable until; finally, after three hours they were able to escape.

Their stay in Rome was over and after the car was, yet again, repaired, they were en route along the coast road lined with '*palms and other sub-*

tropical fruit' and reached Pisa where, suddenly encountering *'what looked like an abandoned piece of masonry,'* they realised they were looking at the Leaning Tower. Pressing on they crossed back from Italy into France and made for Nice where although they found a cheap hotel and had a good meal they were frustrated in their efforts to swim in the sea that night by a notice saying that swimming was forbidden. The next morning they were delighted to see plenty of people ignoring the notice and having joined them they then drove on to Cannes where they spent further time swimming in the perfect calm and warmth of the Mediterranean Sea.

Christopher managed to contact some friends who recommended a small hotel in a village called Saint Basile in the hills above the town where they spend a couple of nights and eat a splendid three course meal described in the diary in minute detail including drinking not a house wine but Chateauneuf, *'which was quite good'.* Next day, in between long periods of sunbathing, swimming and sand-castle building, Harry found time for something more intellectual, Balzac's 'Femme de Trente Ans', *'it is in the true French analytic tradition unfortunately one constantly feels Balzac dropping his characters into the pigeonholes he has constructed for them.'*

Next morning September 13th, after a final swim, they set off on the northward journey home. Then 208 miles later, having found a cheap enough hotel in a village called Sanlieu the diary, once again, abruptly stops.

There is a sad coda to this adventure. Having been out of touch for well over a month, they must have sent a telegram to Harry's home when they landed in Britain, to say that they were on their way, because when Christopher drew up at the house they were greeted by 14 year old Jeremy, on the look-out by the garden gate, with the news that Sandy, Harry's father, had died on September 19th. His death was indirectly the result of the rheumatic fever he had contracted while serving in the trenches of the First World War which had affected his heart so that, unexpectedly, at the age of 56, he had had a fatal heart attack while out driving with Mugie, Harry's mother. Harry was home in time to help Maurice, one of Sandy's brothers, and someone very close to the family, organise the funeral. It must have been a traumatic time for them all but Jeremy, above all, would have been

34

relieved that he no longer had to shoulder the main responsibility.

Sandy may not have lived long enough to see the fulfilment of his ambitions for his son, the publication of the first book, but at least he will have known that Harry had been made a Scholar of the House and on the road to successful academic achievement.

Chapter 4

From then onwards, for just over two years, until the end of Harry's time at Trinity it is more difficult to chronicle his progress; his closest friends, Cecil Jenkins and Frank Davis, had graduated before him and although he maintained contact with them they have been unable to help me with personally observed information although they and others have, when I approached them, kindly tried to plunder their archives and memories. There were, moreover, no personal diaries but some information was available from the two literary magazines, Icarus and TCD.

But outside the time spent academically and in literary and debating pursuits, there was an interesting development in his personal life. Almost certainly as a result of further involvement in acting activities his name started to be linked to that of a female undergraduate, Kate Kelly. Noel, his brother, having as an adult changed from his given name of Jeremy, remembers their mother receiving a letter with the announcement that he is engaged to be married. The letter seems not to have been preserved and there does not seem to have been any later correspondence on the subject so that was the last they ever heard of the matter. That it was a fact was corroborated some few years later when Harry told me, his new fiancée, of the former engagement and added that it had been amicably ended. Indeed Christmas cards continued to be exchanged for many years. Further evidence comes from TCD in their miscellany column, *Bells, Books and Candles,* which contained many references to H.R.F. Keating, Scholar, but also as a caption to a photo, *'Harry 'Kiss-me-Kate Keating' having descended from his exalted positions—monasticism being one of them—seen queuing to see the latest Hollywood epic. His new modus vivandi being almost on the ordinary human level.'* Nor did Kate escape the teasing comments, being referred to as *'Kate Kiss-me-Harry Kelly'.*

There does not seem actually to have been a production of 'The Taming of the Shrew', so this must have been the product of the correspondent's rather flowery and over-active imagination. But there are plenty of mentions of them both, singly and together, indicating involvement in drama productions. In June of 1951 there is a review of Shaw's 'You Never Can Tell' in which Harry played the elderly lawyer. His performance was said to be *'exaggerated to just the right degree'.* A later review concerns scenes from 'Measure for Measure', the compilation of which seems to have been largely Kate Kelly's responsibility and in which they both performed. This article ends with a general round-up of the season suggesting that there was no lack of acting talent and goes on to name five people, two of whom were Harry and Kate, and concludes, *'While there may be no star Players, we have plenty of those honest, hardworking performers who must be the backbone of any amateur production.'*

Did he ever consider life as an actor? If so, this was, probably, not a very serious option. For all his imaginative leaps he was a realist and must have known his own limitations. He did continue to enjoy addressing an audience and later, when he gave talks about writing or when one of his books was being launched, he would invariably include a reading, which was always very well received, in large part because his own relaxed enjoyment was quite evident. Nature, despite the opprobrium of that earlier BBC official, had endowed him with a pleasing voice which he used to good effect. He added to this an innate sense of timing. On one occasion I remember a woman in the audience saying, *'Before I ask my question I just want to say that I love your voice, I could listen to it forever.'*

But however much he was seduced by the greasepaint and footlights of those college days and however lured by the headiness of successfully entertaining others, he remained steadfast to the literary scene. A large proportion of his spare time went on editing and contributing to the magazines. Harry owed a huge debt to Cecil Jenkins for being far-sighted enough to include him on the initial editorial board of Icarus and for his courage in founding the magazine in the first place. Unlike TCD, where there was a policy of anonymity with everyone writing under grandiose pseudonyms and only the editor having to be named for legal reasons, the contributors to Icarus were totally accountable. That did not stop it being very upfront in its commentary as well as contributing its share of undergraduate satirical humour, something Harry would have relished.

But nor did he neglect the more conventional TCD whether on the editorial side or as contributor. On one occasion having visited and enjoyed an exhibition of paintings by the Dublin artist Neville Johnson he not only found the money to purchase one of them but also wrote a glowing review. This had unexpected repercussions some fifty years later when the artist contacted Harry to ask him if, as an art critic, he would be willing to have those words quoted in the catalogue for a new exhibition he was mounting. In replying, after renouncing any claims to art criticism, Harry agreed. At the same time he invited Neville to visit him in his London home where he could see his earlier work in pride of place over the mantelpiece.

There was something of curiosity in the invitation because Harry had heard that at some point Neville had become dissatisfied with everything he had done and had, in consequence destroyed anything he could put his hands on and Harry wanted to see what reaction the earlier picture would evoke. Somewhat to their surprise the Keatings, now in their late seventies, heard from Neville, in his nineties, that as he now lived in London, he would call on them one afternoon.

Watching for his arrival out of the first-floor drawing room window they saw a very ancient figure wander past their front gate, quite obviously lost. Once rescued he safely negotiated the uneven front path and steps up to the front door of the Victorian terraced house, but he still had to cope with two flights of stairs to the room where the picture was hanging. He sank thankfully into a chair where he sat for quite a time collecting himself. After a while he got up and shuffled over to the fireplace, above which, impressively framed, was his work. He stood for a few minutes, then, with a muttered, '*Hm, not bad*,' he returned to his chair. Perhaps a predictable comment because it was also known that when Neville resumed painting, after the conflagration, he appeared to be producing work that bore a marked similarity to the earlier collection. However, now, when no further comment was offered, Harry was able to reassure him that over the years 'Cocotte' had been much admired. Everyone who saw it, finding, as he himself had done, all those years ago in the Dublin gallery, that the subtle tones of the painting of this folded paper shape, this Cocotte, and the positioning of a small painted ball in the top right hand corner gave the whole a pleasing perspective and made viewing it a calming and satisfying experience. Harry was very grateful for this trip down memory lane, particularly as Neville died not long after.

Searching through the stacks of Keating documents left behind in the study cupboard, provided a neat postscript to this story. He had preserved the catalogue of the original exhibition at which he had bought the painting which gave the asking price for the various pictures. He had paid £22.10 shillings, which, even allowing for inflation over the years was not a large sum but it was nonetheless an astonishing amount for a student on a £4 a week government grant to find. Perhaps the Historical Society's silver medal award in 1949 for his essay on 'poverty' had had a small cheque attached or maybe the money prize for the competition short story awarded by TCD provided the extra cash. The essay on poverty, some 8,000 words long, set out to prove that the solution to universal poverty lies in a belief in God. Whether the case he argued was right or not, buying that picture was in the nature of Manna from Heaven for him because it had certainly enriched his spiritual life. It was undoubtedly one of his most treasured possessions.

Without any daily record to help us it is impossible to know whether, in those final two years, with his leisure hours divided up between acting, editing and writing and canoodling, he still found time for anything less cerebral such as going on bike rides or having a daily swim. These were the two forms of exercise he enjoyed, according to the earlier diaries, but whether he still found room for them we will probably never know. To be thoroughly uncharitable probably not because by the time he graduated he was no longer skinny being a sturdy thirteen and a half stone, but then that could also be attributable to Guinness. What is certain is that he did a prodigious amount of study because he graduated with First Class Honours. The surviving certificate, also found in the study cupboard, states that '*Henricus Raimundus*, (after which the traditional classicists had to admit defeat) *Fitzwalter Keating........Examinatoribus in Litteris Recentioribus Anglicis et Gallicis.....Moderatores Primae Classis relates est.* And so ended four years largely devoted to study and decisions had to be made on what was going to happen next.

Chapter 5

Had careers advisers been as readily available then as they are nowadays, they would undoubtedly have recommended one of two options to the successful graduate. The first would have been to remain at college and do a PHD with a view to a career in academia. The second might also have started with the advice to do a PHD but would have suggested that this could lead to his becoming an author. But, apparently lacking outside advice, he decided for himself to do neither of these things. He must have considered both, but when asked later he said that he could not envisage himself spending the rest of his life cloistered in a University, that he was not 'Don' material. He seems to have been good at recognising what he would not have been good at, a repetition of his time in the army when he recognised he was not officer material. Quite bizarrely, however, after having devoted so much time to it, he had made up his mind that becoming a writer was not for him either, giving as a reason that he had nothing to say. Somehow the knowledge of all that he had achieved during his four years at Trinity, not to mention the self-confidence he had acquired, seems to have deserted him and without a belief in his own abilities what was he going to do?

The trouble was that without the University ex-serviceman's grant he would have absolutely no money to live on. A living had to be earned. He could have followed in his father's footsteps and become a teacher but that does not seem to have occurred to him or if it did it had no appeal for him. There was really only one obvious option, journalism. Surely with his college magazine experience he could manage that, and, thankfully he appeared still to have his love of words. Accordingly, he applied for and got a job as a graduate trainee with The Westminster Press, a company who owned several provincial papers. He was given a six-month trial period in Swindon where he would learn how to become both a sub-editor and a reporter on the daily Evening Advertiser and the weekly Wiltshire Herald.

Swindon itself was a town in transition. It had been a great railway centre, not only as a major station but also manufacturing the component parts for the rolling stock. Now, with a more modern approach to trains in general, the industrial side had moved elsewhere and so far not much else had been put in its place, so the town was marking time. It had always been a place of two halves with the industrial half lying in a rather dreary huddle at the bottom and the older, more picturesque part perched on the hill above it, the utilitarian terraces below being in sharp contrast to the more gracious living in the top half. For Harry it was back to living in digs after the cushioning comfort of college rooms, but he was fortunate in finding a friendly landlady with a house in the Old Town.

Arriving at the newspaper offices in early 1953 he found he was kept busy by whichever paper needed him most, doing the jobs no-one else wanted. This included all the excitement of the 'Cat stuck up tree' news story; the dreary routine attendance at a local funeral to list the mourners or, even worse, sitting through the end of term performance at the local dance school, writing flattering words about their darling off-spring to induce the parents to buy the paper. Perhaps the words he found to describe these banalities impressed the editor because, after a while he was given what turned out to be a more congenial job reviewing the professional productions of the local Repertory Company. The theatre occupied the building that had been home to the old Mechanics Institute in the lower town and could have done with some cosmetic refurbishment, but it was capacious both back and front stage. It had previously been used for the recreational activities of the railway workers. The stage, behind a traditional proscenium arch, was fully equipped, allowing the productions to be well and amply lit. The gently 'raked' seats that had been installed in the auditorium, ensured reasonable visibility and the acoustics were surprisingly good.

Every Monday night Harry now had a regular outing. The rep was a weekly one, a new play each week, which meant that it was necessary for the review to appear in the Tuesday evening paper in order to entice people to come and fill the seats for the remaining shows. There were eight of those a week, nightly from Monday to Saturday and matinées on Wednesday and Saturday afternoons, so each Tuesday, a paragraph would appear in The Evening Advertiser above the initials HRFK. He was not given a great deal of space so his reviews would concentrate on what was good in the production with only the occasional need to mention what was not quite so successful. On the whole he was a tolerant reviewer but there were times when the banality of the plays made it difficult not to be judgemental. It helped that he genuinely thought the standard of acting from the majority of this particular company was above average and was delighted to be able to help publicise an artistic endeavour in a town that was actually a bit of a cultural desert. He was probably helped by his own college acting experience which had at least introduced him to some of the pitfalls of acting.

There was another staff reporter who reviewed the rep productions for the weekly paper. Between them they covered all the performances given by the amateur societies. These societies, at one count, numbered seventy-five and that in a town whose population was a mere seventy thousand. It might have been thought that this would at least generate large audiences for the Repertory company but in fact few of the amateurs attended their local professional theatre. There was, however, a regular 'Playgoers' club whose activities basically kept the 'Rep' afloat, generating enough money to pay the actor's small salaries and the production costs. This was in the days before such theatres had any sort of government subsidy and budgeting was always a major headache. What was certain was that the regulars thoroughly enjoyed seeing the same seven or eight actors who made up the company, transforming themselves each week into an astonishing variety of parts. By way of forward publicity Harry would add a sentence or two about the following week's play to the bottom of the current review, which would also indicate how the company would be enticingly deployed in the following weeks' production.

But these evenings were the icing on the cake and there was a fair amount of journalistic grind to be got through in the rest of the working week. In those days before new technology made it easily possible to record interviews, a reporter was expected to write it all down and for this he needed shorthand. It was back to the classroom for Harry. In his case the resulting squiggles never attained the conventional text-book ones recommended by 'Pitmans' but they served their purpose and the skills he acquired stayed with him for the rest of his life. The bulging notebooks he filled with research and planning before writing any of his subsequent books are filled with shortened versions of everyday words and symbols and signs to denote things like paragraphs or changes in punctuation. These together with a tracery of lines like a mini traffic system that decorated the pages of a first draft, when he needed to shift a passage of text from one area to another, make those pages collector's items.

Even more tedious were the classes to give him a basic knowledge of legal terminology and most importantly of the laws that governed libel as well as the rights of anyone he interviewed. There were many pitfalls waiting to ensnare the rookie reporter. He does not seem to have found any spare time for creative writing at this point, which, as he had said he had nothing to say, was not surprising.

In a short while the editor, being somewhat peeved that he had allowed a previous graduate to escape once he had finished his six month trial period, took steps to ensure that Harry would remain with them long enough to pay for his apprenticeship. Before that six month period was over Harry had to sign up for a further three years. Given his lack of qualification for other jobs he had little alternative but to bind himself to Swindon until the autumn of 1956. As a result of a development in his personal life—about to be revealed—he secured work abridging books for serialisation on BBC radio, which he fitted into his spare time and earned him much needed extra money. Abridging is a job requiring not only good filleting skills but also sensitivity and while akin to sub-editing, something he was already doing, it is rather more creative. For a fifteen episode serial an average length book had to be reduced by about 2/3rds. In so far as is possible the plot and characters must all be retained and, most tricky of all, the abridged version must convey to the listener what the author intended when writing the book.

He hardly had an idle moment but, as just indicated, his personal life was about to change. One Monday evening taking his seat before curtain up—these were the days when stages still had proscenium arches with a velvet curtain which would rise or draw back at the start of the play—he was probably thinking only of the words he would have to write for tomorrow's paper. This week's play did not look very promising, but then they seldom were. The company needed to find something new each week, something to keep their regular audience happy. On the whole classics and anything too experimental were not popular and attendance would drop, so there were a lot of 'drawing-room comedies'—the 'whose for tennis' or 'jolly hockey sticks' plays, beloved of the time—or plays with a detective such as those by Agatha Christie However this one, *Dark Summer,* turned out to have a good story and just sufficient sentiment to engage the feelings without being too cloying. It centred round a blind man who was being cared for by a young Jewish woman. The review would really write itself, a brief summary of the subject matter without giving away too much of the plot and then space to praise the skill of the actors.

At the end of the performance with jotted notes that would ultimately be transformed into printed copy, stuffed into his pocket, Harry made his way to the front of house bar where, over a glass of beer, he would be given the necessary information about the following week's production. That evening, when he had got what he wanted, he took a last swig of his beer and was about to leave when the young Jewish actress came in. She was clutching a copy of Andre Gide's *Strait is the Gate,* an author Harry knew well. He was intrigued. From his lofty intellectual heights he had not expected someone involved in provincial theatre to be interested in serious reading. He changed his mind about leaving and offering to buy the actress a drink, embarked on what he hoped would be a few minutes of enjoyable conversation. Here was someone whose performance he would be praising in his review and now it seemed that she was intelligent enough to read Gide as well. The ensuing conversation was lengthier than he had expected.

Euphoria apparently enveloped him that night as he set out to climb the hill to his digs until a terrible thought assailed him. Catholics were prohibited from marrying Jews. Quite a few evenings were to be spent in the theatre bar before he managed to work the conversation round to religion and race. There was just the chance that she was not Jewish. Acting a Jewish part and having a nose a little on the large side were not necessarily conclusive, but it would have been rather brash to ask straight out. Had he done so he would have saved himself a few weeks of anguish. I am not, as it happens, Jewish.

During this time money had begun to be a real problem for the theatre and the actors were asked to take a cut in salary in an effort to keep it afloat. The huge backstage area was surmounted by a vast raised gallery that not only held the dressing rooms but quite a few other empty ones as well. Some of the company who were living in digs decided to move in, hopefully saving enough money to be able to exist. I, Sheila Mitchell, the non-Jewish actress, was one of them. This had an added advantage because each night after a drink in the bar and a hasty supper, there were lines to be learnt for the following day's rehearsal. Harry, having become almost a nightly visitor, was roped in to help me by hearing those lines. There was not a lot of free time for an actor in weekly rep. Each week, after the Monday first night, rehearsals for the next week's play would start on Tuesday morning and would continue morning and afternoon every day except when there was a matinee, so if a relationship was to develop it had to be fitted into this busy schedule. Even Sunday, particularly for the women, had its tasks. Whatever personal wardrobe an actress possessed had to be adapted to suit the new character she would be playing. There was a lot of creative designing needed to make last week's slightly frumpish long dress, suitable for a maiden aunt, into an alluring Paris gown to fit next week's siren. It was a relief when occasionally the production was a period piece and a costume would be hired. The same applied to hairstyles because it was rare for the budget to run to the hire of a wig. There was, however, one occasion when I wore an outrageous red wig with plaits coiled round the ears and Harry refused to talk to me after the show until I had removed it, so repulsive did it make me he said.

Things continued in this routine for quite a few weeks. Then it was decided that the production for the week which would contain the Queen's coronation would be devoted to a revue, performing it non-stop on the day of the coronation itself. One of the items was to be a monologue written by Harry in which I would play a governess looking after two young minor royals watching the event from a balcony. This new working relationship seemed to tip the balance and mid-way through May 1953—some three months after the initial meeting—the engagement was announced.

The rep survived and Harry continued to burn the candle at both ends. His journalistic duties were demanding and his days were often long, working quite unsocial hours. But plans went ahead and the wedding was scheduled for early October. My mother was initially horrified, having had a Scottish Presbyterian upbringing, that her daughter was considering marrying a Catholic but was, eventually, persuaded that there was nothing she could do about it and organised a splendid reception for a couple of hundred people at the Basil St. Hotel in fashionable Knightsbridge, being close to the Catholic church off Sloane St. where the wedding took place. The flourishing Evening Standard, was published six days a week and was on sale in the early afternoon of each day Monday to Saturday on October 3rd 1953 chose to include my photo with the caption 'Actress is Today's Bride'. If any of this reached the ears of Harry's editor in Swindon it would have given him pause for thought because when Harry had told him he was marrying an actress from the local Rep his heavily inuendoed comment was, 'I suppose it will be a very small wedding'. One repercussion was that what had become a weekly event for Harry—a cosy supper with the editor, his wife and two eligible daughters—became a thing of the past.

Our honeymoon began with a night in Paris and continued in the South of France, not St Tropez or Cannes but further along the coast in unfashionable Sête, which was no more than a picturesque fishing village. Nowadays, after a severe mosquito problem had been dealt with, it has become a flourishing port. But at the time the mosquitoes made the place affordable for us, even if they were liable to bite. What could, however, have been an equal annoyance was Harry's asthma which was still quite troublesome. This could be particularly acute following a stressful event, so it would not have been surprising if he had had an attack after the wedding day. But, miraculously, he did not which was fortunate because he had placed his 'puffer' (the old-fashioned, large and bulbous forerunner to the modern inhaler) on the mantelpiece in the Paris hotel where we spent the first night and in the morning failed to pack it when we left to catch the train to the South. Fortunately, and miraculously, the honeymoon was asthma free. We spent a few days in Paris on our way home, where we met up with old college friend, Cecil Jenkins, at that time doing post-graduate work and we were greeted by his words, *'Abruti par le bonheur'*. The French have some odd turns of phrase but there can be no doubt that happiness—it is hoped not too brutal—was the predominant feeling radiating from us, the newly married couple.

Apart from the prevalent mosquitoes, the only other snag in the South of France was a problem attached to the theatre we should have left behind in Swindon. I knew that when I went back I would immediately start rehearsals for Rattigan's 'Deep Blue Sea'. The lead part, Hester, required not only a lot of line-learning but also much study of the complex main character. A character driven to suicide by a failed marriage and subsequent failed liaison was hardly the most suitable subject to occupy someone trying to enjoy an idyllic honeymoon, but Harry was very supportive and our old occupation of line-hearing became part of the daily routine.

Essentially it was a fortnight spent leisurely in each other's company with no journalistic duties and no, apart from line-learning, theatre worries. Perhaps many marriages in those days were a gamble, not, on the whole, having had the opportunity that modern morality gives to couples to get to know each other by living together beforehand. However the sun shone, the food was amazing, and the wine flowed and, fortunately for us, our instincts in choosing each other seem to have been right.

When we returned to Swindon it was to a modest flat that Harry had found before leaving. It was the top floor of a two-up, two-down terraced house owned by a couple of spinster sisters who lived on the ground floor.

Relaxation over and, perhaps with the thought of returning to work, not to mention married responsibilities, resulted in Harry having a massive asthma attack that Sunday evening. With no 'puffer' to help him, he sat at the open window gasping for breath as I looked on, helpless and terrified, never having seen him so incapacitated before. Harry managed to reassure me, more by gesture than by speech, that all would eventually get back to normal. 'By the grace of God', as perhaps Harry said, and by visiting the doctor next morning to get a new inhaler, the asthma thereafter was kept at bay. We embarked on our new life. Harry had to leave for work first thing in the morning and not long after he got back in the evening I would be setting off for that night's performance. Of course our existence was much easier, for one thing we had our own bathroom and kitchen, but the actual 'ships that passed in the night' style of living was strange.

But no sooner had we become acclimatised to this routine than the financial writing was, once again, on the wall for the theatre. No further cuts in salary could be made and just after Christmas the Rep closed its doors. There was little possibility of finding more theatre work while still living in Swindon but fortunately I had established a link with BBC Radio having, among other work, read a great many short stories and books for them. So I applied to BBC Bristol, the nearest place producing Radio drama. I was lucky and started to get free-lance work there.

We frequently discussed our individual ambitions and Harry came up with words to describe himself, words which have often been quoted in articles about his life and were based on his decision not to write books because he felt he had 'nothing to say'. He found a phrase that was typical of that side of himself which not only liked to tease but was also slightly romantic. He wanted to be, not a failure but 'a gentle failure'. What is also on record is that I would have none of it and urged him to *write one of those detective stories you are so fond of, they don't say anything.* Stupid words which he would have had every right to throw back in my face, but it seems that when you are in love anything, even inexactitudes, can be forgiven. And I think posterity can be grateful that they were sufficient of a goad for Harry to return to the typewriter. In fact I am sure that there had not been much

49

need for persuasion from me, once started the floodgates were open.

Even in those early days Harry wrote fluently and fast but perhaps not with quite the dedication that later became his hallmark. He also, through contact with one of my radio producers in London, began the abridging of books to be serialised on Woman's Hour and Book at Bedtime. The money we earned between us was just about adequate for our fairly modest needs. The 1950s still had a residual austerity after the war years, some things were still rationed, and many of those who had grown up during the war did not expect to be surrounded by luxuries. It was still quite common to live, as we did, without a refrigerator let alone the dish washers or indeed the clothes washers and driers which are part of the newlyweds' necessities these days.

This was still before TV came into the home and our chief entertainment was the radio but just occasionally we would spend time in relatively near-by Oxford where we could go to the theatre. To do this a bit of extra cash was necessary and as we had both brought our collection of books with us there were duplicates which could be sold in one of Oxford's second-hand bookshops. We were both in our late twenties and were happy with this low key domestic life. But inevitably when I became pregnant in the early summer of 1954 we realised the one-bedroomed flat would be too small, and it was necessary to house-hunt in earnest.

Chapter 6

Wiltshire is full of charming villages and we hoped we could find somewhere affordable with perhaps a garden but the problem was that there was not much public transport connecting them to Swindon. We had no car and even if we had, neither of us had a driving licence. The solution that presented itself was the Bond Mini car, a low-slung, racy-looking, three wheeler which could turn around in its own length and consequently had no reverse gear thus enabling it to be classed as a motor-cycle. Added to this the test required for a motorcyclist to gain a licence could be taken on an auto-assisted pedal cycle. Harry was fairly expert on a pedal bicycle so he borrowed one with an auto-cycle attachment and set about mastering the added mechanical bits.

All of this took a while to organise and in the meantime we scanned the local press for advertised properties. Taking what buses were available we started to look for somewhere to rent. Harry booked his test and the very friendly examiner, who, as he lived opposite us, knew Harry by sight—was indeed on nodding terms with him—decided to pass him despite having to have more than one shot at the question about the order of the red, green and amber of the traffic lights.

Triumphantly we took delivery of the Bond and were able to drive out to view a remarkably cheap and large half of a top floor of an Old Vicarage in a very small village called Broad Town, not far from Wootton Bassett. As soon as we saw what was on offer, we knew that we wanted to live there and there was the added bonus of the landlords. Mrs. Taylor and her husband had sold their farm and invested their money in this large property. There were two

51

flats to let on the top floor and they themselves lived on the ground floor. Mr. Taylor, known to all and sundry as Charlie, did a daily milk round. Mrs. Taylor was never happier than when she had children around her and once they heard a bit of our history and that we were expecting our first child in the following March, we were welcomed as if we were family. The flat was furnished, so moving in was quite straightforward except for the fact that there was a bat spread-eagled in the wash-hand basin in the bathroom but once that had been coaxingly banished all was well.

To add to the sporting car image, the Bond had a soft top and Harry would set off for work in the mornings, hood down, wearing a hand-knitted green and yellow pom-pom hat and a pair of protective yellow tinted specs. Indeed, sometimes on the downward slopes of the larger roads he contrived to reach the car's maximum tearaway speed of 50mph. A feature of the Bond was its disproportionately long bonnet and some said that they thought Harry had no difficulty imagining he was on the circuit at Brands Hatch. He certainly had an imaginative approach to the art of driving. Once, coming back over the exposed Marlborough Downs, having had supper with friends, the fog came down and having removed the side windows for better visibility, I observed uneasily that I thought he must be on the wrong side of the road. Harry replied, 'Yes I know it's much easier to see the verge from this side.' While being undeniably true, the dangers, to most of us with a different sort of imagination, were fairly evident. On another occasion, after a slight memory lapse, about which was the accelerator and which the brake, the long bonnet ended up embedded in a reinforced concrete fence but fortunately both of us were unhurt. It is good to say that for the three years we owned the vehicle there were no major incidents.

Evenings were now regularly devoted to writing. In that article about writing an autobiography, Harry sketches out the plot of the first which he set in a repertory theatre and ends up telling us that no publisher was interested. Like so much else the manuscript has subsequently disappeared. Whatever its fate was he embarked on a second, and this one an agent liked very much but after fifteen publishers had rejected it, he sadly returned it. Both these books have totally vanished and Harry later said about them both that he was not surprised at their rejection because they were *'hopelessly formulaic'*. Presumably, although disappointed, he had become hardened to rejection, or perhaps the demands of journalism and being a new father left him no time to mourn. Simon John Ford (three initials in the best family tradition) was born on the 22nd of March 1955 and after a period of adjustment in sleep patterns, Harry began a third novel.

But this time it was far from formulaic. 'Death and the Visiting Fire-men' was based on his own experience when, shortly after joining the Swindon Evening Advertiser, they sent him as their representative to join other journalists carrying greetings to the Queen on the occasion of her coronation. They travelled in a coach and four and dressed in appropriate period costume. Although the new novel resembled that Coronation journey, it had nothing to do with Royalty but involved a publicity stunt using a coach and four. It was about a group of visiting fireman, representing 'The American Institution for the Investigation of Incendiarism Inc.', the delegation was being met off their ship by the coach and would continue the journey to the London convention by road. The style of the writing was bizarre. Many sentences lacked a verb altogether which gave the narrative an entirely intentional staccato urgency, but there was also an ulterior motive. Harry hoped that the originality of the style would arrest the attention of a publisher. However, with family life taking up more time, this book did not get written so quickly. It was still unfinished when the Westminster Press contract came to its end.

Harry was determined to get out of Swindon, indeed out of provincial journalism altogether, despite his older colleagues shaking their heads and telling him it would be wise to gain more experience in the provinces before applying for a job in Fleet Street. Fortunately they were wrong and he was proved right. In a surprisingly short time he got an interview with the Editor of The Daily Telegraph. They were advertising for a sub-editor. Harry maintains that he actually landed the job because the Editor was rather proud of his knowledge of French and, seeing the degree the applicant had obtained, conducted the interview in that language. In June 1956 it was good-bye Wiltshire.

Arriving in London accompanied by a wife and fifteen month old Simon, had its difficulties. We had nowhere to live. We were saved by the generosity of a friend who had quite a small flat in a mews off Church Street in Kensington. Clare Foden had been at drama school with me and subsequently had been the final Artistic Director of the ill-fated rep in Swindon and, an even closer tie, she was Simon's godmother. She endured this invasion of her privacy for three months while Harry settled into his new job and we searched for a flat that we could afford. This was, incidentally, the beginning of our association with Kensington Gardens, which was within walking distance of the flat, and which later were to become such a feature in our lives, ultimately resulting in a book of short stories, 'In Kensington Gardens Once'.

We found a large two bedroom, two living-room flat in between Cricklewood and Willesden overlooking Gladstone Park. The area in NW London was Gladstone country and, in accordance with his principals, it was a 'dry mile', not a pub in sight. There were not many amenities apart from the park itself and the nearest shop was the best part of a fifteen minute pram-push away. The flat was unfurnished and, with very little spare cash, the Bond Mini car had to be sold. In many ways it was a relief, it was no fun being inside such a miniature vehicle sandwiched between huge double-decker buses whose drivers tended to show their contempt by leaving as little room as possible. But, without a car, a lot of walking was done. Admittedly much of this was to achieve the three hours of fresh air and exercise, which was recommended by the popular baby specialist of the day, Dr Spock, whose book had become our bible.

With that money and the help of an enormous second-hand furniture repository called Simpsons at the top of Tottenham Court Road which sold extremely cheap beds, tables and chairs we were able to move in. The old 'sewing' table, which cost two shillings and sixpence, and at which Harry sat to continue writing *Death and the Visiting Fireman,* remained with us when we moved to our next and final house. And the old typewriter as well as its electronic successors rested on this 'desk' and was an essential to each and every subsequent book that Harry wrote up to the time of his death and still remains in the study.

It took a while to settle in with Harry having to undertake his least favourite activity, DIY. Electrics, from his BBC days, were fine, but carpentry and plumbing were anathema. He did both, fairly inexpertly, but with great gusto, and we both tackled the decorating. By the New Year a pattern began to establish itself. Mornings, for Harry, were spent at the old German typewriter and, by myself and Simon walking at toddler's pace in the park or pushing up to Cricklewood Broadway to do the household shopping. The mid-day meal was the main one of the day because Harry would not be there in the evening and shortly after that had been consumed the family would walk to Willesden Green underground station for Harry to catch the train to Fleet Street where his hours of work were 3 p.m. to midnight. Saturday was the only exception as there was no Daily Telegraph to get ready for the next day. Writing in the morning and sub-editing in the afternoon and evening was ideal because he was at his freshest when he was being creative but still had enough energy to tackle the cutting and editing of other people's work later in the day. The only creative side of sub-editing, headline writing, came naturally to him and his wit in their composition became quite a legend at the Telegraph and later at The Times, where he moved after about a year.

Although grateful to the Telegraph for enabling him to move to London, the political stance of the paper was a bit too far to the 'Right' for him and he was delighted to be moving to The Times, then thought to be more impartial, to say nothing of also being The Thunderer. This was long before the move to Wapping when, still in their ancient Fleet Street office, the subs ascended by the miniscule and ancient, rope-operated lift and sat round a magnificent table in a room heated by an open fire. The same table at which a then unpublished Graham Greene had sat when he too was a sub-editor. Indeed Harry is said to have occupied the same chair.

As well as the move, life was further interrupted by the birth of our second child, a daughter, Bryony Mary (only two initials like her mother not three like her father and brother) on September 30th 1957. The name Bryony had been decided long before her conception when, dining with friends in Broad Town, the naturalist Geoffrey Grigson strode into the room, exuding health and *joie de vivre*, and declared, *'The bryony in the hedges is wonderful this year.'* Glancing at each other Harry and I had a moment of telepathy, as we both thought, 'What a lovely name for a daughter.'

The first draft of the third novel was not finished until 1958 but a few months after that, when revisions had been made, it was sent off to the friendly agent. This time it did not spend months making the rounds of fifteen publishers, the agent replied with genuine sorrow that he did not think he could find anyone who would want to publish such an eccentric novel. This was, of course a crushing blow but at least it was put into a drawer and not consigned to the waste-paper basket. When some time had gone by and the numbness had worn off a little, Harry sensibly decided that it was absurd to give up on one agent's say-so. Having always admired the crime novels that appeared in the bright yellow dust-jackets of Victor Gollancz, he sent it directly to the great man himself. Common sense was vindicated. In Harry's own words. *'On the day of the Feast of the Epiphany, January 6th, 1959, as I was hurrying off to Mass (I was still then a practising Catholic), I stopped to tear open a letter that had dropped onto the doormat. It was from Victor Gollancz himself, he wanted to publish my book, if I would make a few changes.*

In any one lifetime there will be one or two golden-moments and this was one such for Harry. After all the trials and errors, after all his own uncertainties, he was going to be published and moreover by such a reputable publishing house. The changes asked for were not enormous and did not present any particular problems. The contract was signed. The advance was a minimal £100, not an unusual amount for a first-time author and par for course for a Gollancz publication. Then, out of the blue one morning, the telephone rang. The instrument hung on the wall by the front door and I remember, vividly, the incredulity of Harry's voice after he had realised who was on the other end, Victor himself, and even more strangely, because it was totally untrue, Harry remembers the strong middle-European voice. The only possible explanation must be that Harry had always assumed that anyone with a name like Gollancz would not be English and the extreme euphoria of the moment allowed his imagination to roam free. The purpose of the call was purely routine, to establish contact and arrange for Harry to meet the man who would be his editor. This turned out to be the delightful Hilary Rubinstein, Gollancz's nephew. A man with whom there was an instant rapport and who, over the next few years, made the process of transforming a manuscript into a printed page as pleasurable as possible.

It was not until September 1959 that publication day arrived. By then we had moved again, Willesden station was a thing of the past and on the way into work at the Times that afternoon, the family accompanied Harry to a nearby bookshop in Praed Street near Paddington station. We were rewarded by a truly astonishing sight. There was an eye-catching window display of *Death and the Visiting Firemen* by H.R.F. Keating. Between the title at the top of the yellow dust jacket and the author's name at the bottom Gollancz had written a longhand sentence, *'a detective story with one of the most enjoyably outré opening scenes you will have come across for years.'*

Chapter 7

The seeds of Harry's life were rooting themselves firmly in fertile ground. After what might be described as the fallow time at the BBC and the disagreeable uncertainties of the army, University had provided the conditions which allowed him to flourish, after which journalism had offered him a way to earn a living, enabling him to marry and start a family and finally he was a published author.

Earlier in 1959 we had taken a momentous decision. We moved away from rented accommodation and bought a house. As Harry said later it was the best investment he had ever made. His childhood friend Christopher O'Brien had recently moved into the down-at-heels Notting Hill area. This was 1959 just after the race riots and the house was in the racketeer Rachman's territory. Northumberland Place, a quiet terraced street built for his retainers in the 1860s by Prince Louis Bonaparte while living in exile in his palace just round the corner in Westbourne Grove, is architecturally charming. Although built some years into Victoria's reign with much of the neighbourhood consisting of terraces quite heavy in design, this one was more elegant, having been constructed from Georgian plans. However, in 1959, the surveyor employed to assess the property for a possible mortgage said that, although the house itself was sound, he would not recommend any financial assistance because it was primarily in a slum area.

In many ways this suited Harry who hated the idea of being in debt. Indeed this hatred extended to having an abhorrence of having an overdraft, something he managed to avoid throughout his life, although, as we were lucky enough to be offered small short-term, no-interest loans from relatives on both sides of the family we were briefly in debt, but this lasted only a year. To be able to live for evermore rent and mortgage free in a part of London where property values rose astronomically year on year was an amazing and lasting bonus. Expenses that come with a growing family are, obviously, a burden; Simon would soon be five and a school would have to be found. Both Harry and I had been educated at public boarding schools and both knew that was not what we wanted for our children. Ideally we wanted to use the State system but there was the added complication that Harry thought it right that as he and the children were Catholic they should attend Catholic schools (and as a non-Catholic I had had to agree that any off-spring would be brought up Catholic) but unfortunately the Catholic primary schools in the area seemed to be of the hell-fire, doom and gloom variety so we felt an alternative must be found.

The French came to the rescue. There was a Lycée in nearby South Kensington—in France that would have meant it was only a secondary school, but in London six years of primary education were also on offer. Although Catholic religious studies were not part of the curriculum which did not include the teaching of religion at all, this was available, outside school hours, from visiting Catholic priests. As we were not French, we had to pay fees, which undoubtedly put it under the heading of private education but with a little ingenuity we convinced ourselves that it was a state school even if not an English one. Having studied French at Trinity Harry thought being brought up with more than one cultural background would be a plus. To this was added the fact that from the age of four or five they would learn another language—only French was spoken in the class-room and small children are very receptive, so that a pupil would automatically be bi-lingual after a very short time—and, the final bonus, the fees at that time were only £19 a term.

We had moved into the new house in May 1959 with a lot of odd-jobbing and decorating to be done and this was, inevitably, a slow process. Harry was using all his spare time in the mornings writing a new book. It was his agent at A.D. Peters, Michael Sissons, who had suggested that the next book should be begun shortly after delivering the manuscript for the previous one and this was the pattern he adhered to from then on. The six months from March to September seemed to go by in a flash. Simon started at the Lycée and shortly after that it was publication day.

Following the euphoria of holding the actual book in his hands, came the amazing number of reviews. Every major national covered it as well as the provincial press and magazines. Fortunately Harry decided to keep all reviews, good or bad, and such individual letters as he received, in the flap of the dust jacket of the first edition. These show a sharp division of opinion, ranging from a letter from an outraged schoolmaster complaining that Maurice Richardson, of The Observer, must have had a brainstorm to have written, *'Don't miss this scintillating debut. Written in crackling telegraphic style, and, although highly artificial and contrived, grips as a really good set of false teeth should.'* The schoolmaster could not believe that anyone who wrote, *'He smiled. With charm. For the first time on the trip.',* was a writer worthy of attention. He was scandalised that sentences with no verbs, that flaunted all the rules of educated English, something his pupils might get to read, should be praised in a prestigious newspaper. An interesting footnote occurred some years later when Harry was asked for his permission, and indeed was paid a small sum, to allow an examination board to use an extract from this book as one of their questions. Pupils were asked to re-write the passage in correct English inserting missing words and punctuation.

But the good reviews were very good and written by names that mattered and the book was considered a success. *'This is written in a verbal shorthand. Mr Keating has done it very well but no-one else should ever dare to have a try. For four pages his style is unreadable, for the remaining 252 it is entirely compelling.'* That was David Holloway in The News Chronicle. Julian Symons the doyen critic of crime fiction in The Sunday Times starts off his review, *'A crime story original in manner is rare enough to be greeted with two and a half hurrahs'* and goes on, *'blends a quirky staccato humour of scene and epithet with a delicious formal irony in the handling of dialogue that is somehow reminiscent, at two or three removes certainly, of Miss Compton Burnett.'* And he concludes, *'Mr. Keating hasn't really written a detective story, but has made murder the occasion for a farce of verbal manners, with the talk of every character—visiting American, retired Major, succulent actress, sullen young actor—vividly caught. This must surely be the most enjoyable criminal oddity of the year.'*

With Victor Gollancz as his publisher, Harry had had no difficulty in acquiring that necessity for the majority of authors, an agent. AD Peters was among the most prestigious at the time and the contract was signed. Peter's young assistant, Michael Sissons, who in time became managing director of the firm that is now Peters, Fraser and Dunlop (PFD), remained his agent for fifty-two years.

With the acceptance of this first book, Harry began to realise that he did, in fact 'have something to say', and when Harry came to write his autobiographical article he says of 1959, *'...it came to me that I could do more as a writer than merely produce detective stories in the mode of those I had read as a boy, lapping up from my mother's example the happy simplicities of Gladys Mitchell, E.R. Punshon, Dorothy Sayers (as I then believed, only later realising how much more she did), E.C.R. Lorac, Margery Allingham, names forgotten and names that have survived.'* He recalls, a few years later, that when he was interviewing Margery Allingham for an article he was writing for a literary magazine, she told him what the writer of the Sexton Blake books. G.R.M. Hearne, had said to her, *'They never mind you putting all you've got into this sort of stuff. They never pay you any more for it, but they don't stop you.'* Harry pithily says, *'It went deep.'* Happily he drew on this profundity to find for himself a philosophical theme for all of his subsequent books even if he kept these themes as a background, not letting them hinder the telling of the story.

At this stage he was re-reading Graham Greene and in the process Greene was elevated to the status of, *'beau idéal'*. Harry explains that, *'This was not for the religious content of his books, but for his relentlessness in going for the truth, in writing, as he says in 'Ways of Escape', truthfully enough for the truth to be plain.'* Long before this re-appraisal he had copied into his writing notebook a quote from Greene's 'A Burnt-out Case', *a writer doesn't write for his readers, does he? Yet he has to take elementary precautions all the same to keep them comfortable.'* Harry himself, in print, or when lecturing about writing crime fiction went even further insisting that the prime necessity was to engage, to entertain the reader, and that, however important the underlying theme, if the narrative was not lively enough to carry the story forwards, the author would lose the reader.

Another quote from the autobiographical article tells us that Simenon too served as a role model, '*an exemplar of what it is possible to do in crime fiction. I have never succeeded in achieving his splendid simplicity of style, and, indeed, I think with my innate tendency to have reservations about almost any plain statement (call it tolerance or inhibiting conscience, as you will) a sentence structure not without parentheses is my way. But Simenon's search for the truth of people, that, yes, he makes me aspire to.*'

And it was the importance of truth which was to be the centrepiece of the next book. He had been brought up to believe that it was a sin to tell a lie but he recalls an incident from his childhood when a lie was told, and told by his father. Harry and an uncle had been passengers in the car when his father, distracted while chatting to them, had shot a red light and, although stopped by a policeman, apparently got away with it. What followed remained indelibly impressed on the young Harry's mind. Returning home, the traditional English tea was laid out under the big cherry tree on the lawn, naturally with childhood's perpetual summer sun shining, and there the incident was told to his mother. It was told, however, in a manner that in no way resembled the truth. In this version he had not been distracted by chatter but had daringly shot the light in order to avoid some imaginary collision. '*A lie had been told. Uttered by God. Or, at least by my God. My book sprang directly from that sun-soaked teatime. Its theme of lies and lying, an obsession ever since that day, arrived at, I cast about for a subject, a background to the murder puzzle that would constitute my story and let me put forth attitudes to the telling of lies, as many as I could find. Soon I hit on that subject. At that time Zen Buddhism was all the intellectual rage, and I saw I could seize on it to give me a nice topical touch. I read a few 'First Steps' books and saw that Zen with its paradoxes, such as getting a bird out of a bottle simply by saying, 'There it's out', led me beautifully into lies and lying, truth and deception.*'

Using what had become a favourite setting for detective stories, the country house weekend, he turned it on its head by making the gathering not an upper class jolly but a week-long adult course in Zen-Buddhism. He was able, through research, to gain a working knowledge of the basic principles of Zen philosophy. The tutor on the course, Mr. Utamaro, a Zen master, is the voice which constantly reminds the reader of the contradictions that underlie the teaching. The assorted students are immediately asked a typical Zen question, *'What is the sound of one hand clapping?'* None of them is able to find an answer and it hangs hovering over them until later a murder has been committed and more pressing questions have to be answered. When the police arrive, the Superintendent in charge warns Mr. Utamaro that he may well call upon him for co-operation, to which the Zen master replies, *'You may call but shall I answer?'* When reminded of his duty as a citizen, the reply comes back, *'But you see, Superintendent, I have trained my mind to the point where such things as the idea of justice, the notion of a citizen's duty, the concept of illegality, all mean nothing to me.'* The policeman is adamant and threatens to take action if information is withheld and this time the answer is even more provocative, *'That is tomorrow and tomorrow the murder may not have been committed.'*

But, as always, Harry knows that to keep the reader engaged the mysticism must not be overdone, it must be laced with reality. While wrestling with birds emerging from bottles and one hand producing the sound of clapping, his characters, the seven people on the course, reveal themselves. All are recognisably fellow human beings even if most have quirks and foibles not often encountered in the daily round. They reveal themselves through the dialogue, there is little narrative description. Any narrative necessary is cut to the minimum by using a couple of 'au pairs'. These delightful young German girls, hoping to perfect their English while doing the domestic chores, act as a running commentary on the action.

Receiving the manuscript towards the end of December, Gollancz wrote to say that Harry had quite made his Christmas which was apparently a difficult thing to do and that he found it, *'the freshest thing of its kind I've read for years.'* The publisher was etching his way into Harry's heart. On balance it was very well received in this country but neither of these first two books sold to America. For an author to make any sort of a living this was essential. Not only was the USA an infinitely bigger potential market for crime fiction but its citizens were enormous fans of the genre. Selling rights was usually the job of the agent and as AD Peters had an understanding with an agency over there it is strange that at this time this did not happen.

When the book was published in July 1960 the loans for the house purchase had been paid off and by careful management the income from journalism and books was adequate to allow for modest living. In addition to the weekly job at the Times Harry was working as a sub-editor on the Observer each Saturday night and he was teaching journalism two mornings a week at the Regents Street Polytechnic. Even using part of Saturday and Sunday in addition to the three free week-day mornings there were hardly sufficient hours for writing if he wanted to make sure he produced a book a year. Another momentous decision was about to be taken. We had definitely made up our minds that bringing up a family was to be my priority and my acting career had been put on hold but even with the loss of income this meant, we still felt that we could manage if Harry left The Times. He gave in his notice and apart from the Saturday subbing and the two mornings spent teaching, he became a full-time writer.

The timing was not perhaps ideal. What was thought to be a biological blip of some sort turned out to be a third pregnancy and on top of that Harry got the sack from the Observer. No reason was ever given but he remembers having a drink with his immediate boss in a very noisy pub where it was almost impossible to hear what was being said with the result that his side of the conversation was confined almost entirely to a random and optimistic 'yes' or an equally random and pessimistic 'no'. He reckons that his guessed responses must have been wrong and he had in consequence given offence in some way, anyway he was out. But the die was cast and after all it would give him all of Saturday free.

By this time book number three was already on the stocks, had indeed been planned and largely written before reaction to the second was known so it must have been quite a relief to read the reviews Zen had produced. Not everyone was, as yet, a convert, but enough people continued to encourage with highbrow comments like, *'His writing is brilliant and his use of the Joycean cathacetic and catalogue technique is a new departure in thrillers',* that from the Irish Press. *'This is one of those books where a fairly good plot is made into a first-class book by the brilliant writing and humane understanding of the human beings who act it out',* that extract and the following piece come from a magazine interview/review, *'...he bent and transformed the usual grammatical rules of sentence structure into a method of self-expression that can only be called Impressionist.'* The Illustrated London News ventured, *'If Mr. Keating knows his stuff about this fashionable form of mysticism—and I dare swear he does—the result is quite brilliant. It is, in any case, excruciatingly funny.'* In The Observer, Maurice Richardson, perhaps a mite grudgingly, allowed himself, *'Might be by a bright young quinquagenarian don out of Agatha Christie which is not such a bad pedigree.'* With encouragement from the established literary world for his quirkiness, Harry would have been pleased that he had already chosen the next arresting background and indeed written the next book, set around the vicious world of croquet.

Once again the location was a variation on the country house. This time the mansion was a private school but in holiday time. The assembled company are known to each other because they meet annually for their croquet tournament but it does not mean they love each other, in fact they are almost united in their dislike of their host, the head-master. This was possibly the only occasion when Harry was on the borderline of using too much of the expert knowledge he gleaned from a family friend, Maurice Reckett, who was a king-pin in croquet circles. But he firmly resisted the temptation to make the book a croquet manual and used the croquet foibles of the various characters to ratchet up the tension of the story.

There can be no doubt from the reviews of this third book, with a title from croquet parlance, *A Rush on the Ultimate,* that Harry was gaining a firm foothold in the hierarchical tree of crime writing. There were constant references in the reviews to the brilliance of his writing with Maurice Richardson saying in the Observer. *'the dialogue crackles all the way'.,* and the Scotsman commenting, *'Mr. Keating will go far. Out of a conventional plot he has made a highly original and entertaining novel, especially in the matter of dialogue.'* But there began to be a divergence of opinion about the style of book Harry was writing: was it a comedy thriller or was it a whodunit? Apparently this was important to some reviewers, if the former then he was allowed to get away with being *'vastly entertaining, with wit and humour.',* but if the latter, *'he should have paid more attention to plot.'*

As Harry had set out to cut through the barriers imposed by categorisation it is unlikely that he cared too much which label was attached to him, but he always described himself as a crime novelist which neatly covered all eventualities. But so long as Julian Symons in the Sunday Times, continued boosting his reputation, *'...as the most eccentric crime writer in the business.',* with the added personal comment, *'It's all really criminally indefensible—I enjoyed it.'.* Harry felt justified in writing more of the same.

But before that book was published Piers William Hervey was born. He made his entrance into the world not around the 9th of December as expected but a fortnight later on December 23rd, 1960, which caused complications. The Dutch au pair who should have been there to help with the domestic chores while I was out of action—all the Keating children were born at home, not in hospital—had never been a success, and after, for the umpteenth time refusing to undertake some simple task, had been given the push. So close to Christmas it had not been found easy to make other arrangements and Harry was left to cope with five-year old Simon, three-year old Bryony and all the Christmas jollities, including cooking the traditional dinner. There were no disasters and mother and baby flourished after an earlier, middle of the night panic. Contractions began with ferocity at 2 a.m. but on the phone the midwife said *'don't worry it will be hours yet'.* After an hour and a half she had still not arrived and Harry decided to call the GP—this was 1960 and we had an exceptional GP in Dr Stuart Carne who always visited when summoned—and he arrived within a quarter of an hour. Piers made his appearance, but with the umbilical cord wound round his neck, some ten minutes later. Thanks to Harry's instinctive reaction and the GP's expertise all went smoothly. As a fellow sub from The Times said, *'Everything runs so smoothly when Harry's in charge and there's a crisis.'* Harry always regretted that for different reasons he was never able to be totally in attendance for the actual birth—this time because there had to be someone outside the bedroom in case the other two children were woken by the undue activity.

Things got back to normal in the New Year especially when the statuesque, middle-aged Spanish help arrived. Rafaela spoke virtually no English so the Keatings developed rudimentary Spanish and a creative skill in communicating through drawing an object that was pertinent to the job that required doing. Peace and quiet was restored and Harry got back to the fourth book which Gollancz, on the dust jacket, was still calling a thriller—this time with some justification. The country house was banished; Ireland, with Trinity College at its centre, replaced it. Although there was underlying humour, the word 'comedy' no longer prefaced the word thriller. In its place we are told in the blurb to expect, 'pursuits and escapes, or pursuits and captures, and the brainwashing....' Gollancz, in a press release confesses to being a Keating fan which is probably par for course when a publisher is speaking of one of their own authors but there is more than that—a genuine warmth—in the question he asks himself, *'But can he really go on and on like this, doing something, every time, absolutely new? The answer is that he can....*

But his agent was getting more and more unhappy. Michael Sissons was appalled that the advance remained, to his mind, ridiculously low. However Harry was not to be moved, Victor Gollancz had made him into a published author and moreover he plainly loved the books. A loyalty was demanded. Then there was Hilary Rubinstein who had continued to be a delight to work with during the editing process. 'The Dog It Was That Died' remained with Gollancz. Although the title was very apposite it was not Harry's. He had offered an equally apposite one, 'A Worm for His Brain', reflecting the major part brainwashing played in the story. Gollancz thought it repulsive, that it would be a turn-off for some readers and consequently would not sell, so Harry bowed to the inevitable. The Oliver Goldsmith poem, which was already quoted in full at the front of the book, and from which Gollancz's title was taken, contains these two couplets:

```
'The dog, to gain some private ends.
Went mad and bit the man.'

'The man recovered of the bite,
The dog it was that died.
```

There is a dog in the book who boasts the splendid name of Cuchulain and is as important as any of the human characters, which is strange because Harry himself never owned a dog. But the animal is most affectionately treated and did nothing as heinous as biting his owner. Indeed he dies nobly in place of his master. But the title was appropriate enough and after all Harry had originally prefaced the book with the poem.

But far more important than the question of small advances in Harry's mind was the lack of a sale to America. Something had to be done. He put the problem on the back burner and addressed himself to what he would write next, and this was mid-way written at the time the almost universally ecstatic reviews for 'The Dog It Was That Died' came out. The book had turned out not to be more of the same, but a book with rather more underlying seriousness. But still no offer from the USA. Julian Symons in The Sunday Times said, *'Our native surrealist crime writer is in danger of descending into logic...but Mr. Keating remains a highly original writer.'* While the Yorkshire Post found it, *'Exuberant and witty, with appropriately macabre undertones.'*

It pleased Harry to be able to write about Dublin, but Trinity was transformed from his joyous undergraduate heaven into a murky place where mistrust festered. Moreover one of the people working in the sacred portals was linked to an extremely dubious, government-backed intelligence organisation which worked out of Leeds. The boss of this institution is visiting Dublin and is a grotesque, lubbery, character whose bulbous fingers are described as *chipolatas*, revolting enough to match a man who has abduction and brain-washing on his mind. One reviewer suggested that the old, overweight, sinister Hollywood actor, Sydney Greenstreet, would be excellent casting for the part. Another was reminded of the rotund GK Chesterton. As a coincidence the Daily Herald thought that the book itself was reminiscent of Chesterton's masterpiece 'The Man who was Thursday'.

Music to Harry's ears being compared with one of his early idols. The crime writer, Nicholas Blake, the pseudonym of the famous poet Cecil Day Lewis, declared he had written a 'broth of a book.'

Perhaps to have given Gollancz four sparkling books was all that could be allowed because 'succés d'estime' was not enough. Profitability, for a full-time writer, was also essential. Harry regretfully agreed that the next title should be offered elsewhere.

The new publisher chosen was William Collins and Harry would become one of the authors in their Crime Club series whose editor was Lord Hardinge of Penshurst. It should be incontrovertibly stated that George Hardinge was a pearl among editors, intelligent, inspiring, thoughtful and caring. Harry knew at once that if he had to leave old friends behind his new mentor was going to be an admirable replacement. That first novel with them, which they made a Crime Club Choice, was to prove more of an interlude than anything else because of what was to follow it.

Chapter 8

'**D**eath of a Fat God' was probably the most conventional of the books he had written so far. It is set in a provincial Opera House with as temperamental a group of opera folk as can be imagined. Harry was plainly enjoying himself with an appropriately larger-than-life International cast. The Irish Independent said Collins *'had made a good choice. The author not only has a first-class knowledge of the opera and its staging; he has an excellent sense of humour and the gift of imparting his information about back-stage activities, the feuds and quarrels of the temperamental stars.* It is worth noting that the 'first-class knowledge of the opera' was only partly true. Harry never claimed even to have a toe in the musical world, although he loved attending concerts and opera, but as with all the backgrounds he used, his research was profound, enabling him to sound like an expert.

He also invented a new sort of detective, a charlady called Mrs. Craggs who is sharply observant and has an acerbic tongue. Antonia Sandford in The Spectator sees her *'in her intransigent square hat as a match for every high-falutin' actor. Her dry comments make this tragedy hilarious. Keating has a marvellous ear for conversation and uses it with skill to illustrate character through dialogue.'* This ability, to let characters reveal themselves through what they say, was apparent in all his novels and he seldom indulged in more than the briefest physical description if he could avoid it.

It may have seemed more frivolous than before but there was, as usual, an underlying serious theme. This time it is an exploration of pride. Of course this is admirably demonstrated in the ego-consumed behaviour of more than one of the characters but the point is not laboured and although one of the seven deadly sins it does not seem to have weighed very heavily with him. But perhaps this lack of emphasis caused some of the more highbrow reviewers to give less space to the book than previously, dismissing it as a romp, although they did concede it was a good romp. Two reviews interestingly refer in a similar fashion to Mrs. Craggs and her lugubrious fellow char, Mrs. Milhorne; one of the reviewers sees them as, *a kind of clown's chorus*, and the other as *a rather unimpressed Greek chorus.* Mrs. Craggs remained a diversion and she never became the central character of another novel, although there are many short stories about her some of which in 1983 he collected into the book, *Mrs. Craggs, Crimes Cleaned Up.* Mainstream publishers were, indeed still are, very wary of doing short story collections and it was due to the enthusiasm of a young couple who ran a small publishing house, Buchan and Enright, that the lady had a further life between hard covers. Earlier she was even the central character in a series of short stories specially commissioned to kick off an experiment. The Radio 4 mid-morning story moved to be part of the disc jockey, Jack de Manio's programme on Radio 2.

The original morning slot had been fifteen minutes long but this was now cut down to just ten minutes of early afternoon air time. It was quite a challenge, to tell an interesting story in so few words, but as usual Harry rose to the occasion and produced 'The Five Senses of Mrs. Craggs'. Each story had her using one of the senses, seeing, smelling, hearing, touching and taste in turn. The producer, Barbara Crowther, was someone I had often worked for so I got the job of reading them. One of the ideas behind moving the short story readings from Radio 4 to a DJ's slot on Radio 2 was to create a cosy atmosphere with the reader apparently sharing the studio with Jack and reading the story as much for him as for the listening public. Each day when the story drew to a close he would say much the same thing in his warmest, most appreciative manner, *'That was lovely, Sheila, I'll look forward to tomorrow',* while, in fact, the story had been pre-recorded in another studio and Jack probably never even heard it as he would slip out for a quick break leaving the story to be transmitted by the engineer. A very innocent deception and all part of the mystique every DJ creates but the effusive flattery never sat easy with Harry and me as we listened at home.

But on the whole the time taken to write five very short stories was time well spent because Harry's name was being put before a different public, all of whom could be potential readers of the H.R.F.K. books. Meanwhile reviewers of the opera book had continued to do their bit. James Dillon White had this to say about it in Trade News: *'This I can thoroughly recommend as a witty exposé of the feuds and jealousies of a travelling company of opera singers. Mr. Keating writes with a sardonic tongue-in-cheek assurance which I find irresistible. When I tell you that there is also an excellent plot you will see that this one should be a winner.'* Actually the company was not a touring one but was assembled for a one-off season, but that is a minor point, and even if his assessment was a bit kinder to the book than it deserved, Harry had very plainly enjoyed writing it. But the high-brows were probably correct, it was in the 'romp' category. Perhaps this was understandable because all through the planning and the writing Harry was also concentrating on the burning question of how he was to generate enough income from writing full time. He had to find a way of getting published in America.

Looking back, I realise that I was not more than peripherally aware of how much time Harry must have spent worrying about this. On the whole he preferred to work things out for himself. Of course we talked about his having to change publishers and to some extent we discussed money matters and what a difference it would make if America bought the books but the hours from 9 a.m. to 6 p.m. that he spent in the study were his affair. This had not always been so. At the very beginning he would discuss with me which of the many ideas jotted down in his notebook he should choose as the subject for the next novel, but this stage did not last long. Quite soon he was ready to choose for himself. Also at the beginning I was allowed to read what he had written each day. This gradually changed to seeing the work chapter by chapter, until before too long I would not see anything until he had completed the first draft. As his confidence grew he had no need for any stage-by-stage opinion other than his own and this applied even more in his search for the magic formula that would capture the American interest.

When I recently asked the children if, when they were small, they ever found it strange that their father wrote books for a living instead of leaving the house to go to work each morning or indeed if they ever wondered what he was writing, their reaction was unanimous—total acceptance and no curiosity. As they grew up they got used to books being part of the furniture and if they existed then someone had to write them, so why not their father. Three of them also respected the sanctity of the study, only the youngest, Hugo, daring to disturb Harry if he felt the need to talk to him. For whatever reason this did not provoke anger and even his brothers and sister accepted the fact that Hugo could get away with behaviour that would not be tolerated in them. I do not think it occurred to Harry that he treated any of them differently but there can be little doubt that Hugo's ability to ignore convention and stamp out his own path in life gained Harry's admiration. When Hugo spoke at Harry's funeral he acknowledged that he had always felt that if he needed him, his father would always be there. But for the rest of us the study was Harry's kingdom where he reigned in solitary supremacy.

When writing or talking about this time later he said that word had got back to him that, for America, the bizarre settings for which he was becoming known in this country were the very thing that America found too British and he began to wonder if he should go outside Britain. But what other part of the world would necessarily appeal to an American? Letting his mind drift around the globe, he paused at India. It had been in the news quite a lot lately what with the Beatles seeking out mystic Ashrams, to say nothing of the rapture to be found in smoking pot, all part of the swinging 60s, and there was Louis Malle who was in bad odour with the Indian government for his candid portrayal of the sub-continent in his documentary films, and this had been much publicised the world over. Then there were the historical connections between America and India, particularly the missionaries who had gone there in their thousands to convert the Indians to Christianity. Surely there would be descendants who cherished family links and would enjoy reading about the country that had meant so much to their forebears. All in all India was becoming a distinct possibility. The fact that his own knowledge of the country was limited to being able to count up to five in Hindi, a skill taught him by his cousin Rob Fitzherbert when they were boys, was not a deterrent, he had become used to writing about little known subjects and mugging them up for each new book.

But, of course, it was a mammoth task. First of all, where in India? For his preliminary research he had started to read Indian newspapers, then he had found a second-hand bookshop which had a good stock of Indian books written in English, there were, as well, Indian Art films which would be shown at places like the Nehru centre in London's Belgravia. He also tracked down cinemas where he could see products of India's unique film industry made in flourishing Bollywood. He was delighted to meet anyone Indian and soon made friends with a journalist, Victor Anant, and his Pakistani wife, Zuleikha, with whom the family spent many happy hours, especially enjoying Zu's wonderful and subtle curries, but also in the early days providing an opportunity to talk about India and its diverse regions and cities but particularly about Bombay, a city Victor knew well. As the country's centre of commerce it was also notorious for its great divide of rich and poor, a place teeming with possibilities for crime. But where on earth did that city lie in the Indian sub-continent? Such was his ignorance that he actually had to get out the world atlas to find out. Having orientated himself, he started to assess its suitability in more detail.

On many occasions later, when he was giving talks on crime writing, he would give the advice 'write about what you know', which might seem strange advice for him to give except that by the time he started writing a book he did 'know' his subject from meticulous research. But on the face of it he certainly had no first-hand knowledge when he decided to make India the next off-beat setting for a book. But then he had also included in his autobiographical article that he was at his best when writing *at a distance* and although that mainly meant emotionally, it could also embrace physical distancing. He certainly never entertained the idea of visiting India, for one thing he did not have the money to get there, but no-one was better at exploring unknown territory through research than he was, enabling him to write about it so that readers were convinced he was an expert, as had happened with the opera in 'Death of a Fat God', so surely an unvisited country should not be impossible.

Another reason for choosing India had been that *'he had it in mind to write a crime story that would be something of a commentary on the problem of perfectionism, and one of the few notions I had about India was that things were apt to be rather imperfect.'* That is an extract for something Harry wrote much later in the introduction to his 1989 book, a collection of short stories, 'Inspector Ghote His Life and Crimes', and he went on, *'Then, out of nowhere, into my head came this man. Or some parts of him. A faintly worried face. Certainly a pair of bony shoulders. A certain naivety, which should enable him to ask questions about the everyday life around him to which my potential readers might want answers. And he also brought with him a name: 'Inspector Ghosh'. Oh, gosh, he would keep saying, wide-eyed.'*

Whether he was to be called Ghosh or not, the naivety was an essential part of the character's make-up, a quality or a fault, depending on how people react, which Harry himself shared to some extent. However it was probably just as well that the Inspector was not ultimately called Ghosh allowing him to indulge in what would surely have been an intensely irritating repetition of the similar-sounding word. The change of name was entirely due to one of those coincidences that sometimes occur. A writer friend, Stanley Price, was giving a party at which a fellow guest was someone who had just come back from working in Bombay. Harry was telling him about what he hoped to do and this man, Wally Olins, was enthusiastic but pointed out that if the book was to be set in Bombay the policeman should not have the Bengali name of Ghosh. The regions were hundreds of miles apart, as far apart as France from Russia—Harry later said, *'It would be like calling a French Inspector Ivan Ivanovitch.'* But Wallie suggested the similar but more appropriate Maharashtrian name of Ghote. Harry says in the same introduction, *'So, from birth, we had advanced to christening or, more correctly, to the naam-karana, the name-giving ceremony.*

But as well as endeavouring to write a book that would get him an American publisher, he had to get it finished in time for it to be published by Collins in 1964, a book a year was his necessary financial target. Fascinating as it was proving to be, research could not go on forever. He started to write. On schedule, 'The Perfect Murder' was published that year, the title being, among other things, a reflection of the acknowledged theme, perfectionism. There was, however, no thought of this Indian venture being more than just the sixth in a series of books with odd-ball settings. But all this changed when it won the Golden Dagger, the award presented annually by the CWA, the Crime Writers' Association, for the best book of the year. In those days the panel who judged the entries was drawn from those who reviewed crime fiction, so Harry probably benefitted from the esteem generated by the earlier books.

Harry heard the good news when he was languishing in bed with influenza. The front doorbell rang and I took delivery of a telegram, the quick means of communication in those days, sent by George Hardinge. A miraculous and immediate cure came about the moment the envelope was opened and he heard about the award which may not have been as prestigious as a Nobel Prize but it was to change the course of Harry's life. After this piece of good news there followed probably the best news of all: America was conquered. E.P. Dutton bought and published it a year later in February 1965, reprinting in April of the same year. The author photograph—a very young-looking clean-shaven 38 year old—on the back jacket, was by none other than Stanley Price, obviously moonlighting from the day job. Moreover Dutton was able to include in the list of quotes from reviewers one from the prestigious and foremost American crime book reviewer, Anthony Boucher, 'A beautifully plotted mystery... Please E.P. Dutton, more Keating.' Boucher actually named it his book of the year. There was no question that what Harry had thought would be a one-off had to become a series. There were in the end twenty-five Ghote titles appearing over forty-five years, the last of which was published in 2009.

The reviews were, as usual, good but only The Sun predicted the future, ending with the words 'There'll be more of Ghote.' but perhaps one of the most appreciative came from fellow crime writer, Anthony Price, in The Oxford Mail. The piece started by saying that he found Keating '...one of the most original whodunit writers at work today. This time he almost outdoes himself with his enchanting Indian police inspector who is desperately trying to solve a murder which isn't a murder and a theft which isn't a theft, with an earnest

Swede from UNESCO hanging round his neck like a great blond albatross. At first the story goes agonisingly slowly, but the agony (craftily designed?) gives place to fascination as the eccentric atmosphere grows. I don't know whether the Keating India exists, but I don't care: the book is a delight.'

A quote from Harry himself in his 1989 autobiography article is not only typical of him but also undeniably true. *'Yet looking back now, I see that, with the simple luck which the novelist V.S. Naipaul once said was what a writer needed most, I had found a hero through whom and in whom I could express my every thought, or most of them, and who is someone also, perhaps by virtue of springing from my innermost self, who is a recognisable, three-dimensional, multi-faceted human being.'* This absolutely bore out his theory of being at his best when writing at a distance. He had created a character who lived his life in a totally different environment and was outwardly his antithesis but who, internally, thought his own thoughts and felt his own feelings, freeing him, Harry Keating, to explore aspects of himself in a way that he would have found impossible if he had been writing in the first person.

Of course before it was actually published and had won its awards, there was the first draft of the following year's book waiting to be revised and sent off to George Hardinge. It has a title which is probably as typical of Harry's 'parenthetical', quirky mind as any he ever dreamed up: 'Is Skin Deep, Is Fatal.' The subject is a beauty contest. It is possible that he had had to cover one of these when he was a journalist in Swindon but it is far more likely that a small news story had caught his eye at some point and he had stored it in one of the many notebooks as a fun subject for exploitation at another time.

It is tempting to deduce that even if it had not been the intention to make Ghote into a series, the writing of 'The Perfect Murder' and the research that it had entailed, was still very much with him, even if temporarily buried, and that there was a desire to know more of India, to explore, in detail, this exciting culture so very different from his own. It certainly seems that something was exercising a pull on his subconscious, that he was not as deeply immersed in the world of beauty queens as he might have been, because, as some of the reviews suggest, there is not the same depth or even the same expertise in plotting as in the previous books. Some, like the Glasgow Herald, would have liked Superintendent Ironside, the detective assigned to the beauty contest murder, to become a series detective but that was never on the cards because a great point is made of his being on the verge of retirement. Anyway Harry, until Ghote, had not wanted to have a series detective but, of course, Ironside was created before Ghote appeared. There were, probably, more reviews than ever before, but some, like The Cork Examiner, showed clearly from the previous titles they quoted, that they confined their reviews to the books that emanated from specific publishers. 'A worthy successor to 'Death of a Fat God' and 'The Perfect Murder'.—my guess is that this was written by a 'Collins' man with no time for any of the titles that appeared between the yellow covers of Gollancz. Surprisingly few, however, made any comparison with The Perfect Murder although some did acknowledge its existence. But only The Irish Times suggested that the prize winner was the better book.

But the literary world outside crime fiction had already begun to notice the existence of H.R.F. Keating. In the early 1960s came the Pilkington report which looked into the creation of a second BBC TV channel. Those in charge of putting together a package of what were expected to be more intellectual programmes, began a search for young writers who might be of use to them. They asked publishers to suggest some names. Gollancz suggested Harry. A jolly gathering was planned by Huw Wheldon, one of those setting up the programme and Harry was among those invited. There he was to meet other up-and-coming writers, Tom Stoppard, Austin Mitchell, Julian Mitchell and Stanley Price, at whose party he subsequently met the just-returned India buff Wally Olins. Stanley and Harry had much the same reaction to the rather pompous BBC gathering but spent an agreeable time getting to know each other. The friendship lasted a lifetime.

Moreover some work did come his way when Huw Wheldon started making programmes. That great winged hope of British and French aviation, Concorde, was about to take to the air, and BBC 2 made a documentary about how it had arrived at this point. Harry was recruited onto the team to write the narration which Michael Flanders would be speaking. This was a fine example of his ability to find words for any subject flung at him. At the outset he knew nothing about the construction of aircraft and very little about the significance of ultrasonic flight, but a few hours of studying the briefing papers were quite enough to give him the facts and it was his job to find words—which he did—that would arrest the viewer's attention when spoken by the charismatic Flanders.

This same ability to cope with any writing assignment that might be flung at him was the reason why, when the Radio Times wanted to publish articles that would provide background information about forthcoming programmes, they commissioned Harry. The then editor of the magazine obviously liked the way Harry wrote and in consequence he found himself—not a racing man—sent to Ireland to interview the racehorse, Red Rum. Which seemingly impossible task he managed by a lot of convivial chat in the pub with all those concerned in the training, grooming and general well-being of the horse.

There were other articles of a more serious nature; such as the one investigating the plight of miners left, at the generally premature end of their lives, in a miserable state of health due to contracting pneumokoniosis through inhalation of mineral dust when down the pits. Visiting Wales to interview these men was extremely harrowing but it is to be hoped the ensuing article helped in the campaign to get compensation for these tragic victims.

Just as serious was another problem being investigated: adult illiteracy. Probably not something that was widely known about in the 1960s and talking to those who had to find ways round this lack of a skill most of us take for granted, Harry was in for a lot of surprises. The ingenuity of the solutions found by those who could not read ranged from the obvious, 'I've left my specs at home could you read it to me', to the slightly more subtle plea for help, 'could you explain what is written here?' It also struck him forcibly how often the problem was completely hidden from other people. Many of the illiterates were intelligent human beings who had been let down by their schooling and one of the objects of the programme was to urge an overhaul of how literacy was approached in primary schools and to make every effort to ensure that any child of normal intelligence was wholeheartedly encouraged to read.

A writer spending most of his time shut away in a world of his own can become very distanced from reality and there is no doubt that Harry welcomed these contacts which, obliquely, kept his own natural humanity alive and, in turn, informed how he wrote about the characters he created. On a lower level, the Radio Times paid its writers very well and extra cash was a constant necessity.

By 1962 Bryony was five and just before her birthday, in September, she joined seven year old Simon at the Lycée where he was rapidly becoming bi-lingual. One thing that became apparent to us quite early on was that it was one thing to talk French at school, but it was apparently unthinkable for an English child to speak to his English parents at home in anything other than his native tongue. This was not of major concern, but it did tend to erect a barrier between life in school and life at home, and it was something that had not been envisaged when choosing the Lycèe. Apart from this hiccup we did not find too many faults with it as a school and although the fees had increased from the exceedingly low £19 to around the £30 mark and this was now to be multiplied by two it was still good value for money.

And then, at the end of that memorable year, 1964, Harry again had to cook the Christmas dinner. Our fourth child, Hugo Oliver Fitzstephen, arrived a month early, most inconveniently disrupting plans for celebrating the fourth birthday, on December 23rd of his older brother Piers. He was a noisy baby and one way and another the house did not immediately settle back into the calm that was necessary for the nine to five writing routine. Although a family of four was what we had all along planned, a slightly different pattern had been envisaged: two followed by a largish gap and then another two, but things don't always go according to plan.

Another plan that went wrong concerned my career. A chance meeting with an old school friend, Ruth Ferdinando who was by now married to BBC producer Cedric Messina, resulted in Harry and myself being invited to supper which in turn resulted in my being offered a small part in the popular series *Dr Finlay's Casebook*, one of Cedric's programmes. This was a wonderful opportunity for me because TV had hardly existed when I had stopped acting in the 1950s and I needed to learn a whole new technique. It was a fascinating experience and led me to seek interviews with TV directors after which I landed rather a good part in another very popular series, *Z Cars*. It seemed as if my career was being re-started rather sooner than we had expected. But it was not to be.

Z Cars was one of the last programmes still being broadcast 'live' which for someone of my limited experience added to my nervousness. But I did not expect that I would feel quite so sick on the day we were due to go on air with the episode. It was when I continued to feel ill after it was all over that I began to suspect a different cause. The sickness went on for eight months—Hugo being a month premature—and for a time I felt no inclination to think about acting. In the meantime poor Harry bore the brunt of it all and we both struggled with a baby who did seem to scream an awful lot. It was, perhaps, another reason why writing about beauty contests did not engage him fully. My return to acting was deferred for another few years and we resumed our slightly hand-to-mouth existence.

But ways to augment the family income did arise from time to time. For instance Stanley Price, as well as very successfully writing novels and plays and film scripts also worked as an editor on literary magazines and was able to put work Harry's way. At one point he was given the job of interviewing well-known crime writers, one of whom was Julian Symons, for the glossy publication About Town. Apart from being delighted to meet the man who had championed him from the start with encouraging reviews, Harry greatly admired Julian's own books, so it was sheer pleasure to be able to write an article about him. The added bonus was that Julian and his warm-hearted wife Kathleen became lifelong friends. Although over the years Harry and I made many friends among crime writers, the bond that was formed with the Symons was undoubtedly the closest.

Harry was not actually a gregarious person but it was with shame that he realised that he was not a member of the association that had awarded him the Gold Dagger. Since his days at Trinity when he seemed to have been a member of any Society with a connection to the Arts, he had not joined anything, but in 1964 he did, belatedly, join The Crime Writers' Association and indeed by the end of the 60s he was on their committee, becoming the annually-appointed chairman in 1970. Becoming a member meant that he started going to the monthly meetings in London and quite often to their annual conferences which were held in different UK cities and even once or twice abroad.

It was at the first of the American ones in New York that Harry, needing to spend as little money as possible, opted for a shared bedroom in the designated hotel. He and Peter Walker, the Yorkshire crime writer, were allocated to each other, and fortunately hit it off. Because we lived so far apart and also because we always tried to live economically without the luxury of a car, we did not leave London very much, so the friendship, although remaining warm, never became really close. The same could be said about many of the other crime writers that he got to know and to like over the years.

The blame for that must, to some extent, be laid at Harry's own door. He was essentially a private person and the assessment he made of himself as a writer, 'indelibly a viewer from a distance' could equally be applied to how far he would go in human relationships. There can be no doubt about this and yet ask anyone who ever had any dealings with him and they will say, to a man, that he was a very warm person. The solitary personality that perhaps came from his genes or maybe developed from the circumstances of his boyhood when he lived as much in his imagination as in reality was absolutely fundamental, but he still had another side even if buried deep down. Perhaps becoming a successful writer and a family man allowed this side to emerge and meant he was able to enjoy the company of others when occasion demanded. It is more than probable that without the hours he spent in the enclosing solitude of his study, he would have found it difficult to let this side of his nature develop. But thankfully as the years advanced a balance was achieved.

He was essentially not a clubbable person and never joined the sort of club where men—more men than women—would go for a friendly drink or meal and perhaps, quite often, simply to get away from home. I am sure that this was partly because he disliked the pomposity he saw as inherent in 'the gentlemen's club' and he was a great debunker of pomposity. When he was invited to have his name in 'Who's Who' he deliberately chose a trivial 'mind-your-own-business' entry under the heading Hobbies, writing, 'Popping round to the post' which should really have been changed later to another equally absurd hobby which was quoted on the cover of one of his books, 'Not quite going to India'. And he certainly said on more than one occasion that it was a good thing he did not belong to a club because, hating rows as he did, if tempers got a bit inflamed at home and he chose to walk out of the house rather than indulge in a shouting match, he would always, in the end, have to come back, having nowhere else to lay his head. The peace of family living was what he wanted above all and, despite the occasional stormy interlude, it was what he got for the fifty-seven years of his marriage.

There was one club he did join, with alacrity. In 1966 he was invited into the elite Detection Club. It was a club without a home and only met to eat rather sumptuous dinners but its members were meant to be the crème de la crème of the crime fiction world. It had been founded in the 1930s by such dignitaries as G.K. Chesterton and Dorothy L. Sayers with the original intention of having occasional meetings of like minds to discuss subjects related to their interest in crime fiction. It gradually evolved into something more formal and by the time Harry became a member the club had a President and met for three dinners a year, one of which was a formal black tie affair at which new members were initiated.

Sayers had always insisted that the ceremony of initiation which happened—indeed still happens—in eerie, if romantic, candlelight and had an elaborately-written script, was to be kept a total secret, but after her death details began to be known to those outside the club and nowadays you can find it on the internet. But lack of secrecy has not, subsequently, prevented this annual piece of high camp—devised originally by Ronald Knox with help from Chesterton and Sayers, now slightly abbreviated—from being performed. The new members swear an oath, placing their hand on Eric (a genuine skull, lit by a torch from within), to abide by the very specific rules of the club as to the high standards they should aspire to when writing their books, at the same time declaring an object that they held sacred. While Harry in 1966 chose, in proper Hindu mode, to hold the Cow sacred, others are often more serious, although wit is always welcome.

In the 1930s G.K. Chesterton had been the first President, then E.C. Bentley, followed by Dorothy L. Sayers and very briefly Lord Gorell sharing with Agatha Christie until he died after which she continued with kindly, barrister and fellow crime writer, Michael Underwood, shouldering any of the work that needed to be done, then, when she died, Julian Symons took over. Julian, the first not to die in office decided to resign after nine years. This was in 1985 and he proposed that Harry should succeed him. Apparently no-one opposed the idea and he inherited the post as well as the massive red cloak, made for Chesterton originally, which is worn at the initiation ceremony. This had been duly passed down the line, at least it would have been had it not, at some point, mysteriously, got lost, so that the one Harry had to wear—equally large—was only a meticulous replica.

As President he entered wholeheartedly into his role as controller of the revels for sixteen years, but then, at the age of 75, he decided to hand on the baton. He had begun to find the responsibility of searching out interesting guest speakers quite onerous. Even worse, if more mundanely, having to arrive with cloak, candles, matches and the batteries for the cheating torches needed because no-one could read the script by candlelight, had all become a step too far and he too resigned. In 2001 Simon Brett took over and apart from being an excellent host and organiser, enjoyed the play-acting just as much as Harry had done. At Simon's suggestion the club very generously offered not only Harry but myself as well, free dinners in perpetuity.

Chapter 9

B ut long before any of that came to pass, the fourth book that Collins
would publish in 1966 was to be the second Ghote. The planning of
'Inspector Ghote's Good Crusade' involved a lot more basic India
research, obviously not quite the major task that had preceded 'The Perfect
Murder' but nevertheless very important if each Ghote title was to have
its own individuality, if Ghote himself was to develop as a character. The
underlying theme of the book, in Harry's own words, is '*An exploration of the
impulse to be kind, its benefits and drawbacks.*', something that fully illustrates
his and his character's need to look at each side of every question.

Ghote's task is to find out who killed Frank Masters, an American
philanthropist, who established the charitable Masters' Foundation with
the purpose of helping the tough young vagrants inhabiting the streets
of Bombay. George Hardinge, in the publisher's blurb on the dust jacket,
neatly encapsulates what the Inspector encounters while investigating the
murder, '*Harried from above by unscrupulous superiors, mocked at from below by
a witheringly clear-sighted gang of urchins, poor Ghote strives to hold to the path
of rightness.*' Masters' generosity sprang entirely from the man's kindness
and the book examines how this has generated its own problems. Ghote
obviously has to assess not only the actions and reactions of those Masters
worked with but also how involved he had become with several known
criminals. But above all he had to make contact with the urchins themselves.

As is the case with all Harry's underlying themes, they are just that, they
are meant to do no more than give depth to the action and are not intended
to intrude or slow the pace of the story and this book can certainly be read

on more than one level. It can be taken at face value as the reviewer on the Northern Despatch put it, *'It is a superbly written novel. Keating really excels himself in a thrilling 'whodunit' and even the most ardent amateur sleuth will find himself on edge until the final chapter.',* or, as a pleasurable experience, as the Irish Independent said, *'Keating takes us into a strange world and makes us accept it as if we were there.'* Another piece, in The Guardian, is addressed to the aficionados of the genre. It is ever so slightly snobbishly intellectual, first of all expressing the reviewer's relief that the *'tortured'* style of the earlier books has been abandoned and praising it as, *'very good indeed'* but then goes on to see it as an example of modern crime fiction, *'a succession of facts is duly detected, but none of them having relevance towards solving the crime—until suddenly the whole truth is revealed to the detective in one flash of inspiration. Easier to write than the old type, but perhaps, too, even more readable.'* That was actually written by an older crime writer, Francis Iles, much admired by Harry. From this random sample it could be said that Harry had achieved what he had set out to do—write an on-going, compelling story with no-one specifically mentioning that this is obviously a book about the effects of kindness, although he would certainly have hoped that for some, this had been subliminally recognised.

With each new Ghote book there was more general Indian research to be done and there is abundant evidence of this for Harry would put the typewritten copy of the first and sometimes the second draft, with marginal handwritten annotations, into a large envelope, together with pages and pages of notes he had made before and during the period he was writing the book. These files were stacked up in his study cupboard once the book had been published. Included in the bundle there would also be a small notebook specific to that title which would have gone everywhere with him in his jacket pocket which enabled him to comment on the work in progress while he was away from his desk.

Inside the bundle for 'The Perfect Murder' there was even an old sixpenny London transport bus ticket—a flimsy strip of paper which is a museum piece in its own right—with, enigmatically scribbled on the back, *'It is a muddle; accept it'.* In fact this first bundle was not given even the protective covering of an envelope but was simply tied together with an old shoe-string. The notes for this book were not as numerous as subsequent ones, presumably because all the research he had done before beginning to write about India had been documented in separate notebooks and files which he then realised he would need to refer to with each new title so were kept separately.

'The Good Crusade' envelope contained a long list of possible variations on that title, including what he thought he would originally call it, 'Dead Gooder' and also a letter from a doctor friend, a friendship that had started when the Keatings were living in the village of Broad Town in Wiltshire and John Maskell had been the assistant doctor at the nearest General Practice in Wootton Bassett. Modern and part of the comparatively new NHS in the mid-1950s, there was a whiff of past times with the extremely elderly senior partner still visiting his patients on horseback. In fact horses featured strongly in the life of another of the doctors in the practice who was called in for the last stages of Simon's birth, coming straight from the hunting field. Harry recalled hearing him exhorting me to *'Hup girl, hup'*. But John Maskell, the doctor whose letter was in the file, was an altogether different breed, and his wife Rosalind became part of a close but small circle of friends, and it was a friendship that lasted right up to John's sadly early death and continued after that with Rosalind. John was an exemplar of what everyone wants from their GP, but having subsequently joined a practice in Hampshire, he was no longer our doctor. He was, however, always happy to verify medical detail when it was required in a book. The letter in 'The Good Crusade' envelope is the response to a request from Harry for details about poisons, how long they would take to act, what they looked like, how difficult they were to come by etc. and the information turned out to be pivotal to the plot.

There are also a mass of scribbled pages with information about the geo-graphical whereabouts of the locations he would be using, what could be seen from the windows of a hotel that would feature in the story, where individual roads joined each other and what direction they would take. There were lists of significant landmarks such as *'Victoria Terminus—imposing, domed.'*

Sometimes the note would be no more than an exhortation to himself, for instance in the envelope for the third Ghote book—'Inspector Ghote Caught in Meshes'—were these three sentences: *This is a fairly weighty book. It is about loyalty. It will need to be powerful.'* In this case he had written in a separate exercise book, in well-spaced-out longhand, the plot for the whole book. His pocket notebook had LOYALTY written on the inside front cover in block capitals with underneath that, *'think about it every time you start to write.'* As a good chef would assemble all the ingredients he needed before starting to cook the recipe he had chosen, so Harry gathered his facts, mentally preparing himself before launching into the actual creation.

In this third outing, Harry tests Ghote's loyalties to the hilt in what he described as *'my nearest approach to the espionage novel.'* Ghote is seconded to an obscure branch of military intelligence, called the Special Intelligence Agency because the murder is that of an American CND supporter. He then becomes closely involved not only with the victim's brother but with the Anglo-Indian girl who has been set to spy on the brother by the politically inspired India First Group, resulting in Ghote finding himself with half a dozen different allegiances and so gets 'caught in meshes'. It is possible that Harry felt a little that way himself because there is an author's foreword to this book which is a thing he very rarely did. In this he says, *'The nature of this story has made it necessary to venture here and there into fantasy. There is no such thing as "The Special Investigation Agency" (though there is a Federal Bureau of Investigation, but that is in another country.) There is no India First Group and the secret it protects is equally imaginary...'* The laws of libel almost certainly demanded this disclaimer but it almost reads like a sigh of relief that, with the book in print, he is able to lift a burden from his shoulders.

Almost unanimously the reviewers were delighted that Ghote, the *endearing Inspector,'* was back. One exception is Edmund Crispin in the Sunday Times—another acclaimed crime writer also much admired by Harry—who does not so much criticise the present as bemoan the past. He longs for Harry to return to the eccentricity of the early books, which he very much enjoyed, but nevertheless finishes the review with the words, *'here is how to write a strongly absorbing crime story without the least sensationalism.'* One of the papers welcomes in Ghote, *'a refreshing touch of human fallibility'*, while another praises the inspector's ability to *'move on'* if his first theories are proved wrong; a major example of this is demonstrated when he discards any notion that the murder has been committed in the process of robbery by dacoits and begins to search for political motivation. Anthony Price—as loyal as anyone could wish—says, *'It is good to learn that Mr. Keating can handle a thriller as skillfully as a whodunit'.*

Probably the short review in The Northern Echo encapsulates the majority view of the book: *'Sensitive, intelligent, human Inspector Ghote of Bombay, tangled up with security after murder of an American, whose brother, a famous physicist, becomes his peculiar charge and companion. Series of murderous attacks, while whom to trust is a bedevilment. Ghote's own loyalties, too, are confused, and as it turns out he is not alone in that dilemma. Good surprise finish. Strong local colour as usual, and Ghote is the most endearing of detectives. Take up with him if you haven't already.'* How difficult it must have been for Harry, reading all this adulation, to remain level-headed but, as has already been noted, Ghote and his author had a great deal in common and both kept their feet firmly on the ground, even if they tended almost to tip-toe through life with a diffidence which is indeed endearing.

But there was no time for indulgences such as basking in praise, the next book had to be completed, to say nothing of the peripheral professional jobs that would crop up intermittently. On one occasion he found himself involved in the newspaper world again. A journalist friend, Desmond Albrow, had been appointed Literary editor of The Catholic Herald but needed someone to stand in for him until he was free to take up the position. As was typical of Harry, normally so intolerant of any interruption to his writing routine, that he was happy to do the job for Desmond who himself was a caring and kind man in a profession not necessarily known for these qualities, and after all it was only for a month. Desmond, later on, obviously felt that one good turn deserves another because he offered Harry the job of TV critic, something that could be done from home, mostly in the evenings. He was by no means a pushover as a critic for most of the programmes he watched and he never pulled his punches. When Sir Michael Redgrave was narrating a weighty BBC documentary series with, as Harry thought, too 'tremulo' a voice, he said so. He was astonished to receive a long, closely written letter from the great actor explaining that the 'tremulo' was entirely due to a cold he was suffering from at the time. What was surprising was that someone as exalted as Sir Michael should even have seen a review in The Catholic Herald let alone have paid any attention to it.

This was by no means the only addition to Harry's timetable at that time. In 1967 The Times decided to overhaul its Arts coverage, and announced their plans in advance. Harry at once saw an opportunity and suggested that in their new pages they should have a regular crime book reviewer, proposing himself as that person. With alacrity Michael Ratcliffe, the literary editor, agreed to a column of around 500 words every two weeks. All the books submitted to the paper would be available but the choice of what he should review was left to him. The format was also left to him. He decided that he would write at some length on one or at the most two titles and use what remained of his allocation of words on pithy 'shorts' of twenty-odd words each. Wobbly towers of books mounted up in the study and would remain there until that column was written when most of them would be sold to make room for the next batch. Harry would board the bus, carrying a battered and heavy suitcase, and make his way to one of the bookshops that regularly bought review copies for around half the published price. The bookseller would sell them on to customers, as review copies in good-as-new condition, at around two thirds of the published price. This was common practice for those, like Harry, whose fee for writing the column was not high and who welcomed the additional income.

It was a pleasurable job and one that suited him extremely well, exercising the skill he had demonstrated in the past at Trinity and the seeds of which were sown in his early diary days. But he could not have had the least idea when he suggested doing it that it would open so many doors. Gradually he got known as an expert, taking his place alongside, among others, Julian Symons. His views would be sought when a programme on radio or TV was being compiled. He started being asked onto Arts programmes like Radio 4's Kaleidoscope and from there he progressed to TV; publishers would ask him to write an introduction when they were doing a reprint and some sort of foreword seemed appropriate. Gradually he had become accepted in the literary world not only as a fine writer himself but as one whose opinion was worth listening to. This was, of course, gratifying but it also enabled him to crusade.

Crusading was necessary because there was an element of the literary establishment that, not to put too fine a point on it, looked down on crime fiction and its writers, seeming to believe that 'genre' fiction could not, of its nature equal main stream literature. Harry would not deny that some crime novels were trashy but then so were some main stream ones but he said on more than one occasion, when being interviewed, that good crime writers think more about their readers than 'straight' novelists, many of whom write for themselves alone. Of course the greatest, like Grahame Greene, Dickens, and Trollope knew that however much they wanted to put over a message they also had a duty to their readers to entertain them. And this is exactly what Harry maintained crime fiction was capable of doing. He wanted crime literature to be taken as seriously as any other branch of fiction. Now, with an occasional platform, he was able to make his case.

But it should be said that it was low profile crusading, the gentle drip that wears away the stone rather than street corner oratory which was not in his nature. He had some admiration for the real fighters and in his time joined campaigns on some of the larger literary issues like getting Public Lending Right, something that did finally happen and gave authors some remuneration for the frequent use of the same copy of a book being borrowed from a Public Library. But throughout his life he was able to use many opportunities to further the cause of crime writing.

In the meantime there was that target of a book a year. The one that was published in 1968 was to be a departure for Ghote. In 'Inspector Ghote Hunts a Peacock' he comes to London. Many people, including his publisher, had been urging this on him but he was a bit reluctant to leave what had become the cocoon of India itself. In the end he hit on a compromise: Ghote would come to London on legitimate Indian police business but when he arrives he would be hi-jacked by a distant Indian relative and forced to live among, and get involved in, the Indian community living there. The reason for the journey was typical of the put-upon-life that Harry created for Ghote. His superior in Bombay was due to attend an International drugs conference at London's Scotland Yard and to deliver a paper on drug-trafficking, but at the last minute he had had a fall and broken his hip which meant that he could not travel. Ghote, with no time to prepare, was ordered to go in his place. Not, of course in his own right but simply to deliver the already written paper. In an almost Chaplinesque manner, carrying a woefully battered cardboard suitcase, an exceedingly nervous Ghote steps off the plane at Heathrow. On landing he is seized upon by a voluble fellow Indian who turns out to be the husband of a distant cousin of his wife, Protima. The man is insistent that, the English police having failed, Ghote has got to find his young seventeen-year-old niece, known as The Peacock, who has disappeared. It is useless to protest that he has more urgent business and the whole book has the poor man battling for time to prepare the important paper for the conference while at the same time spending hours and hours traipsing around dubious areas of London, interviewing thugs and pop stars in his search.

The book came out to almost universal praise and there was an interesting development with the subsidiary rights; it was bought by the BBC to be shown in the sixth of what they called their Detective series in 1969. It had to be adapted to fit into the allotted hour and a half. Not a lot of time to cram in the intricacies of such a plot. The adapter chose what, on the face of it, could be the obvious way of dealing with that. He virtually ignored Ghote's reason for being in London and centred the script on the search for The Peacock. Although the result made acceptable viewing it destroyed the purpose of the book, which was Ghote's state of mind and left nothing but a stereotyped comic Indian. It is seldom that an author gets a lot of satisfaction out of TV adaptations, most will say you just have to take the money and turn a blind eye. For, not only does the extra income make it easier for a writer to exist, but it also provides that gold-dust—publicity.

It is not surprising that the TV maker's attention was drawn to the book because the reviews were not only plentiful but in many cases picked up one of the things that Harry had set out to do, let the reader see London through Ghote's eyes, an idea the Birmingham Mail said, *'fell little short of genius.'* This is backed up by RM of the Oldham Evening Chronicle, *'The fascination lies in seeing Britain through the eyes of an Indian fed on British propaganda.'* Many of the reviewers comment on Ghote's reverence for all things British and how this is severely tested as he meets up with some of the seamier and tougher sides of London life and the characters involved in the low life he has to investigate. Most reviewers, including Edmund Crispin, felt that *'In the end Ghote escapes with his Anglophilia undamaged. But only just.'* What was extremely heartening was that Crispin concludes his review, *'Mr. Keating uses his realism with great skill, not letting it either swamp the plot or be stifled under it. His achievement has been not just to create a specially likeable detective, but to avoid letting the likeability get out of hand, with inevitably disastrous effects on the narrative. He deserves his success.'* This from the man who the year before was hoping for a return to the earlier Keating eccentric books perhaps even leaving Ghote behind.

Harry's approach to characterisation, which was all part of his vision for crime books, was picked up by Violet Grant in the Daily Telegraph: *'One of the few thriller writers who trouble to put real life into their characters'.* This was very welcome because there was a worrying tendency to liken Ghote to the Indians being caricatured by the popular comedian Peter Sellers, whose notion of portraying an Indian consisted of much wagging of the head and a curious, singsong approximation of 'Indian' speech, which many found hilarious. It was with horror that Harry was told by his agent that there was interest in making a TV series with Sellers playing Ghote. Fortunately the project foundered so that travesty never happened.

All in all, after just three years being a full-time writer, there was reason for optimism which was given an extra boost when The Society of Authors, at that time the only writer's Trade Union, undertook a survey of author's earnings. The overall findings were quite depressing. Only 6% of those people claiming to be writers, to whom the survey had been addressed, were deemed to make enough money solely through writing to make them eligible to call themselves full-time writers. For Harry it was rather heartening news, he just scraped into that 6%. He could feel justified in having given up the day job although he knew he could not afford to give up on his self-imposed discipline. For one thing by 1968 all four children were at the Lycée and the fees had become rather larger than they were in 1960.

'Inspector Ghote Plays a Joker' sees Harry, on his own admission, climbing up onto a moral high horse. For all his ability to write with underlying humour and his personal enjoyment in playing regular and rather successful, April Fool's jokes on his long-suffering family, he felt that he wanted to address, quite seriously what he saw as the *'too absorbed frivolity of the times'.* This was never going to be a crowd-puller at the best of times and perhaps he allowed himself to be too influenced by the need not to sound too much of a kill-joy. Perhaps he needed to be more of a preacher to put across such anti-hedonistic philosophy. But there was the rub, preaching played no part in the way he crafted his books, quite the opposite. Everything he ever wrote about the ideal crime novel emphasised the need, if you had something serious to say, to do it subtly. Any message should reach the reader subliminally. It seems that this time he failed to find the middle road.

Certainly the reviewers, and there were many of them, while still finding Ghote himself as absorbing as ever, did not universally find the plot and the sleuthing as praiseworthy as usual. One, Anthony Price in the Oxford Mail, who had previously nailed his colours to the mast as a Ghote lover, wonders, *'whether there always has to be a murder?'* Was he suggesting that just writing about Ghote and India without bothering to have a major crime in the story would be enough? It is probable that Harry, although enjoying the freedom that would provide, would have felt he was short-changing his readers. But some were content, Books and Bookmen finding *'above all a very strong, somewhat unusual, plot given superfine, expansional treatment.'* But there were lines from two reviews to treasure. First from the Scotsman, *'Surely the most likeable fictional detective.'* and second from David Irvine in The Coventry Evening Chronicle, *'Ghote stands four-square in my book with Maigret, Poirot, or any other of the great detective heroes one cares to name.'*

The slightly puritan aspect of Harry's personality which he revealed in this book certainly existed, even if few who knew him were aware of it. It could have been the result of growing up in an atmosphere of austerity that meant expenditure had, largely, to be confined to necessities. Even before the war started and everyone had to tighten their belts, his family had not been affluent, and this necessity to count the pennies continued with him for some years after graduating and for quite a chunk of his married life. This did not prevent him thoroughly enjoying himself on many occasions and if he had agreed to be part of a celebration he would make every effort not to be a damp squib. Later, when things had eased financially, he would happily be very generous, particularly towards the family and from early on there were a handful of charities like Penal Reform and Shelter and Oxfam all of which he supported throughout his life by regular direct debit payments. Although, when the children were younger, he had delightedly played the Father Christmas role he increasingly found that commercialism was ruining the true spirit of the festival. The mountain of presents under the Christmas tree was wonderfully exciting, and with four children it was an Everest of a mountain, but it was also a reminder of how materialistic society had become and this was anathema to Harry. To counteract these frivolous extravagances at Christmas he would send a generous cheque to one of what he felt was the most deserving charities like Medicins Sans Frontiers.

It was at this stage that he was faced with a difficult decision. In the October of 1968 which was after the publication of 'Hunts a Peacock' and 'Plays a Joker', George Hardinge came to the end of the road with Collins and left to set up a crime list for Macmillan, naturally taking some of the Collins authors with him. For Harry the decision was agonising because he felt his usual loyalty to a company who had served him well, increasing his sales considerably, on the other hand all his instincts were to stay with George who was such a good and sympathetic editor. He almost certainly made the wrong decision and it seems he had to make it without much guidance. Naturally no-one can say with absolute certainty that things would have followed quite a different path if he had left Collins at that point but given the changes he made in publishers in later years and what can only be described as missed opportunities, it is a strong possibility that George would not have allowed these to happen.

Having made his choice it was time to consider what he would write about in the sixth Ghote novel. He came up with a book which put aside the personal disquiets of life becoming too frivolous and returned to the violence of humankind which had been the theme for 'A Rush on the Ultimate', naturally not this time the English upper class world of croquet, but in a small town in India. 'Inspector Ghote Breaks an Egg' has Ghote being required to impersonate a chicken-feed salesman pedalling his wares literally from a bicycle. To make his disguise more credible he carries with him a prize box of preserved eggs. His task is to solve a fifteen year old crime with his superiors thinking they already know the murderer. In order to investigate these suspicions he has to delve deep into politics and make sure that he charges the present, all-powerful and ruthless Chairman of the Town Council with the long-ago murder of his first wife.

Without exception the reviewers not only empathised with the much put-upon Inspector but found the plotting admirable. Things were looking up for the status of the crime writer, the Financial Times, of all papers, published a short list for that year's Golden Dagger award and Harry was on it. This time he did not win, but in a way it was less important because, although the added publicity for the book would have been welcome, he was already safely ensconced as one of the foremost crime-writers of the time and the books were selling in America.

As usual he preserved the reviews, whether good or bad. This time, together with Peter Philips comment in The Sun, *'Harry Keating writes so vividly that you can smell the mud in the Indian town',* there were some letters from Indians. Mostly they were appreciative but a couple were critical over his choice of names. One letter points out that the name Patel for the doctor would have been more geographically correct than the variation Harry chose, Patil. Another was from an irate gentleman with a political axe to grind who weakened the main reason for writing the letter by including a snide comment about the central villainous character in the book obviously being a portrait of a real-life member of the present ruling party. But the main thrust of the letter was his outrage that the names of some real and greatly revered Maharashtrian personalities were mentioned and being associated with a story about poisoning would assuredly tarnish their reputations. He must have been over-sensitive on their behalf because no writs were issued. It must be admitted that the picture drawn of the chairman and the corruption in the town, together with unacceptable violence generally, is not flattering to India. The Times Literary Supplement even wonders *'if the books will be banned in India as being prejudicially realistic'.*

Interestingly this has never happened, although it should be remembered that when Ismail Merchant bought a film option on 'The Perfect Murder' not long after its publication, commissioned a script from Jonathan Miller and engaged Anthony Shaffer as the director, had even got as far as finding suitable locations in and around Bombay, the Indian government refused their permission to make it, raising seventy-three objections. Perhaps they had a case because at one point Harry has the villain in the story says these words, *'those lovers of their own mothers, Bombay business men.',* which might seem to be cause for a legitimate grievance, particularly when, although spoken by an Indian, it was written by an Englishman. Ismail did not take the objections seriously and was confident they would be withdrawn in due course. He was wrong and the film, at this stage, did not get made.

A writer's life can be full of these near misses and the Indian government did not seem worried by such slurs when they were in print, it was only if they were transferred to celluloid that they exercised a veto. Obviously a disappointment but, looking on the bright side, six years on from the first published Ghote and firmly established as the crime fiction reviewer for The Times, it surely must have seemed, to outsiders, that, against all the odds, Harry only needed to continue in this vein to be able, when the time came, to retire in comfort.

Chapter 10

That Harry was not satisfied to rest on his laurels was in part due to a long-held private ambition to write a book or books that would ensure him a lasting place in literary history and with crime fiction being labeled by many as a lesser genre he thought he should write a mainstream novel that stood the chance of reaching a wider audience. But it was also due to a neighbour, Tim Manderson, who was a Director of Heinemann, the publishers. He was in fact the sales director, but with a difference, in that as well as being extremely good at selling, he had a passion for books which in fact was probably exactly the reason he achieved such good sales figures. He believed that, on the evidence of what he had read of Harry's books so far, something written across a broader canvas, not so easily categorised as genre fiction, could be made into a best seller. With these combined spurs of fame and fortune Harry had for some time been considering a suitable subject.

As soon as 'Inspector Ghote Breaks an Egg' was delivered to his agent the planning became a reality. His basic theme was to be *the true nature of strength of personality*. His first idea was to write a story of domestic conflict, all was grist to Harry's mill, even his own occasional rows with his wife. Was the seemingly stronger personality—in our case the one who had the ability to shout loudest—necessarily always dominant? He argued with himself that, whereas it could be seen as a sign of weakness to walk away from an argument, the action could, conversely, be seen as a sign of strength. In reality a cooling-off period often achieved a more reasoned solution. It was strange that Harry, with his love of formal debate, actively disliked getting into an argument and very often would walk out if it got heated.

These earliest plans for a setting were soon discarded as being unlikely to result in a book with enough depth. Probably another reason for discarding a domestic background was that Harry might have found himself getting too close to the subject. Although the autobiographical article had not yet been written he had already decided that he wrote best at arms-length. Among Tim Manderson's greatest successes had been Wilbur Smith's adventure series and with this in mind Harry turned his thoughts towards adventure and to Lord Acton's power dictum, *'All power corrupts, absolute power corrupts absolutely.'* and under what circumstances could this be best explored. Imagination being one of his strong points he decided on an imaginary island with strong Celtic overtones. There was to be an evil dictator in power and his protagonist, the Strong Man of the title, a peasant by origin, would organise the rebellion.

Harry gives the impression in a later article that a sizeable proportion of the reviews were not good, but in saying this he does himself an injustice. To begin with the sheer number of reviews, often by critics who had not previously noticed him, meant that the Keating name became known to a far wider audience. It is true that there was a small percentage who deplored the island being imaginary saying it made the story unconvincing. Among these was his staunch champion Julian Symons who also found Keig, the strong man, *'too much a model of virtue'* and certainly the Daily Telegraph critic Christopher Wordsworth's words, *'...readable, forgettable.',* drove Harry, in the article, to utter this succinct comment, *'That hurt'.* However those in favour were mostly wholeheartedly so, with two of them comparing the exciting narrative to *The Count of Monte Cristo*.

There is probably more physical violence in this book than he had attempted before and on one occasion during the time he was writing it, he called out as he left the house that he was *'Just going round the block',* which he did, returning to rush straight back to the study. The explanation was given later that evening. He had found himself so repelled by the violence of the scene involving napalm and the horrendous damage it inflicted, that he had needed physical exercise to pump up his adrenalin levels sufficiently to catapult him into writing the scene.

The published version, under Tim's guidance, had undergone some cutting from the original and it is sad that, unlike the meticulously kept manuscripts with notes attached for so many of his books, there does not appear to be any record of the first draft. It is interesting that 'The Strong Man' ended up by being a mere 336 pages long—just a pamphlet when put beside the length of the tomes published today. It is tempting to speculate about those lost words—did they contain material that would have turned the book into the run-away success it did not become? Undoubtedly Tim would have found it of paramount importance to keep the pace up, not to allow the story to be diluted, but with hindsight is it possible that if perhaps some of the sub-text was of the kind that made the Ghote books so compelling, that might not have moved the book away from straight adventure to a major novel?

Harry's own words are probably as good an assessment of how far it was successful. *'I do not know to this day quite how good it is...in that it failed to find an American Publisher, it must be considered a partial failure at least...I think probably I was unable to give it the power it ought to have had. But was this out of an inherent inability? Or was it simply a failure of technique? A series of misjudgements? I cannot say. But when every now and then I come across someone who remembers the book my heart leaps up. That is, after all, what one aims to do: to plant in another mind something memorable. And in that in a few minds here and there I appear to have done this I am happy to regard the book as a success, a small success.*

As I have said many of the reviewers were different from the regular crime fiction ones but quite a few mention that Harry is better known for Inspector Ghote and that this is a move into a different field. Neville Braybrooke in the Sunday Telegraph hoped that both styles would be kept running side by side and the Cambridge Evening news thought *'that it will enhance his reputation'.* Heinemann must have had a substantial market in South Africa because many of their papers noticed it, with The Cape Times saying, *'Highly satisfying adventure story with subtle overtones'.* The overall picture from the reviews is that it is a very readable book although not becoming the best-selling success that had been hoped for. It is a tribute to Harry's tenacity that once he was over the initial disappointment he was able to put it behind him and get on with the usual writing routine. Of course by the time it was published in January 1971 the next annual crime novel was almost ready to be delivered to his agent.

There were to be two publications that year with Collins bringing out 'Inspector Ghote Goes by Train' in November. Here we are given '*A hymn to the huge and fascinating Indian railway system*,' and in the same breath Harry tells us that it is an examination of the merits of '*going by train steadily, as Ghote and I do, as against 'flying', as my villain in the book metaphorically does, and as the world's high-fliers do.* This time the theme of the book is not so much a universal ill to be investigated, but more of a private vendetta. Flying was definitely one of the problems that had come into Harry's life with his success. It was not so much the actual aeroplane as the bureaucracy of airports which upset him, engendering such an unacceptable level of chaos and noise and bustle that the whole experience became an anathema. Whereas others experienced excitement from this atmosphere, it deeply depressed him.

Conceiving the notion that Ghote is to be dispatched to Calcutta to bring back to Bombay a notorious fraudster being held there in custody, gave Harry, as it were, the opportunity to go by train, albeit at second-hand in the body of his Inspector. Ghote, enamoured at the thought of the long peaceful journey in air-conditioned first class, volunteers to use some of his leave as a way to cover the cost of the extra hours incurred through not flying. Those who knew Harry would have recognised this gesture as something he himself would happily have made.

Most of the, once again, large number of reviewers were happy to travel with him, particularly The Times Literary Supplement. '*Here at last is the Inspector Ghote book we have been waiting for. The perfectly shapely tale...Many a crime story set on a train has been a classic: there is something about a train that brings out the best in a crime writer. This new book will certainly rank in that special and delightful class.*' But not all were universally happy. There were problems for those who wanted more action—and for this the reader has to wait till the end. But when it comes Ghote is on the roof of the train in spectacular form. But many were content to travel from Bombay to Calcutta and back with an author who, as Sarah Raikes of the Durham County Advertiser put it, *'really knows how to gradually unravel a plot while maintaining throughout the mystery and suspense and at the same time bringing his characters brilliantly to life...I really felt I had travelled a long way across India in a hot crowded train.'*

It must have been a relief for Harry after all the violence and action of 'The Strong Man' to put his energies towards mental dueling in what The Eastern Daily Express calls *'The battle of wits that goes on all the way there and all the way back, a serious matter for the inspector and his quarry, but great fun for us.'* He admitted that he, himself, had derived a great deal of pleasure from writing it and he ranked it among the best he had written. For some reason it was not until this book that Ghote acquired a forename, Ganesh, which in fact, was seldom used. Somehow this revelation meant that, over the years, representations of Ganesh—the elephant God—began to appear on every surface of the family home, mingled with straightforward elephants made of ebony, teak, brass, jade and ivory. There is even a huge wall-mounted Ganesh, high enough up on the stairs to appear to be cast in a heavy gold metal although in reality it is made from gilded papier-maché. But undoubtedly one of his most cherished possessions was the sculpture done by his daughter, Bryony who, disliking the head of the model her group were meant to be sculpting, and had replaced it with a splendid Ganesh elephant head and trunk.

Speculating in the autobiographical article he wonders whether the formality of his writing style—and hardly ever using a forename was part of this arm's length approach—was one of the reasons for Ghote, not being overwhelmingly acclaimed. Harry could not provide an answer, perhaps because what he was hoping for was almost unachievable. How often is anything as subjective as a book universally admired? There must be a thousand reasons why an individual reader does not sympathise with the particular character being depicted. In this case for every reader who loved to read about India there were almost as many who had no interest in the sub-continent, people who were out of tune with the very different Indian approach to life. The 'distancing' style that Harry chose undoubtedly gave the books their distinction. There is no doubt that he would have been capable of getting more personally involved, as he did in later books with protagonists who were not extensions of himself, but many would say this would have harmed the overall enjoyment, that the objectivity was part of the charm. The undeniable fact was that Ghote was Harry's alter ego and for anyone as introspective as he was this meant he had to tell the stories obliquely. For all that, in an interview on French TV, he quite shyly admitted, 'Inspector Ghote, c'est moi.'

Some of the reviewers of 'The Strong Man' had pointed out that, strangely, in the year of writing this 'straight' novel without the usual crime to be solved, he was in fact the Chairman of the Crime Writer's Association (CWA). He had been elected to the committee in 1969 and had been elected Vice-Chair in order to fulfil the requirement for becoming the Chair in the following year. Occupying this position meant that he was able to use every opportunity to promote crime fiction. This was something which he cared strongly about. For instance the year he won the Gold Dagger, 1964, not a single newspaper devoted even one line to the Dagger awards although these were the major accolades for crime writers. Of course he did not immediately change things but undoubtedly he sowed very fruitful seeds. From these beginnings the CWA was able, in the end, to get splendid sponsorship from the jewelers Cartier. This sponsorship meant that winners got a sum of money as well as the prestige of winning and, if it is not too cynical an observation, once money was involved, the press began to show an interest. Little by little the battle for recognition of the genre was being won. Many of our foremost crime-writers, like P.D. James, Peter Lovesey, Simon Brett, Ian Rankin and of course Julian Symons just to name a few, were tireless in promoting the genre. They all, Harry included, began to feel that they were achieving respect for the crime novel, even from some of the established literary world.

'The Strong Man' publication year, 1971, was also the year when 'Inspector Ghote Trusts the Heart' was being written, and it was also to be the beginning of a new image for H.R.F. Keating. He started to grow a beard. In the series of family holidays the aim of each of which would be to use a different form of transport, it was the turn of the horse-drawn caravan in Ireland. In this back-to-nature vehicle there was of course no electricity and as Harry used an electric shaver he thought the only solution was to stop shaving. By the end of what in itself turned out to be a remarkable week, it seemed a shame not to let this quite impressive growth continue. Although he did trim the accompanying moustache, the beard itself was never cut for the remaining forty years of his life and, turning grey and then white, it developed into a truly magnificent feature, earning comparison with Tolstoy or, for others, made him resemble an old testament prophet or even more appropriately an Indian Guru.

While it was little more than 'designer stubble' the family wrestled with their equine problems. These began when there was no horse to put between the shafts of the vehicle ear-marked, by the hirers in Sligo, for the Keatings. The previous renters had mistreated their animal in some way and it had had to be sent to the vets. We had to wait a few hours while they found a substitute. Unfortunately, when it eventually arrived it turned out that they had chosen one that was too big for the shafts so that, as we went down-hill, the caravan knocked against the poor beast's legs, resulting in a mutinous but quite understandable refusal to budge. Being Saturday it was necessary to get to the first stopping place as quickly as possible in order to find a blacksmith who could reposition the holes in the shafts that night because the next day was Sunday, and in God-fearing Ireland, no-one would be working. Harry ended up walking beside the horse's head and more or less dragging him forward by the bridle, brutal perhaps but necessary, and the destination was reached before nightfall, allowing the repair to be done. Matilda—so christened by the family in the apparent absence of a real name—was safely turned free in a field belonging to the farm designated as the first stopping place. There were already quite a few other horses browsing in the field from other caravans which had arrived before us.

The instructions for the morning were to put some oats in a bowl, stand in the field and call your horse's name. Harry saw this as his job. Disaster number two struck. Can all the animals have been christened Matilda? In no time at all Harry was marooned in the centre of hungry horses with no hope of enticing any one of them, let alone the right one, to follow him back to the caravan. He threw the bowl in the air and with a cry of, *'That's the last I have to do with the b...y horse',* and returned on his own to the caravan.

None of the family, and that included Harry, was experienced with horses but Simon aged sixteen volunteered to take over trying to capture Matilda. This was eventually accomplished and he and I set about the next process, the grooming. It was then that disaster number three became evident. Simon's eyes began to itch and stream as did his nose. It was obvious that he had a previously unrecognised allergy to horsehair. At sixteen he had been quite reluctant to come on a family holiday at all but had finally agreed and now he was faced with this. It says something for his sense of duty that for the rest of the week he continued to catch and groom the horse but having fulfilled those duties he distanced himself, either walking ahead of the caravan or several feet behind it with head, once the eyes had stopped streaming, buried in a book. Harry continued to control the progression of the party from the driving seat with delighted help from thirteen-year-old Bryony, ten-year-old Piers and six-year-old Hugo. The sun shone and we all—with the possible exception of Simon—enjoyed the care-free, romantic West of Ireland countryside.

That was until disaster number four struck. Perhaps the caravan-hirers did not know, and certainly the information was never passed on, but it soon became apparent that Matilda was a bolter. She did not like being put into a strange field while lunch was being eaten or when the day's travelling was over, and she escaped over fences or hedges and clip-clopped away down the road whenever she could. Mostly the recapture was accomplished reasonably easily and more secure pasture found without too much disruption to the family plans but just once she managed to ruin a dream. The route we had been taking was the one recommended by the owners. But then Harry saw a signpost pointing to Innisfree. Yeats fan as he was he was unable to resist the temptation, and we turned off. The plan was to camp somewhere with a view of the 'lake isle', find a farmer willing to house Matilda and then have lunch, after which Harry and I would swim out to the island perhaps at the same time even managing to recite a line or two of the poem. But no sooner was the lunch on the table than the familiar 'clip-clop' was heard. This time it took an age to get Matilda back and when we did the farmer told us there was nowhere else for her to be pastured so back she went into the shafts and with lunch eventually eaten so to speak on the hoof, we sadly returned to the recommended route.

We did come away with a delightful memory from that remote Irish farmstead. While their father was being located to ask his permission to pasture Matilda we had chatted with his two quite young children. When the question was put to them about the nearness of their school and how they got there, the reply was that they walked the three and a half miles there and the same distance back but that the return journey took them rather longer because 'We do dally on the way', a phrase that seemed to symbolize the Irish attitude to life and served, perhaps, to underline for us the importance of relaxing when faced with any sort of trouble.

Undoubtedly those two small girls had their effect on us and anger and allergies were put into perspective. At least the younger members of the family probably have happy memories of that week. There were only one or two other unforgettable incidents such as when Piers and Hugo were out walking on their own and Hugo jumped into the centre of a bog, mistaking the bright green for a verdant patch of grass. Fortunately the bog was shallow and Piers was able to haul him to safety. But all in all a week was quite long enough and we were ultimately quite content to hand Matilda back and make our way to County Galway where we were going to rent a cottage in the small village of Rosmuck for a further five weeks. It was unprecedented for a family holiday to be so long but urgent and quite lengthy alterations—undertaken by Noel, Harry's brother—were being made to the London house, dividing rooms so that all four children could have their own bedroom and we needed to be away while the work was being done,

The Galway village was in no way modern—to use the telephone the receiver had to be lifted off the hook and a handle vigorously turned to contact the exchange. The telephone was Rosmuck 4 which the literary editor at The Times found so endearing that he was determined to use it with the excuse of keeping in touch about the delivery of the review books and any queries about the columns that would be written. Harry had, of course, not been able to do any writing during the caravan week but was determined to get back into as near his usual routine as possible. He did agree to limit writing to the mornings, leaving the afternoons free for swimming, immensely long walks and fishing.

It is astonishing that the book that was being written, 'Inspector Ghote Trusts the Heart', did not suffer in any way. In fact, for many, including Harry, it was regarded as the best of the series so far. Certainly there was a glowing batch of reviews. There was however one error-finding letter from an Indian who had not been able to afford the hard-back and wrote only after reading the Penguin paper-back version, too late for corrections to be made. He pointed out that Harry had got his sums wrong in the matter of how many 100 rupee notes are needed to make up a lakh of rupees and that he had used 50 rupee notes three years prior to their being in use, bad enough errors for someone used to getting his facts right, but fortunately not harmful to the plot. This hinges on the mistaken kidnapping of a poor tailor's son in place of that of a rich man who, nevertheless is still asked to find the same large ransom for a boy not his own. Ghote has not only to locate the kidnappers but try to persuade the rich man to pay up. This time, as the title suggests Harry was exploring how much you should trust your heart and how much your head.

Stephen Craggs of The Northern Echo probably encapsulates much that is repeated by other reviewers, *'Inspector Ghote stories have a way of taking a hold of you. You feel at one with the irrepressible Indian detective for he has a style that allows him to look at the human and not only the professional side of things...He grabs hold of your heart as well as your mind and relieves the tension for himself and the reader with occasional eccentric lapses which provide welcome shafts of humour. Set against the exotic backcloth of Bombay, the scene is richly painted by Mr. Keating who based his exciting story upon a real-life Japanese case.'*

Andrew Hope in The Evening Standard raised a philosophical point concerning the difference between Eastern and Western attitudes when it comes to the sanctity of young lives, no matter how rich or how poor. A fine debating issue but one that did not occur to anyone else and does not seem to have stopped him appreciating the book because he concludes his review, '*Ghote's frustrated hunt for the kidnappers mounts to a fine climax and his relationship with his elders and betters is comically apt.*' Matthew Coady in The Guardian states what has been said over and over again down the years, '*Demonstrates yet again that disaster-prone Ghote is an ideal candidate for a TV series.*' Although this transition to the small screen has not happened yet there have been many options acquired by producers over the years. None have so far come to fruition but at the time of writing this there is still perhaps a possibility that it will happen.

Back in London the full day routine was resumed which, of course included The Times reviews which had to be fitted in including all the reading that entailed. Harry was not a slow reader but faced with those toppling piles in the study he wished he was a bit faster. Then he saw an advertisement for Tony Buzan's Rapid Reading Course that guaranteed to increase not only your speed but your comprehension by three times what it was when you started, he decided to give it a go. Those attending a trial evening had been invited to bring along a chapter from a book or equivalent length document which three bright young women, who had already completed the course, would be given five minutes to read after which they had to answer any questions that were thrown at them. This they did faultlessly. Once embarked on the course it very soon became evident that a forty-year-old man did not possess the mental agility of a young graduate. It was six weeks of hard slog and intensive brain-washing. There were two classes a week and in between there was an hour's homework each day to help you perfect the new skills you were learning. Among these you were required to forget the usual habit of reading from left to right, line by line and substitute whole page reading. There were various stages to be gone through; reading from right to left; dragging your finger from top right to bottom left absorbing the words on the way; using the same dragging movement down the centre of the page. Added to this there was to be no inward vocalisation of the written word, something the majority of us do without realising it.

Harry would do his homework sitting up in bed at night and the sound of a rubber fingerstall grating its way over the page was almost as irritating as the proverbial squeaking of chalk on the blackboard. At the end of the six weeks everyone was individually tested. Harry failed. He was somewhere around two and a half times faster, not the required three. The terms of the agreement said that if you did not pass you could do a further three weeks free of charge and sit the test again. He did this and was successful. He was still capable of the more leisured read but using the system not only took up less time but also meant he was able to cover many more books.

That there was no actual publication in 1973 is not surprising. There had been two in 1971, 'Trusts the Heart' in 1972 and there were going to be two more in 1974. Also sandwiched into 71/72 Harry had found time for his first editorial publication, a collection of true crime pieces written by members of the Crime Writer's Association, working with George Hardinge at Macmillan. It was based on the assumption that anyone writing crime fiction would almost certainly have at least one notorious real life crime that fascinated them and it was entitled 'Blood on My Mind'. Harry invited the CWA members to submit ideas they would like to write about and he chose nine from those suggested and then added his own macabre choice—the case of Eugene Aram, the eighteenth century schoolmaster hanged some fourteen years after the event for clubbing to death one Daniel Clark, shoemaker. The collection ranges far and wide both historically and in background. One takes a look at how far Cicero was involved in a murder committed in 52 BC, another examines what actually happened in Canterbury in 1170 to Thomas á Becket while others were perpetrated in the twentieth century and were to do with everyday folk. This was a rare undertaking for Harry who preferred his crimes to be fictional.

Perhaps it was just as well he was able to have a year without a book coming out because my campaign to go back to work produced a result. I was offered an amazing job playing Lena in Athol Fugard's 'Boesman and Lena' and that meant I was touring Great Britain from January to April, not always getting home at night. Fortunately that time coincided with a period that Harry was doing research and not actually writing so that having to break off to shop and cook was not as disastrous as it might have been. It is often said that women are much better at multi-tasking than men and there are indeed many instances of female novelists managing to write and look after the family simultaneously. Harry was quite certain that he could not do two things at the same time so without doubt he was unable to put in as many hours in the study as usual. But he was, if anything, keener than I was that I should resume acting and tackled his new responsibilities very successfully. Simon was at University but the other three were still at school and it was as well that Bryony was by now sixteen because Harry was very grateful for all her help.

One of the 1974 books was breaking entirely new ground and once again had required a great deal of research. It was a second straight novel. No more imaginary islands, this time. 'The Underside', he tells us, 'was set *at a favourite period of the past, the years around about 1870 when Victorian England was perhaps at its apogee.'* Harry explains that he had had the idea in mind for some time and had even written some passages in between the first and second drafts of whichever was the current book. *'I read widely for it, especially as its hero was to be a painter (=writer) called Godfrey Mann (=Everyman). Its theme was the value that should or should not be given to the underside of our nature. Its story took Godfrey to the highest and the lowest depths of Victorian London. It was my first attempt to come to terms in fiction with the sexual instinct. I remember to this day the moment when my typewriter, it seemed, spelt out to me the famous four-letter word. I looked at it. I felt it was right in the context. It remained.'*

Harry again took the book to Heinemann but this time Tim Manderson did not think the subject matter fitted in with the adventure titles they were concentrating on publishing. But George Hardinge, who had remained a good friend, even after Harry ceased being one of his authors, was enthusiastic when it was shown it to him. It was not a crime novel so there would be no conflict of interest with Collins provided it was published outside Macmillan's crime list. It appeared on their general list. The partnership between editor and author, once again, was a very happy one.

It could be said that Harry invariably chose a subject or a manner of writing that ran the risk of alienating some readers. Originally it had been the verbless, staccato prose; then the foibles of an Indian way of life not to mention the possible barrier of Anglo-Indian speech; after that imaginary islands, it seemed, were not to everyone's taste and now the decidedly dark side of Victorian life. Obviously he was not deliberately choosing difficult settings but some quirk in his imagination drew him to explore unusual aspects of life.

Reactions, as had been the case with 'Death and the Visiting Firemen' were sharply divided between wholehearted praise and absolute condemnation. In the latter camp Wilfred De'ath in Punch found *the sentences so convoluted as to be unreadable* with the final death blow, *extremely boring, obscene and unpleasant book.* Perhaps, to some extent, the reviews say as much about the stomach of the reviewer as they do about the book itself. In contrast to De'ath was the Sunday Times review where Maurice Wiggins has this to say: *Though in no sense pornographic this is a novel about which the public should be suitably warned. It is a deeply perceptive study of the carnal impulse and has a lot to offer to the student of sexuality. But its description of Godfrey's sexual adventures in the underworld, unsparing and revolting as they are, are not to be undertaken without due warning. That said, I must add that as a description of London's underworld in the Victorian Imperial heyday it has really impressive power.* Francis King of the Sunday Telegraph did not like it at all but George Thaw in the Daily Mirror, with a small reservation, did. *This is a powerful novel. Strongly written and with a good solid ending. Genuine characters and a real feeling for the period make it thoroughly enjoyable, if a bit strong in places.*

Once again, as with 'The Strong Man', the reviewers were mainstream fiction ones but many of them had it firmly in mind that Harry was in some way moonlighting from the day job if he was not writing about Ghote. In many ways this was a good thing because it reinforced his reputation as a front runner in his chosen field but it did little to help him in his quest for acceptance as a literary figure, given that crime writing was still regarded as a lesser genre. American publishers were still happily buying the crime titles but no-one ventured on this one. Just as well that he had his finger on the financial pulse and had not relied entirely on Victorian London to continue putting bread and milk on the table in the coming months.

'Bats Fly Up for Inspector Ghote' was published two months earlier in March of 1974 and has the poor man in personal turmoil and on the verge of voluntarily retiring from the police. He is seconded to The Black-money and Allied Transactions Squad (acronym BATS), and his duties require him to spy on his colleagues in an effort to discover who is the mole amongst them who has been leaking vital police secrets. Suspicion becomes central to his working life. This frame of mind so warps his judgement that it begins to enter his private life, leading him to suspect his beloved Protima of infidelity and young son, Ved, of telling lies. When, ultimately, he is able to get things into perspective and love and trust return, these are the thoughts Harry gives to Ghote: *'Much as he loved Protima, much as he loved little Ved, it had always been his job that came first. It was his life, worked into his veins, and there had been nothing he could do about it.'* Words that are written about a fictional character but also words that were penned in the knowledge that they applied equally to the author. This is a prime example of what Harry meant when he said that if he were to expose fundamental parts of himself in an autobiography he would have had to do it at arm's length, through the books.

The reception was universally good with The Times Literary Supplement wanting to say it was the best ever but unable to do so because the reviewer had so much enjoyed 'Inspector Goes by Train' that he could only make this one second best. It even had The Irish Times calling it vintage Ghote while at the same time admitting that the reviewer had not previously been a fan of the series.

Time was moving on and with Simon, our eldest son, already at University, there was one less mouth to feed at home, but still the parental contribution to his accommodation in Nottingham had to be found. But even if Harry had not yet achieved the book that would assure his literary immortality, it was clear that he was now making a good living as a free-lance writer. However he was not destined to lie on a bed of complacency, his life was about to be thoroughly shaken up.

Chapter 11

One day, by the first post, breakfast time in those halcyon days, there came a letter from Air India. Apparently they had heard that there was this author writing book after book about their country without ever having been there. They would like to remedy this and offer him a free return flight together with accommodation at the Taj Mahal Hotel in Bombay for three weeks. It was impossible to take it in—was it perhaps a hoax? If so it was a pretty elaborate one written on headed note-paper and signed with a verifiable signature. Once having discarded that notion it was time for serious consideration. What if, despite what was always said about how authentic Ghote and descriptions of his country were, that should turn out to be untrue? What if the Bombay he had inhabited and loved was a fantasy? What if, a very real possibility, he was unable to stomach the poverty and the smells? It was true that not so long ago he had nearly gone to India, not to Bombay but to Delhi, where he had been offered a job teaching journalism. The fact that this had not happened, due to the job being cancelled on account of some political emergency, was really an irrelevance because he had been prepared to go then, so why the doubts now?

It did not take long for common sense to prevail—it would after all have been unthinkable to turn down such a generous offer. Meanwhile there was going to be a gap between receiving the letter and the actual departure in order for him to be there when the weather was at its most bearable and he began to make plans for the beginning of October. In the meantime he had to decide what he would write next. It would plainly be absurd to embark on another Ghote when he might be about to discover that he had got it all wrong but he was not quite ready to launch into another mainstream novel. Never at a loss for long, he hit on the notion that he could write a crime story set in the world he had so recently researched, 1870s Victorian England. He would take advantage of the ever-increasing popularity of the upstairs/downstairs life of that bygone era that had been fuelled by a series on TV and base his story round a nouveau-riche household living in Bayswater—his own home territory—but in those bygone days very much the up and coming area of London. The plot revolves around the downstairs element of the house, embodied in the naïve kitchen-maid, Janey, who gets embroiled with Irish Val Leary, the Jack-me-lad labourer with his mind set on acquiring wealth. Val reckons the house would provide rich pickings for a burglar and that through Janey he could gain valuable information. The story introduces us to the highly-organised Victorian crime world with its sordid gin palaces as well as the genteel rule-ridden upstairs life of the bourgeoisie served by downtrodden maids, an irascible cook and a sage butler. By the time October came, the first draft of 'The Remarkable Case of Burglary' had been completed and was put aside for revision and submission after the Indian trip was over.

The long-awaited date arrived and on October the 11th, I, together with two of the children, Piers, by now fourteen, and Hugo, ten, went with Harry to Heathrow to see him safely onto the Air India night-flight to Bombay. After he had embarked we stayed watching from one of the airport buildings until the huge plane vanished into the night. If we felt that the steady centre of our lives was taking off into the unknown it must have been as nothing compared with the turmoil going on inside him. In fact he later said, in the autobiographical article, that he spent a few minutes during the flight deciding the words he would utter as he got out onto Indian soil, *'One small step for Harry Keating, a giant leap for Inspector Ghote'.* This did not, in the end, happen because as he stepped out of the plane he was '...*overwhelmed by the thick, damp heat, I thought simply, "Cripes" and immediately afterwards was summoned back on board by the Air India photographer, who had missed me stepping out, and I had to re-enact the moment. If I had seen India once as a symbol of the imperfect, my notion seemed now to be realised.'*

In the autobiographical article he admits that on his first morning in the city, *'I decided, timid fellow that I am, to take a walk round the block and then retreat again to the air-conditioned safety of the Taj Mahal Hotel. I was waylaid, though, by an agreeable Indian who began to talk to me about the buildings round about. Naïve Harry Keating failed, of course, to realise he was in the hands of a professional guide. But under a stream of implacable discourse, I was led far that morning, saw lepers up against the railings round St Thomas Cathedral and did not blench. I saw much else during that visit that might have disgusted me and did not. I saw, as well, things that happily confirmed what I had written, and I saw some things, not many, that I had got wrong. I filled, of course, notebook after notebook with those little, different touches that make vivid a strange environment to readers of fiction, the women selling bundles of grass beside the holy cows wandering at will in the metropolitan streets, the roadside cobblers, thread held taut round a big toe, ever ready to mend the strap of a frail sandal, the rust red splashes of betel juice from chewed 'paans' on the pavement everywhere, the padlock on the letter boxes.*

Above all he was relieved to find that because he had previously absorbed, in his imagination, the horrors of the beggars and the squalor, he was able to cope with them in reality and over the best part of three weeks he accumulated backgrounds for many of the novels that were to come, among them, the red light district used in 'The Sheriff of Bombay' (*1984*); the burning ghats referred to often; the unreality of India's film world in Bollywood which he used for 'Filmi, Filmi, Inspector Ghote' (*1976*).

Although this relentless pursuit of information was exhausting, he nevertheless felt exhilarated, due, to some extent, to what he described as the high level of cheerfulness he encountered everywhere. Just as well because back home he had straightaway to pick up the relentless writing routine. There was a Times column to be written, with a stack of review books to choose from and after that the second draft of 'A Remarkable Case of Burglary' so that Collins would have their book for 1975.

But once again that had to be put on hold because of even more exciting plans. The BBC had a series with the broad title of *'The World About Us'* and, within that there was a sub-series called, *One Pair of Eyes*. One of their directors, Lawrence Gordon Clarke, undertook the task of taking his small film crew and Harry out to Bombay and making a documentary which they called '*The Search for the Real Inspector Ghote*'. They were happy to forget the trip Harry had just made and let it be assumed that this was his first visit to India. The film took him all over Bombay with an actor playing Ghote, investigating mock-ups of various crimes. One of the most vivid of these tackled the ever present problem of pick-pockets with Harry acting as guinea-pig. They had also had a mock-up made of Ghote's office—a replica of those used by the genuine Inspectors with, on the desk, a Toblerone-shaped block, painted black, with the name **G.V. GHOTE** engraved on it. This was presented to Harry afterwards to bring home. It remained a most cherished possession and sat, proprietorially, on the 'What-not' just inside the front door surrounded by Ganeshes and other Indian brass ornaments.

In the film he is in the background over-seeing these simulated police activities, looking absurdly young for his forty-eight years and sounding tensely high-pitched as the voice-over narrator. But it was in an extraordinary interview with the then Deputy Commissioner of the Bombay CID that the film had its most telling moments. The highly intelligent Superintendent Kulkarni spoke passionately about police work and from time to time talked easily about Inspector Ghote, praising Harry for the invention of an Inspector that he said he would dearly have loved to have had on his force, He praised particularly the character's humanity and his way of arriving at solutions through getting to know the suspects and, especially, for his cast-iron incorruptibility. What made the interview so compelling was the burning sincerity of Kulkarni who incidentally went on in later years to become head of the Indian Police Service.

I was extremely lucky to find that the programme shown just after Christmas in 1975 was still in the BBC archive in 2012 because we did not seem to have a copy of it. With great good fortune, Roly Keating (no relative) a BBC producer who had worked with Harry on book programmes in the intervening years, had, by the time Harry died, become head of the BBC Archive department and very generously made a DVD copy of the film for me.

The notes he made on that visit augmented the first visit and added hugely to Harry's data base. But returning from India that second time he could not at once return to writing about Ghote because he had to get the Victorian crime book to the publishers. Astonishingly when it came out in the autumn of 1975, there was apparently no trace of the impatience he must have felt, no sign that he needed to get shot of it in order to get back to Ghote. It would seem just the opposite was true from what was said in the reviews. According to George Duthie in The Scotsman, *a remarkable example of how hard work, research, attention to detail and fine imaginative writing can raise the crime novel far above anything we can rightly expect of the genre.'* After briefly describing the plot he continues, *'Rapscallion seduces scullion.''Through the dark and steamy Hogarthian splendour of Mr. Keating's scenes runs the bright thread of honest-hearted Janey's love for her rogue. Wonderful stuff.'* Easy to dismiss as just one man's opinion except that the praise is repeated many times by, among many others, Ann Brady in the Sunday Press of Dublin: *'Mr. Keating has successfully recreated a way of life long gone and given us a heart-warming picture of nineteenth century London.'* or The Sunday Times, *'cool yet humane, thoughtful yet fast-moving.'* Personally I would endorse all this from my experience recording the book for AudioGo a few years ago. I read it with great attention to detail three times during the preparation time before going into the studio and discovered more sub-text each time making it a very rich experience.

Happy that at least George Duthie of The Scotsman felt that crime writing could, on occasion, climb out of its genre and join the mainstream, it was however time to get to work and explore the jungle of information from his new-found India. The Times helped him to order his thoughts by inviting him to write an article for its Saturday Review about himself and Ghote. The first paragraph sets the tone of faint self-mockery.

'And there it was Haji Ali, the mosque that projects at the end of its long causeway into the Bombay sea, just as I had known that it would look. So I pointed it out to the driver of the car bringing me in from the airport, (Well, he might not have known.)...Haji Ali was heartening. It promised me that I had got a lot of it right,

117

and soon indeed I was able to confirm that I had done better than just getting the buildings in the correct places. I had, thank goodness, captured the atmosphere.

But, again, no great miraculous feat. Those other writers I had trusted had simply proved trustworthy, even down to such humble practitioners as the creator of the comic strip from whom I had learnt that Bombay pillar boxes have tops domed like tin hats. Though I had not learnt, thanks to the maddening obscurity of almost all illustrations, that the boxes are fastened by padlocks. In fact padlocks are great fasteners of things Indian everywhere.

Other details, too, of course, I had never got quite clear. Yes, I knew that 300,000 Bombay lunches are brought in each day from wives in the suburbs, by boys carrying metal containers in wooden racks. But until one afternoon when I walked along beside a returning trio of such dubbawallas I did not know exactly how long those racks were (6ft), how many went to a handcart (10), or just how each container got to its right luncher (painted letters and figures on the lid). Nor had I appreciated the cheerfulness of the striding dubbawallas. Here was something new: the high level of happiness in this city of patchily dreadful night.'

He details some of the things he had got wrong like the scratched and whorled state of Ghote's desk—in fact a description of the old sewing table he himself always used—when it should have been smartly topped with green leather. Some of the things he had not known such as the fact that the Bombay CID crime clear-up rate in 1973 was better than that achieved by Scotland Yard or that the prohibition laws had almost been abandoned allowing something called the Colaba Wine Mart to trade. He admits that, *'The sheer wild volume of it all threatened to sink me. The office of the Chief Inspector of Steam Boilers and Smoke Nuisances, I know just where it is, and the New Gentleman Restaurant, and the Moon Winding Works (specialists in re-winding fan motors). Oh, and yes, I can lead you, and diligent Ghote, straight to the shop that advertises "Surprised Contracts Are Undertaken". But heaven preserve me from too much easy quaintness.'* But he also acknowledges that much of what he saw he could never have imagined. He admits that he would never have been able to grasp the public acceptance of magic, astrology, palm-reading and the affect this had on people's lives. Although he already knew that cows wandered the streets he had actually to see them for this to become a reality. Things like the post-monsoon heat which he calls, 'bathroom humidity', or the actual sight of lepers and the maimed beggars on their trolleys were difficult wholly to imagine without, 'seeing, hearing, touching and smelling'. He was totally able to accept that an Indian may have beliefs not necessarily held by Westerners because all these things were, 'simply and naturally all around one.' but at the same time found it difficult to know how much he could put himself in their shoes and believe with them.

He concludes the article in philosophical mood. 'Such pieces of the pattern and others, will perhaps, eventually underpin half a dozen crime stories. But a last doubt enters. If it was all a giant leap for Inspector Ghote, did it take him in a mortally dangerous direction? Certainly he escaped death by bludgeoning under a rain of blows intolerable to his begetter's sensibilities. And he may have grown all the sturdier for his creator's new confidence after finding much of his acquired learning and some of his wild guesses justified, as well as for errors now happily correctable and for new nuggets stored away and incredibilities made at last credible. But Ghote's dangerous journey will not be finally done till he reaches the safety of a finished typescript. He could still be set upon and come to a sticky end suffocated under a feather pile of crowding facts. Other heroes have been stunted by their creators knowing too much. Just a little I tremble.'

But all his misgivings remained within himself to be battled out in the solitariness of the study even if, plainly, it was not altogether straight forward, as he tells us in the autobiography article, 'I found I had got myself into quite unexpected difficulty. I had decided to test the new Ghote on a short story. It began, as many of his adventures do, with a summons to see the head of the CID. Only, with the BBC camera crew, I had spent hours myself in his very office. I wrote a description of it right down to the names of the police dogs on the crime board behind the desk. It took pages and Ghote still had not been sent on the mission that was to constitute the story, "The Noted British Author." (Such I myself had been called in a Bombay newspaper piece.) I saw the error of my new way, and I hope afterwards did not allow myself to be dragged down by sticky facts from the real world instead of being buoyed up by airy ones passed through the transfiguration factory of the imagination. As an interesting footnote, thirty-eight years later in 2012, the year after he died, that same short story appeared again, this time as a tribute, in a Crime Writers' Association collection edited by fellow crime writer, Martin Edwards. The inclusion of the 1975 story in a 2012 publication is a reassurance that the words live on after the hand that wrote them has left us.

The first toe-in-the-water safely behind him it was time to tackle a full-length Ghote novel. Bollywood had often occurred as a possibility but it was good that it had been postponed until after he had actually visited and seen for himself this larger than life, thriving industry. The comment Harry made was predictable, *'out-Hollywooding Hollywood at its most absurd...In many ways it exceeded my most riotous imaginings with its marvelously self-absorbed stars, its shift system by which they make as many as forty films at a time moving from one to another from morning to evening, its playback singers voicing for the dancing stars the obligatory songs that interrupt even a story like the "Maqbet" I invented as a typical rip-off from Shakespeare's tragedy.'*

Among the reviews kept inside the flap of the dust jacket there is an article included with a review of the book but not written till much later. To the article is pinned a card from a Peter Henson of Rupa and Co., with a message sadly too faded to read. But the article is from India Today dated February 1981, the year Harry had revisited India for the third time, and it quotes something he had said to the interviewer—maybe Peter Henson?—obviously in disbelief at the reception he has had in India, *'There you are quietly writing away at your desk, and you produce this little book. Your wife likes it, but she's an interested party. Your agent approves, but he's also an interested party. Then you come 5,000 miles from home, and people stop you on street corners to tell you how much they love reading your books. Isn't it wonderful?'*

Between finishing it and publication day he had time for one spin off from 'A Remarkable Case of Burglary' as well as his first non-fiction title. The spin off was an adaptation as a radio play which, for some reason the BBC chose to call 'The Affair at No 35'. This went out in the Saturday-night Theatre slot on Radio 4, and in those days it went out 'live' which meant that after rehearsals the play was performed at the actual time of transmission, with no possibility of stopping and starting again if something goes wrong, which is, of course, what happens nowadays when everything is pre-recorded. It also meant a strict adherence to one of the golden rules for actors in those days that there must never be any 'script noise', the listener must believe that the characters are really speaking to each other and not reading the words written on a page, so there must be no tell-tale rustle as a page has to be turned. Part of the technique was to choose a moment during someone else's speech to face 'off mike', turn the page silently and then be back facing the right way for the next cue. Just one of the minor, but many very different skills that a radio actor had to learn, skills which are quite separate from those required by a stage actor.

Of course scripting a radio play is also different from writing a stage one but this was not Harry's first experience of radio, having had three original Ghote plays produced by the splendidly eccentric John Scotney who was a stalwart of the now defunct BBC script unit. These had been quite chaotic productions with the studio filled to capacity with a host of Indian actors particularly in the case of the one where Ghote, disguised as one of a group of hopelessly ill-prepared illegal immigrants, was expected, on landing, to revert to his job as a policeman and expose them to the British police. It can only be hoped that, in the end, the dialogue achieved a level of audibility to allow an understanding of the plot.

In contrast this Victorian play was a model of orderliness. Harry adapted the book himself and was on hand in the listening cubicle with the director, Norman Wright, and the technicians, throughout the rehearsals, ready to make any alterations to the script. Possibly his days 'copy-tasting' in the subs room at the Times were a help because he was very calm and quite able to make whatever changes were necessary. Once again Harry was instrumental in giving me employment, this time I played the down-to-earth, martinet, cook. It was a happy occasion and undoubtedly good for Harry to realise that creativity could possibly happen away from the strict privacy of his own study.

The other task—the non-fiction book—happened because an old college acquaintance, Alan Synge, was starting up a small publishing house with the charming name, The Lemon Tree Press. He was interested in doing a book about The Golden Age of crime fiction. Harry had many times addressed this subject in talks and articles about crime writing but this was a chance to examine the work of those who came to prominence in the half decade leading up to the second World War. Some, like Agatha Christie and Dorothy L. Sayers, are still in bookshops today; others such as Nicholas Blake, better known as poet laureate Cecil Day Lewis, Margery Allingham, Edmund Crispin, Michael Innes, Josephine Tey and Ngaio Marsh are, perhaps less available but nevertheless acknowledged as masters in the field. They and others were the authors that Harry was reading when he was growing up and borrowing the copies his mother got from Boots lending library. And although his own books were stylistically very different, he never had any doubt of the debt he owed them. While many literary critics tended to under-rate Agatha Christie in particular, he would always point to the immense pleasure she gave to millions of people around the world, praising her for providing a diversion for those in need of comfort or those who were lonely, capable of providing hours of relief from their troubles.

He called the book 'Murder Must Appetize'—deliberately an echo of Dorothy L. Sayers well-known Lord Peter Wimsey novel 'Murder Must Advertise'—and the first words of the book are also deliberately light-hearted: *'Is there anything, when life gets a bit much, as comforting as a detective story?'* He immediately answers himself, *'Well yes of course there is. Drink. The love of a good woman. The attentions of a bad woman. Yet,'* he continues, *'for many of us the quintessential detective story does have a warm inward-spreading cosiness that can expel any number of everyday horrors.* In 1981 a revised version of the book was reprinted by The Lemon Tree Press and Otto Penzler, owner of the The Mysterious Press. He also produced a beautifully assembled, limited boxed edition. Otto has been a fixture in the Keating family life for many years, not only as a friend but as a publisher and not only is his name to be found elsewhere in these pages, attached to other non-fiction titles, but in the early 1990s he was responsible for the American editions of five novels, 'Dead on Time', 'The Iciest Sin', 'The Rich Detective', 'Cheating Death', and 'Doing Wrong' and to this day is still including reprints of some of Harry's short stories in the anthologies he is producing.

But 'Murder Must Appetize' was the first actual professional connection between them. Inside the cover of one of that limited-edition is the typescript of a Cincinnati radio broadcast, delivered by Walter Shepherd, a devotee of the traditional 'mystery'—the word used by the Americans when we say detective story. He said in his broadcast, *'The balance of the book is an amiable, leisurely, not-too-critical examination of how a mystery with such powers is written. He provides numerous examples of his points.'* Then he quotes Harry's words in the book itself, *"Evil was not allowed to triumph. And it is this affirmation that underlay the whole genre's popularity."* There were several further critical books to come over the years but this was an introductory song from the heart.

Another quickly fitted in job was quite bizarre. Sometimes a paperback publisher decides that there's money to be made from turning the script of what looks like being a successful film into a book. The actual film script would be sent to a chosen hack and it had to be ready in around three weeks to coincide with the release of the film. In this case the film was 'Murder by Death' scripted by the well-known American playwright Neil Simon. With Harry's journalistic background the speed required was no problem except that, in this case, when he came to read the script there were unexplained blank pages, the characters' names were written down the left-hand side but there was no dialogue. When he asked if these gaps could be filled in the reply came back, 'You know which actor is playing the part and the way they speak and where the story has got to go so you will be able to imagine what they said.' It is to be hoped that Harry guessed right. Nobody complained and as the film was not a run-away success probably very few people bought the book. As far as any writer of such a mish-mash of a book is concerned they would receive a not ungenerous one-off payment for two or three weeks of work and that was the end of it.

These 'side-shows' were a way of making a bit of extra money and they filled in the odd minutes between planning and writing the first draft of whatever the next Ghote was going to be which, it must always be remembered, would have been completed before the publication of the last one. When the reviews for *Filmi, Filmi,* came out they showed that the first visits to India seem neither to have cramped the style nor, what would have been even worse, have led to extravagant over-indulgence in painting the background.

The Times in their review—not, of course, in Harry's own regular column but written by someone else—tried hard to find traces of difference, but could not, *'The atmosphere, as always, is spot on, Ghote is as endearing as ever, and there are some good Shakespeare-wallah jokes. The Birnam Wood lines have been translated to the "Banana groves coming to Dehra Dun".'* Harry would have especially relished finding the echoing rhythms for 'Birnam Wood be come to Dunsinane' and the transposition of 'B's for 'D's and his own fun was echoed by what could perhaps be interpreted as the delighted chuckle which pervaded all the reviews. William Weaver, in The Financial Times, credited the Bombay visit for the success of the book, calling it, *'unusually rich and irresistibly funny.'* While Edmund Crispin in The Sunday Times draws attention to the, *'convincing portrayal of the combined glamour and tat, posturing and hard work which characterises filmdom everywhere.',* something he knew at first hand because he wrote the scores for many films.

Filmi. Filmi—Harry tells us the word is a Hindi hybrid—had been written to amuse. It was a way of easing himself back into writing about India and he calls it a comic Ghote. It was almost as if he thought of Ghote's extraordinary escape from reality into this fantasy world as an interlude in the Inspector's life. Both author and character could be said to be relaxing before embarking on the next, much more serious, task that awaited him.

Chapter 12

The next book in the series, 'Inspector Ghote Draws a Line', was not intended to be in the least degree frivolous, for it was to *portray a figure that, with increasing age, had begun to fascinate me, the former idealist turned realist, the liberal who had moved quarter-inch by quarter-inch to conservatism*. It is interesting to put that phrase 'increasing age' that he applied to himself, into the context of the 1970s when reaching the age of fifty weighed more heavily than it does now. Harry was fifty-two when he was planning this book yet, although actually the article that quote comes from was written some ten years later, he was already in 1978 thinking of himself as advancing in years. But the character he chose to help him to explore this idea was considerably older; he was a retired judge living in an isolated house in the arid countryside somewhere outside Bombay. Ghote soon finds out that the judge is viewing with contempt the threat to his life which he has recently received. Ghote's superiors, alerted to the threat, have sent him to investigate and forestall such a disaster, but when he arrives he is met with a blunt refusal to co-operate.

Harry was fortunate in knowing an Indian now living in this country, a former Indian judge's highly intelligent daughter, Roshan Horabin, who had done a legal side-step and become England's first Indian Probation Officer. She was able to give him details of the very different life a judge on the sub-continent would have led in the dying days of the Raj as well as talking about the sort of man her father had been. Not intended in any way to be a portrait of Roshan's father, he was able to give the fictional judge many of the characteristics that were apparently common among the early Indian judiciary. Many had the reputation of being harsh and implacable in the way they had wielded their power when sentencing miscreants. Ghote thinks that it is quite possible that the death threats come from the descendants of a group of nationalists who had been condemned to death for conspiring to blow up the Governor of Madras. But there is a vivid cast of equally likely suspects ranging from the extremes of an insane son kept imprisoned in a dungeon on the grounds of the house, to a radiant swami who remains silent throughout the book. The household have accepted Ghote's disguise as a Doctor of Philosophy and that he has been summoned to discuss academic matters with the Judge.

This was always meant to be a contemplative book and while the reviews remained positive, some did mention that the pace was on the slow side with Mathew Coady in the Guardian finding it leisurely, although he concluded, '*subtle personality conflicts, perceptively observed, predominate.*' Alec Spokesman of the Northern Echo coined the phrase a 'who-might-do-it' but nevertheless found it, '*entertaining.*' The Evening Standard thought that, '*a great deal of the interest—and the implicit fun—of this excellent novel is following Ghote's frustrated investigations into who might be doing what.*' Harry, himself, always had a soft spot for the book perhaps for the very reason that it was such a cerebral book and he had enjoyed the intellectual challenge. It is worth noting that he plainly felt secure enough to loosen the usual taut boundaries of his chosen genre

But before it was published in 1979 there were three very different books to be completed. Two of these were non-fiction titles where he acted as editor as well as contributing an article. The first of them had to be put together with some urgency. Agatha Christie died in 1977 and Weidenfeld and Nicholson were quick off the mark and reaped the rewards by publishing that same year the first tribute to her to hit the market. Harry was commissioned to assemble articles on all aspects of Christie's work, not only the world-renowned Hercule Poirot and Miss Marple books but also the pseudonymous Mary Westmacott romantic novels. There were also a vast number of stage plays as well as the films that were made from her books. He found distinguished writers from both sides of the Atlantic to address the phenomenon and he entitled it 'Agatha Christie. The First Lady of Crime'. The publisher left it to Harry to decide on his team and set his own agenda.

The final paragraph of his introduction neatly encapsulates what he set out to do. *'It is fashionable in French intellectual circles currently—and there can be no more intellectual circles than these, nor any more fashion-conscious—to claim that the many-angled approach of many writers is the highest form of biography, the colloquė. I hardly go as far as that in putting forward this combined look at the phenomenon of Agatha Christie, that least intellectual of persons. But it is perhaps true that her mystery is best solved, not, alas, by the lone amateur detective but by the sober and concerted efforts of all the specialists a whole police force can bring to bear.'*

The specialists he assembled were impressive. They included leading crime writers of the time Emma Lathen and Dorothy B. Hughes, both from America, while British crime novelists included Julian Symons, Michael Gilbert, Colin Watson, Christiana Brand and Edmund Crispin. J.C. Trewin, the eminent theatre critic, and film specialist Philip Jenkinson completed the list of contributors.

The piece from Crispin, entitled 'The Mistress of Simplicity', nearly didn't happen. He had not been in very good health and had found it difficult to find the energy to write, so Harry said he would visit him in the West Country where he lived and record a conversation with him. He managed to borrow a state-of-the-art recorder of the type then used by BBC reporters and prepared questions for Crispin to answer which aimed to analyse what made Christie so consistently successful. The dialogue that resulted was very lively because Crispin did not always agree with the answer Harry expected, which, of course, added sparkle. The interview concluded, Harry packed up his machine—they were quite sizeable in those days—and made his way back to the station.

He had a while to wait for a train so thought he would check what the interview sounded like. Sitting on a platform bench he switched on only to be greeted by silence. There was nothing there. Plainly the fault must have been his in some way but the machine simply had not recorded. Feeling very shame-faced—what a thing to happen to an erstwhile BBC sound engineer—he decided he would have to return and ask to do it all over again. It was apparent that Crispin was too exhausted to do the interview a second time that evening. Very hospitably they invited Harry to stay the night and try again in the morning. This time, after meticulously checking all the connections, it was smoothly recorded.

The book was finally assembled and ready for publication in record time and was also published in America that same year. It came out in a generous crown quarto size and was lavishly illustrated but was still able to be priced at a modest £5.

The other non-fiction title that Harry edited came out a year later, in 1978, as a BBC publication simply entitled 'Crime Writers' and sprang from a TV series put together by producer Bernard Adams and writer and technical expert Mike Pavett for the BBC Further Education Department. The series itself was based on Julian Symons' 'Bloody Murder', a study of the golden age detective story through to the more modern crime novel. The book drew on the series where the experts talked about different aspects of crime fiction and crime on TV. After the filming was completed, it was decided that BBC Publications would produce the book to complement the series and Harry was asked to edit it. In his Editor's Foreword he makes the interesting point that although the TV series and the book would be covering the same ground and use many of the same contributors, the approach would be very different. To begin with, the BBC only allowed Bernard and Mike a brief half hour for each of the six episodes, but the book had the advantage of being able to be more expansive. The foreword puts it this way: *'Television has its own way of conveying information: books, even illustrated ones, go about conveying it in another manner. So, although in editing this volume I have kept loosely to the format of the television series, I have expected the authors whom I asked to contribute essays to approach their subjects in a slightly different way.'*

I am very grateful to Bernard Adams and Mike Pavett, who not only unearthed the originals but then transferred them to DVDs so that I was able to re-watch the programmes which, when I re-read the book 'Crime Writers' made this interesting difference very apparent.

The immediacy of the TV is, of course, obvious. Both Julian and Harry act as presenters and are also seen in conversation with other experts like Phyllis James talking about Dorothy L. Sayers or Colin Watson exploring the mores of the upper middle class and Mayhem Parva, and they all make for compelling viewing. Then there are the trips down memory lane made possible through clips of the classic TV series 'Z Cars', introduced by one of the originating writers, Troy Kennedy Martin. Gavin Lyall explains the sharp reality of life which is the essence of Dashiell Hammett and we are shown the sleazy world of Raymond Chandler's Philip Marlowe. By the end of the six programmes, Bernard and Mike succeeded in giving the viewer a history of crime fiction with the bonus of the highlights of TV and film. The time allowed for each episode had obviously condensed the material quite severely but what remains has an extraordinary vividness, an immediacy that it would be difficult for words on a page to achieve, even when supported by illustrations.

But the book, as Harry said, was never intended to mirror the TV, its aim was, as the foreword says, '... *to look at crime and the writer. We have asked ourselves how at various periods the writers of the day tackled their subjects. We have asked what readers, and later viewers, wanted from them. Our approach has tended to be more social commentary than literary history.* The beginning of the final paragraph of the foreword although using only words, does, in fact, paint an even more vivid picture of the job of an editor than any TV screen could do, *'The editor of a book such as this is like a spider. He sits there in the early stages spinning an aerial web of suggestions, promises, even sticky flatteries, and he hopes eventually to catch a full haul of meaty flies, perhaps a succulent bumblebee or a dragonfly for his deep-freeze.'*

Which are 'meaty flies', which 'bumblebees' and which the darting 'dragonfly' it would be difficult to say but the line-up of contributors is very impressive. Harry was quite right to say that, *'I think I have been enormously lucky in the haul I caught'.*

It is easy to understand why Reginald Hill's own books are so masterfully written, showing, apart from ingenuity of plotting and attention to characterisation, a meticulous attention to necessary detail. In the article he contributes he compresses into around five thousand words an analysis of Sherlock Holmes, whom he calls the 'Hamlet of Crime Fiction' and gives us not only a detailed account of the man and his methods, but produces a scholarly dissertation on the world he inhabited. This is linked to a particularly well-argued examination of the policing of those days and the importance to crime fiction of having a police force. He also, briefly, looks at Edgar Allan Poe and his creation, the amateur sleuth, Dupin, whose methods are so similar to Holmes' own, pointing out Poe's influence on Conan Doyle, something the latter happily acknowledged.

In an introduction to Hill's piece, Mike Pavett provides information about the days before crime fiction proper, when what was on offer were broadsheets and ballads to titillate the masses with tales of real violence, and he sets the scene of those days with potted portraits of the villains and newly arrived policemen—some of whom were as much villain as representatives of law and order. His words are plentifully backed up with reproductions of period pictures such as an invitation to witness an execution or the graphic illustrations to the article in the Catnach broadsheet which described the murder of Maria Marten of Red Barn fame. Mike has a further five entries in the book which act as links between the main articles so ensuring that the continuity of the story is maintained. And throughout he has plundered the archives for portraits as well as film and TV stills which appear on almost every page, nudging the reader's memory.

When Colin Watson tackles the Golden Age crime novels, it is not just a list of the best, it is an in-depth investigation into what made the middle classes tick in the years between the two world wars. P.D. James takes over with an appraisal of Dorothy L. Sayers, which gives her the credit for being a fine example of what could be done beyond the boundaries of the conventional crime novel and the influence she had on the genre as a whole, while not glossing over criticisms that have been levelled at her about, for instance, her anti-Semitism. Julian Symons expands on the eventually self-defeating life of the 'Onlie Begetter of the true American crime story', Dashiell Hammett, about whom he says, *Almost everything he wrote, after the earliest pieces, was stamped with a personal mark. He was an original writer in style and approach,*

130

and there are few of whom one can truly use the word. The least of his work is interesting and the best has a permanent place in literature.

Maurice Richardson, having been the crime reviewer on the Observer for thirty-seven years and TV critic as well for a thirteen year period in the middle, was in a strong position to look at two of the major talents in the genre, both of whom he had met, Simenon and Patricia Highsmith. Both are renowned for being enigmatic, and Richardson makes a fine stab at unravelling both their writing and their personalities. Troy Kennedy Martin expands the picture with a look at the multi police TV series, 'Z Cars' before Harry has a concluding article which he calls 'Patents Pending' in which he tries to second guess the path the crime novel will take in the coming years. His conclusion is predictable but nevertheless states what cannot be repeated often enough: *'Crime stories while still acknowledging that they exist first to entertain, that they are written for the sake of the reader and not primarily for the sake of what the writer has to say, have contrived over the years, and I believe will succeed in the years to come yet more, to have their say, to make their comments on our world as it actually is and on the way we mess it about. And at the same time, because they are entertainment, they have kept to the form expected of them and have, with exceptions that illustrate the rule, given their readers a happy ending, have asserted once more that justice ought to be done, but that order can be, if ever so little, if only for a while, attained.*

As editor and contributor, Harry was able to provide space for airing, not only his own beliefs, but also for those eminent in the crime writing world to join the crusade to get the genre taken seriously. A pity that Harry could not hear the comment Bernard Adams made about him when we were talking recently about the making of the series and the subsequent book, *'He was the most modest, accommodating and delightful writer this person has ever met.'*

The second 1978 book was fiction but not a crime novel. The nagging desire was still there—to write the definitive straight novel. And so there followed 'A Long Walk to Wimbledon'. This was as near as Harry would ever get to writing science fiction and it only remotely fits into that category because it is set sometime in the unspecified future. It cannot even be categorised as truly fantasy because the narrated events are harshly linked to reality. His own description of the genesis of the book is not only vivid but is a perfect example of how his imagination could turn a mundane incident into drama. *'I had stopped at the kerb about to cross the road near my home in London's Notting Hill and had seen in my mind's eye a truck, waveringly driven, mount the pavement and almost knock me down. I imagined its driver under the influence of a marijuana-like drug and saw that it might happen in a future London wrecked by the excesses of its own civilisation.'*

This wreckage, and the affect it has on surviving isolated communities, is told to us through the eyes of a man who is attempting to walk, because there is no means of transport, from his home in North London to Wimbledon in South West London—Harry admits he chose Wimbledon as much because he thought Americans would have heard of it, as the fact that it provided a route of about the right length from the North of London through the centre to the South West of the city. His hero is undertaking this task because he has been summoned to his estranged wife's deathbed. He has to fight the clock because he has been told she has only forty-eight hours to live, but he also has to fight his own reluctance to tackle what will be at best a risky journey and at worst could result in his own death. Mark, the central character, is obviously and indeed, on his own admission, Harry himself. Given his reluctance to write anything remotely in the first person, the result is a somewhat hazily drawn character, something that at least one reviewer found a drawback. But others were not put off. David Holloway in The Daily Telegraph finds the story *'Quite plainly an allegory as the title hints, a modern "Pilgrim's Progress." As all good allegory should be, it is also an absorbing story—funny, sad, exciting, depressing.'*

It is plain that the book meant different things to different people because despite Jeremy Brooks, in The Sunday Times, after describing some of Mark's encounters with *'gangs of hippies high on home-grown marijuana, a flopped-out crowd of arrack-drinkers...a strict religious community...a fascist regime...being attacked by wild dogs.',* goes onto say, *'Mark himself, hitherto a coward in hiding, learns the physical and mental tricks of survival. Life, of a kind, even kindness, of a kind, are possible in this new jungle.'* His concluding paragraph, interestingly, disagrees with David Holloway. *'There may be an allegorical meaning here that I've missed; if there is, Mr. Keating isn't pushing it, and I'm all for that. As sheer entertainment the book is hard to beat.'*

Harry had his own comment to make. *'I think the book was a success, if not the overwhelming one in both literary and sales terms I was hoping for. And again, I ask, have I got the right stuff for that in me?'* Peter Tinniswood's review in The Times goes some way to answering this question. He finds the beginning of the work *'brilliantly written. Images of familiar objects (the Archway bridge carrying Hornsey lane soaring above the landscape, the dark and brooding Highgate Wood, Archway itself and Junction Road) poke themselves out of the chaos with stabbing clarity. This is how it should be. Horror, dismay, awe, fascination flood over you as you compare contemporary familiarity with the ghastly picture of the future so bleakly portrayed. When the book sticks to this theme it never wavers for a moment from the highest excellence.'* But—and it is a very big but—Tinniswood can find only one character who is fully rounded: Mad Meg, the old woman he encounters in the ruins of Buckingham Palace who tells him that feigning madness is the recipe for survival and who ingeniously helps him on to the final stages of his journey along the tracks of the old tube lines. It is worth considering whether this lack of deep characterisation was not, in fact, deliberate. Mad Meg was the only person Mark encountered who actually made a major input to the outcome of the story, acting as the catalyst to his own inability to cope with life and ultimately complete his pilgrimage. All the other characters encountered in the course of his action-packed journey have to be more thumbnail sketches than in-depth studies and although vivid and dominant at the time are of necessity ephemeral. They come alive for the moment and then disappear as Mark moves on.

P.D. James, who spoke powerfully and movingly at Harry's funeral, was unequivocal in finding it the best book he wrote. With so much praise, so many comments making it apparent that he was so tantalisingly close to what he was hoping for, it is tempting to add more questions to the one Harry asked of himself: was it indeed a fatal flaw in himself that he found it difficult to write 'close up' rather than at arm's length? Or was it perhaps that he should have allowed himself longer when writing these books which had a larger canvas? Should he not have asked himself if it was still essential to produce a new fiction title each year? Should those at the cutting edge of his life, myself, his agent, his publishers, have involved ourselves more, perhaps urging him to ease up a little? After all, the pace had been relentless for nineteen years. Add to that I had quite successfully resumed my acting career and, although not earning megabucks, was able to make a contribution to the family income. Simon at twenty-three was through University and was earning a living as a stage manager, Bryony was nearly through her Art School degree course with a salaried future beckoning in the BBC's Visual Effects department, which meant earning money was, for us, no longer a burning issue. Admittedly Piers at eighteen was about to go to University with the intention of making acting his career and Hugo at fourteen still had four more turbulent years at school, but the family had no debts and their home was without a mortgage. There was every sign that in Harold Macmillan's 'never-had-it-so-good' years someone as well-established as H.R.F. Keating could look forward to continuing to make a comfortable living from his pen. Perhaps the problem was simply that Harry's confidence, like the 'beauty' in 'Is Skin Deep, Is Fatal' was just that, only skin-deep, and that was, if not a fatal flaw, at least a hindrance. But this is dangerously close to conjecture and as such, Harry would say, is forbidden to the biographer. What is fact is that he continued to drive himself relentlessly forward.

But leaving aside how much of a success 'A Long Walk to Wimbledon' was at the time there is no doubt that he would have been pleased that the book still lives on in new formats. It has recently been published as an ebook by Bloomsbury reader—indeed Amazon used it as a 99p marketing project for a day and sold more than two thousand, five hundred copies in that one day. I personally find it dubious marketing that they chose the opening day of the tennis at Wimbledon to advertise the book because of its title with which it had no connection whatsoever. How many of the two thousand-odd punters actually read the book once they discovered the deception?

It is also an unabridged audio book first recorded by AudioGo (formerly BBC Audiobooks) but now owned by Audible (the audiobook arm of

Amazon) and read by one of the very best readers, Stephen Thorne.

And most recently an option has been taken out by a Hindi film maker to turn it into an Indian language film.

While this was undoubtedly a serious fiction offering, he was also providing Otto Penzler, who was by now looking after the crime fiction for Little Brown in America, with a contribution to the book he was compiling in 1978 entitled 'The Great Detectives'. Each author was required to write a comprehensive profile of their hero. Harry's response, according to the blurb for the book, was *'an hilarious letter from a harassed official of Bombay's Crime Branch.'* This is written in the Anglo-English of the Ghote books and begins by absolutely sending himself up: *'Ha it is BIO-DATA you are wanting? Bio-data on Inspector Ghote? Well, well, no-one here at Bombay Crime Branch is knowing all that much about the fellow. Not at all. He is meant to be working here, but all the time no-one is ever seeing him. Only from those books which that writerwallah in England is always publishing am I at all knowing that Ghote is a colleague of mine only.'*

For some six pages Harry pokes fun at himself and points out how little is actually known about Ghote, making the Indian policeman, who is supposed to be writing the article, express his surprise among a host of other complaints that Ghote did not even have a forename for the first few books and it was not until the tenth book in the series that the name attached to the second initial 'V' was revealed and he could be known as Ganesh Vinayak Ghote. The various other missing details are laid out for us, no physical descriptions other than a pair of bony shoulders; no age is ever mentioned; that originally there was no acknowledgement of how Ghote, a native of Bombay, came to be married to a Bengali which she must be with the name of Protima and even when there was this concession there was still no explanation of how that had happened. Towards the end of the letter the imaginary policeman snaps, *'So why is it then that despite all and sundry Ghote ends up every time successful? Is it because he has to do so for the purposes of Literature only? Or is it because the Gods are wishing to show us that Good always in the end must triumph? Well, if that is the case, it is frankly bloody damn unfair.'* And, finally, a triumphant jibe, *'And there's one thing I can tell you also.*

However, many cases this Ghote fellow tucks under his belt only, he would never rise above inspector rank. Never. Never.

Chapter 13

To come out in the same year, 1979, as 'Inspector Ghote Draws a Line', Harry was commissioned to write a completely different book which neatly married fiction and non-fiction. Thames and Hudson, who although mostly publishing art books, were running a series with the overall title 'The Man and His World', asked Harry, already known for his admiration of Sir Arthur Conan Doyle, to write a life of Sherlock Holmes. Holmes had often been regarded by Doyle's many readers as made of flesh and blood so it might seem a small step to take the fictional character and with a wave of the wand transform him into a living person worthy of a biography in his own right. Deliberately Doyle had made his character shy of any sort of publicity and very few actual facts are known about him, leading previous 'biographers' to speculate in whatever way they chose or, indeed, base what they said on anything Dr. Watson seemed able to divulge. The blurb for the book explains how Harry set about achieving what reads like a genuine life story. *'H.R.F. Keating has taken a new approach. In writing this life of Holmes he has confined himself to the authenticated facts that Dr. Watson alone was in a position to give the world, but to them has added historical facts and documented accounts of cultural events of Holmes's day.'*

There can be no doubt that this was a rewarding book to write; Harry's own enjoyment leaps off the page. He had revelled in the stories from boyhood as well as re-reading them many times since. Moreover they were set in a period of history that he not only found fascinating but about which he had done a mountain of research when writing 'The Underside'. He has a sentence on the very first page which sets the tone for this light-hearted but also totally serious study. *'But conjecture in biography is a sin as deplorable as simony in the Church (though perhaps more often committed) and it will be my endeavour in this portrayal of Sherlock Holmes and his world to avoid it.'*

Just as Harry used to give himself constant reminders, a word or a phrase written in a way to catch his eye constantly while writing a particular book, such as **LOYALTY** when writing 'Inspector Ghote Caught in Meshes', so, maybe, a biographer should have inscribed in capitals, somewhere close to their screen, **CONJECTURE IN BIOGRAPHY IS A SIN**—or at least know where to find the nearest confessional.

Here he does not sin and manages to paint a vivid picture of the late nineteenth century into which he introduces the characters and situations invoked in the stories. The reader is immersed in a bygone world where Britain is supreme, emerging in the 1870s from a long period of Victorian peace into a time of war but also of successful imperialism; a time of order when the trains ran on time and the post was delivered on the same day it was put in the pillar box. He presents us with a picture of the English Gentleman, that upright individual who could always be relied upon to 'do the decent thing', together with the sober hard-working ethics of Carlisle, Browning and Ruskin. And, although this is social history, we are never in the lecture hall, all the information is completely accessible so that as the story unfolds he is able to introduce Holmes and Watson leading their lives as real people, people we ourselves would have encountered had we happened to become embroiled in their adventures.

What could have been a work of whimsy, an absurd attempt to persuade us that Doyle's stories were not works of fiction, becomes instead a gentle, but full-bloodied, introduction to those bygone days told by someone who has undeniably done their research but never rams it down our throats. There were several more non-fiction titles to come over the succeeding years but none had this imaginative formula which allowed Harry, so felicitously, to air his grasp of historical fact while writing about the world of fiction.

Much later in 2008 at the annual Dorothy L. Sayers convention, the book provided material for a talk about Sherlock Holmes and how Lord Peter Wimsey was a link in the chain of great detectives that stemmed from Conan

Doyle's creation. As an honorary member of the DLS Society, Harry had, over the years, delivered a variety of papers at their conventions and after his death Christopher Dean, the Chairman, now sadly deceased, decided to ask a member, Geraldine Perriam, to collate these as 'The Keating Papers' with a generous tribute from fellow crime writer, Simon Brett, as an introduction. Simon has some pithy sentences which capture Harry and his work. *'And all his works were imbued by the same qualities: a strong moral sense, a compassion for mankind and a subversive current of mischief.'* Or, as a comment on his non-fiction books, *'His knowledge of the genre was enviably broad, but his erudition was always lightly worn. He was, above all, an* **enthusiast** *for crime fiction, and that comes through in all he wrote.'* Simon concludes with an anecdote which was incidentally included in a collection of memorable snippets from after-dinner speeches published by The Folio Society. *'He was a man of delightfully understated wit and I remember once sharing a platform with him after an excellent dinner at one of the Inns of Court. He began his speech by saying, "During the meal I was discussing with Mr. Justice Brown the correct amount to be drunk by someone about to give an after-dinner speech...and I've just realised I've got it wrong".'*

After 2008 when his energies started to decline Harry would spend a great deal of his time reading, or rather re-reading, the same treasured books. Julian Barnes' part fact, part fiction account of Conan Doyle's involvement with a young Indian solicitor accused of horse mutilation, 'Arthur and George', was one such. What captivated him was not just the exploration of Conan Doyle's personality but the way in which Barnes told the story with such compassion. It was indeed a quality Harry much admired and always tried to emulate.

But back in 1980 Ghote was given a rest while a book, still set in India, but in the 1930s' days of the Raj, occupied him. This was at the request of Collins Crime Club who were about to celebrate their fiftieth birthday. For once the first edition copy does not contain the raft of reviews which were stored inside the dust jacket of previous titles. This is particularly strange because it was universally admired and gained Harry a second Gold Dagger from the Crime Writers' Association. But even if the originals appear lost, excerpts can be found on the back of 'Inspector Ghote Goes West', the next book in the series, which would be published in 1981. Reviewing this 1980 book, 'The Murder of the Maharajah', a doyenne of critics at the time, Marghanita Laski, said, *'A truly classic detective story...an absolutely splendid book holding up its spine with the best of the genre it pastiches...fictional entertainment at its best.'* Echoed by F.E. Pardoe in The Birmingham Post, *'It really is a delightful story, creating a lovely picture of a world that has disappeared, and the plot is impeccable—with a surprise served up for the very last word.'*

The critic Julian Symons, now really 'emeritus', having retired from his regular slot on the Sunday Times, wrote to Harry about the book and that letter is preserved. It expresses his delight, *'Setting, language, Indian relationships were all splendidly realised and the Maharajah himself a joy...the puzzle was dead clever, and I got it wrong, keeping my eye so firmly fixed on young Michael (excellent) that I missed the clue.'* Interestingly he goes on to say that he is sure it will make a splendid film. Surprisingly that never happened, although someone did take out an option which in the event was not followed through into a production. The irony of this is that it had originally been written as a film outline for James Ivory, Ismail Merchant's director partner. One evening when Ismail and James were dining with us, James had said to Harry that he would love to direct an epic crime movie along the lines of the successful 'Murder on the Orient Express'. Never one to miss a chance like that Harry set about doing a treatment for the Maharajah story but by the time James received the proposed outline he had moved on to something else and having read it, stowed it in a pocket and forgot about it. There can be no more mercurial world than that of the big screen.

It did however make it to a BBC studio some years later when the BBC decided to adapt a series of Gold Dagger winners for the radio. Neville Teller, a master at adaptations, did an excellent script but, for thespian reasons, which it would certainly be unkind to detail, it was not an enormous success. Once again I was lucky enough to have the part of one of the Maharajah's visitors, a formidable American mother, so was there in the studio and I think we all sensed a tension during the recording which did not bode well for the finished product. Most, if not unfortunately quite all, of the performances were excellent and there were some memorable scenes, particularly the dinner party where a solid silver toy train, on its own electric track, circles round the table, allowing the guests to help themselves from miniature trucks containing a variety of delicacies. Typically the train is not just there as ornament but is there to illustrate the Maharajah's love of playing practical jokes, something which is integral to the plot.

Should someone, Harry himself perhaps, have done more to promote a book which had been so well-acclaimed? This is a rhetorical question in the circumstances, but it is surely one that could have been asked by others on two or three other occasions when the reception given to the published book would have warranted an aggressive marketing campaign. However the blame must, to some extent, be borne by himself, but it was not in Harry's nature to take the lead in such matters. He did, often, suggest ideas for publicity but having made the suggestion he felt it was up to those in that department to pursue them.

Although there had been no Ghote title published since 1979 plans had been hatching since the year before about where the next one would be set. From time to time Harry had been urged to send him to America, an idea that did not greatly appeal to him but then in 1978 he was invited to lecture at a conference in California and he realised he could do his research in person. His host at the conference was 'Heat of the Night' crime writer John Ball who very generously offered to drive Harry and another crime writer, 'Green for Danger' Christianna Brand, after the conference was over, up the West coast in his RV (Recreational Vehicle). They set out in this enormous conveyance—not, however, before John had made sure that he had his 'piece' on board. Whether it was feared that they would be set upon by wild beasts or marauding gangs was not made clear but it was obviously intended to fire 'the piece' should anything untoward occur. This added a certain unreality as well as a frisson to the venture.

If Harry was hoping to lap up genuine American speech and attitudes to life, his prayers were answered. But it was as well that Christianna was there because of her ability to find humour in any situation. John was unfailingly kind and hospitable but also completely overwhelming. He planned to give them a lifetime's experience and did it in spades. For instance, to their dismay, they were not allowed to linger in the open air viewing the mighty Grand Canyon, they had to retreat inside to the cinema where, according to John, they would not only be able to absorb far more detail but would be bowled over as the camera explored every nook and cranny of this natural marvel, and, what is more, they would have the benefit of a modern American explanatory commentary. Then there was the excruciating and embarrassing, almost daily, question that he asked them, 'Aren't you having the best time of your lives?'

But perhaps the worst was still to come. Harry had expressed a desire to see an Ashram—already having plans for the Ghote book to show the contrast between the Western and Eastern approach to a contemplative life—and John made that their ultimate destination. But Harry could not have foreseen John's exuberant introduction, 'Hello folks, I've brought you the best crime writer in the world and he's going to write about **you**.' No hole could have been dug that was big enough to swallow up that oh-so-English author.

But somehow they survived the experience and Harry got back to Britain more or less in one piece. It took quite a while before Harry felt capable of tackling the actual writing of the book. The whole episode had to be digested and some way had to be found of utilising the overwhelming all-American experience. If he was going to be able to write objectively, he had to start seeing the story through Ghote's eyes. Above all any resemblance to any of his travelling companions had to vanish. He had no wish to belittle or vilify a host who had genuinely tried to give him the introduction to a world he wanted to write about.

As it was, when the first draft of 'Inspector Ghote Goes West' was finished and Harry asked an American publisher friend to read it to check that he had not committed any transatlantic howlers he received an unexpected response. The friend found one or two minor things to put right but added, without the question having been asked, that the voice given to the private investigator was, unmistakably, that of someone she knew quite well—John

Ball. In her view she had never heard any other American sound quite like that. As this character was, to say the least, not a sympathetic one, it presented a bit of a problem.

Being aware that there were elements of this character's attitude to life and particularly his exuberant manner of speaking, that were taken from life, Harry had made absolutely sure that at least there was no physical resemblance whatsoever. He had hoped that he had done enough to ensure no-one would be able to find a resemblance to a real person. This was something that he had become good at doing in the past and the real people that were the basis for many of his characterisations had never, so far, recognised themselves in the finished story. Apparently my mother, or perhaps I should say Harry's mother-in-law, featured in one book but not even I, let alone she, recognised the finished product which was probably just as well. It was obvious that, in this American book, some revision was called for. The second draft contained dialogue that was slightly toned down although undeniably still over the top. However it seems he did enough because there were no complaints.

Harry himself says that he had some doubts about writing the story at all but saw that he could use the opportunity of having Ghote cross the Atlantic to, his own words, *'comment on the mystical versus materialism, but making the West the centre of mysticism (all those Californian ashrams) and the East the materialistic centre (Bombay is as business oriented as could be). I think that aspect came off.'* Certainly this was the kind of topsy-turvy reasoning that he was good at and that he delighted in. He was almost as certainly on dodgier ground when, into this locked room mystery, he introduced the firmly held Indian belief in translocation. In Harry's own words, *'Some critics jibbed horribly at an incident of translocation of the body.'* There was a part of Harry that had no difficulty in accepting this mystical concept and for the most part it did not seem to be a problem for the majority of the reviewers who were enthusiastic, with Henry Stanhope in The Times admitting that this was the first time he had read a Ghote novel but that the experience had made him determined to catch up with the back list. J.I.M. Stewart (crime writer Michael Innes) paralleled the London book, 'Inspector Ghote Hunts

143

the Peacock', with Ghote's visit to America, applauding Harry on his ability to comment with great perception, both aurally and visually, on life in the different countries through the Inspector's eyes.

An interesting contrast comes from The Oxford Mail who was disappointed but admitted this was unfair because the disappointment stemmed from the high expectations created in previous books. Whereas the Bolton Evening News had no quibbles, *'It's a first-class story with characters and incidents up to the standard we have come to expect from one of the world's crime fiction kings.'* A case of 'you pays your money and you takes your choice'. Len Deighton, a treasured friend, wrote saying, *'Wonderful! I've always said I'd follow Ghote to the ends of the earth, and here he is in California: what a truly inspired confrontation.'* While Harry would obviously have been delighted that the book was well received, he, himself, did not rate it as highly as other titles.

It seems that Harry was as capable of objective assessment of his own work as he was when he was reviewing other people's work and there is no question that while he was rated highly by critics and by readers, he, himself did not feel he had reached his potential and was determined to keep on trying.

Chapter 14

W hile waiting for Ghote's American adventure to appear in 1981, there was ample proof of this determination; he managed to prepare three books which were all published the following year. Two of these were non-fiction and the third was his fourth straight novel 'The Lucky Alphonse'. First came one of the non-fiction titles and must have been something of a chore dealing as it does with real crimes, which, on the whole, had not taken up much of Harry's time hitherto. 'Great Crimes' although garishly produced and lavishly presented in a large format volume co-published by Weidenfeld and Nicholson in Great Britain and Harmony Books, a division of Crown Publishers of America, still showed great attention to accurate detail. The blurb tells us that H.R.F. Keating, as editor, has gathered fifty legendary tales and true stories of history's most notorious criminals and their crimes. The crimes are divided into six categories: Classic Cases, Superb Swindlers, Great Robberies, Crimes into Art, Mass Murderers, and Unsolved Great Crimes. It was plainly devised for the mass market with illustrations taking up much of the space of most of the pages and cross-headings in large and bold type to announce the meat of the paragraph to follow. Once the considerable research had been done it would largely have been a scissors and paste job. In a later list Harry himself compiled of his own publications, he actually names St. Michael as the London publisher which would at least account for it appearing on the shelves of some of the larger Marks and Spencer stores—St. Michael being their trademark name—but the credit must be given to Weidenfelds.

The other non-fiction book was altogether different. At the time there was

145

something called "packaging" in the publishing world and Julian Shuckburgh and David Reynolds were running such a company. They brought the idea to Harry who would not only be the editor and find the contributors but would write the introduction and also contribute articles to most sections of the book. The title was straightforward and comprehensive: 'Whodunnit? A Guide to Crime, Suspense and Spy Fiction' and it was published to great acclaim on both sides of the Atlantic. It is a book that almost certainly Harry would not have attempted to write on his own or even embarked upon without the input of the packaging team who had responsibility for all the technical side.

Some three hundred pages long, it takes a comprehensive look at all aspects of the crime novel. It is imaginatively put together by the packaging team and their designers, who provide informative and charming drawings as well as appropriate photos. Harry writes the introduction in which he is able to voice all his passionately held beliefs about the merits of the crime novel and the difference—and he would say the superiority—of the crime writer over the main stream novelist, contending that, *Crime writing is fiction that puts the reader first, not the writer.* It is interesting to reflect that just over twenty years earlier he embarked on writing crime fiction because it would be a way of using his expertise with words without the necessity to 'say anything'. As has been shown he had very soon found out that he wanted and was able to add a great deal more than he had originally thought. The introduction also confirms what so many people said about him, that he had a well-developed sense of moral integrity. It also states something that he would often put forward when talking about Agatha Christie, that the 'order' that was expected from crime fiction, the contract that the writer has with the reader to make good prevail in the end, has always been a great reassurance to the crime-reading public. And he would always emphasise that one of the merits of crime fiction is the comfort it can give, particularly to those who are alone, and who can use an absorbing book to fill the void, if not with actual people, at least with fictional characters.

The final paragraph is worth quoting in full because it reads like a declaration of faith in his chosen profession. *'And, finally, take note of the way*

CHAPTER 14

crime fiction carries out its share of the novelist's task. It does not work openly. It does not, as the master novelists do, say "Hear me" and risk closed ears. It says instead "Read me". It pledges entertainment, and it provides it too. But, in doing so, often and often it teaches its readers, subtly and secretly, and thus perhaps more effectively. It makes maps for them. It shows them for a little what some of the mess of life looks like. Crime fiction earns its keep.'

It is something of a paradox given his belief that the crime novel could outshine the straight novel, that, in pursuing his holy grail of total success, he, at this point and for the fourth time, abandoned crime to write 'The Lucky Alphonse'. Strangely, considering his inability to keep a note when singing, or for that matter, to read the notes on a musical stave, he very much enjoyed listening to classical music. Opera and chamber music gave him great pleasure but also orchestral symphonies particularly those written by Mozart. He decided to take the basic structure of a symphony and apply it to composing a novel. He then explored his theme, one he deeply cherished, 'The position of being in the middle', over what he conceived as three symphonic movements. The theme is not, of course, a new one and it is illustrated by his methodology and his style of writing in general. Take Ghote himself who is frequently put in the middle, as he tries to look at both sides of a question. Then there is his own sentence structure with those frequent parentheses, those thoughts that come in the middle, which he uses as a way of examining every side of the case he is exploring. I will digress at this point to add, as someone who has recorded many of his books, that his parentheses can sometimes be very challenging if each thought is to be given the right amount of emphasis while at the same time allowing the sentence as a whole to remain clear.

He decided to write the book as three separate novellas, each having as the central figure a man with the name Alphonse but in three different variations—Afonso, an Indian; Fonsy, an Irishman; and Alfons a German, the first two set in their own countries but the last interestingly set in Africa. As this was not a crime novel, he wanted a different publisher and once again he was fortunate in the man who became his editor for this book. David Harsent, himself the author of some taut thrillers but best known for his

147

poetry, was, at the time the managing director of an imprint, Enigma Books, part of Severn House publishers. Harry worked very closely with David who provided sound advice once the first draft was written. The resulting book was well produced with a dust jacket which, although strictly within the budget limits of three colours, was arresting. The designers, credited as Camron Ltd., cleverly put across the fact that there are three different stories in the book. There are three identical images of a man, a black figure against a coloured background, to illustrate the three separate stories, but these figures are also joined down their backs which makes each man face both right and left, thus showing that they are in the middle but being pulled both ways simultaneously.

Unfortunately these same budget limits meant that few review copies were sent out and there was no money to spare for any other sort of publicity which resulted in mediocre sales. Severn House, the parent company, largely produced books for the public libraries and seldom in those days aimed at bookshop sales.

The book did reach some reviewers, among them Andrew Hislop who wrote a very erudite piece for The Times Literary Supplement. He, quite plainly, had delved deep behind the very readable stories to the central theme of what he called "Troilism" and wrote at length on what he was sure must have fascinated Harry, *'the power of knowledge (and ignorance) in the relationship of self to others.'* Although he does admit that *'Keating's almost Sartrean obsession with self and others is more playful than morbid.'* It would be interesting to know how many readers were attracted by such a serious piece of criticism of a piece of writing that was based on, in Harry's own words, *'the punch-line of a well-known dirty joke.'*

The joke is told as a foreword to the three stories. *'A man was staying in a hotel and the name of his room waiter was Alphonse. Seldom when rung for did Alphonse appear. One day after ringing and ringing, the man, impatiently striding to and fro, happened to glance out of the window and there below on a secluded lawn at the back of the hotel, he saw Alphonse lying out in the sun with the Head Waiter and the Chef. Enraged, he seized the telephone and summoned the manager. When the latter arrived, Harry simply pointed down in fury to the scene below. The manager looked out. 'Ah.' He said, 'ze lucky Alphonse, in ze middle again.'* Although Harry is apparently on record, according to The Times Literary Supplement, as finding the joke *'neither very dirty nor very funny,'* he did see its potential when creating three very different stories where the name of each central character was a variant of Alphonse. He decided to set the three movements of his symphony, with the thematic man in the middle, in different countries. In the first of these the Indian diplomat, Afonso Noronha, is being blackmailed by both wife and mistress, and it has a slow-tempo, doloroso, tragi-romantic feel. The second movement has an Irish setting and features Fonsy Noonan, an informer caught between crooks and police, written in the lighter more comic mood of a scherzo. In the third we are given Alfons Neumayr, a German Professor summoned by a former pupil to sort out political problems in Ovangoland, an imaginary South-West African Republic of which he is the ruler. Being the finale, Alfons finds a unifying solution to their problems and restoring the balance of power brings the symphony to its triumphant, maestoso conclusion.

It was only five years later, in the autobiographical article that Harry mentioned, that the book was written as an attempt to use words to emulate music, to write a symphony in print. Almost certainly few will have picked this up of their own accord, although, reading it with hind-sight, as I have shown, all the clues are there. It has given pleasure to those relatively few who knew of its existence in print and may now find a wider audience as an eBook, and it did produce one treasured letter—there for posterity to read among the reviews tucked into the dust jacket. It came from a native of Namibia, an accountant in his sixties called Zwarenstein, in which he says how much he enjoyed the African story *'with the liberal use of literary licence, the dumping together of various countries, the simplification of ideas and doctrines, this story has an undeniable thread of truth about the situation in South West Africa/Namibia.* He goes on to confess that Ghote is a favourite of his.

What a lack it is that Harry kept no personal diary to record how he was feeling while living through these periods of almost manic creativity. Did he ever wonder how he had found the hours to produce enough words to fill those three books? As far as the family were concerned it does not seem as if they realised that any year was different from any other. In December of 1982 the youngest, Hugo, attained his majority, while the other three had fled the nest and I was leading a very active life back in the theatre. Presumably we were all too caught up in our own affairs to be aware that the head of the household had once again shown so much versatility and skill without apparently becoming exhausted. He was of course extremely fortunate that by and large his health had been good so that physically he was capable of working endlessly, but in a way Harry acted as his own generator, creating his own energy so that what he expended on writing was never debilitating. At the risk of being thoroughly fanciful it could be said that words were what pulsed through his veins in place of blood.

Chapter 15

There was certainly no letting up of the pace at this point because he managed to have a title ready for publication in the USA in 1983 and the UK in 1984. Once again, although drawing on past research, the book itself was a new departure, moreover he chose to write it under a pseudonym and an androgynous pseudonym at that. This may have been because he felt the public might be becoming weary of seeing the name Keating on so many books but it is far more likely that he felt it would be appropriate for a novel with a female protagonist to have an author who was possibly feminine. As Evelyn Hervey, the Hervey with an 'e' was his father's middle name, he perhaps belatedly went a bit of the way to right the omission of the Reymond so hopefully bestowed upon him at birth and discarded as an eye-catcher when he chose to write under initials. Without doubt his father would have been delighted at this nod in his direction. Harry chose to revisit Victorian England and this time the protagonist was to be a character who, in those days, lived a genteel life poised between upstairs and downstairs. Miss Harriet Unwin had dragged herself up by her boot straps from the humblest of work-house beginnings to the comparatively dizzy height of governess. He called the book just that, 'The Governess', and in it she finds herself at risk of losing everything she has fought to attain unless she can prove her innocence when she is accused of murder. She is helped in her struggle by a friend from her workhouse days, Vilkins, who, in strong contrast, has failed to gentrify herself and is a robust but engaging scullery maid.

Harriet and the book were well received and surprisingly attracted a reasonable number of reviews considering the writer was unknown. Weidenfeld and Nicholson, the publishers over here, were quite astute to mention in the blurb for the book that the writer was a widely published author writing under a pseudonym. But only colleague Reg Hill in Books and Bookmen speculated that Evelyn Hervey could well be a male. Not surprisingly most of the positive reactions were centred on the authentic period detail and atmosphere, along with praise for the central character. Libby Purves writing her column in 'Living' magazine on the best books of the month, all comers, reviewed two crime novels and liked the fact that this was a *good-hearted, old-fashioned, English thriller, wholesome and blessedly easy to read.*

Doubleday, the American publisher, having bought the last book set in Victorian times 'A Remarkable Case of Burglary' also published this one. There was sufficient interest for Harry to consider writing a follow up and in 1985 there was 'The Man of Gold'. Miss Unwin is up against it again and once more is helped by Vilkins, still as much a rough diamond as she is in the first book. Libby Purvis this time was not so enchanted, finding the plot contrived which led her to speculate whether the author was tiring of the creation and maybe sending it up somewhat. On the other hand Christopher Pym in Punch thought it a, *'most skillfully concocted plot, sedately told and as neatly tied up as any I have rubbed shoulders with this year.'* Which only goes to show how subjective reactions to any form of the Arts can be. The Times, with whom Harry had by then parted company, decided in their review to blow the gaff and reveal that the author was none other than their own former reviewer.

But once again there was sufficient interest for a third outing, gainsaying Libby Purvis and proving that Harry had not, as yet, grown tired of his invention and most certainly was not sending it up. And although 'Into the Valley of Death', with its Crimean War undertones, was to be the last novel featuring her, Miss Unwin was quite dear to his heart and she has survived as the heroine of many short stories. The reviews had many of the writers using the space to pat themselves on the back for having spotted the genuineness of the Victorian setting in the previous two books. How, they said, could it be otherwise when Evelyn Hervey was in fact H.R.F. Keating? But on the whole this final title was considered a good read and, as The Times said, '*Convincing, unhurried manner and dialogue of the period, topped with a convincing plot and surprises en route.*' Harry must have felt that if there were to be no more in the series, which there were not, he was bowing out creditably given this comment from Christopher Wordsworth in the Observer, '*The highly improbable becomes totally absorbing in the hands of a real craftsman.*'

But while Miss Unwin was having her Crimean 'i's dotted and 't's crossed, prior to publication, there came the opportunity of transferring Ghote to TV. Not an adaptation this time but an original play set, not in India, but once again in London. Thames Television was searching for something that would successfully replicate their earlier, highly popular series starring George Cole and Dennis Waterman, called 'Minder'. They had decided to commission six pilots which they broadcast under the title of 'Story–Line'. From these they hoped to find one which they could expand into a series.

The script that was recorded in the summer of 1983 was called 'Inspector Ghote Moves In'. Ghote is officially here to observe Police procedure at Scotland Yard and accommodation has been arranged for him in the Knightsbridge flat of an ex-Indian army Colonel Bressingham and his wife. Inevitably, in the way of crime fiction, a theft occurs at the flat. The plot is neat and satisfactorily resolved but had the added charm of Ghote's involvement with the pukka-sahib Bressinghams and has him very bewildered by their English style of living.

Irene Worth and Alfred Burke were cast as the upper-class couple and Sam Dastor, a Parsee Indian who for many years has lived and worked as an actor in England played an admirable Ghote. It was a success and there was a further commission for a script that would kick off a series. Although dialogue was something that Harry excelled in he always maintained he was first and foremost a novelist and never felt entirely at home in a medium that was so visual and he had to convey all the thoughts normally found in the narration through the words spoken by the characters. But there was no way that he could pass up the opportunity of getting Ghote into

TV so he wrote another episode. Thames liked it but were not convinced that it would attract the massive audience that 'Minder' had brought them and asked him to try again. What they wanted was impossible. It was like asking Jane Austen to write in the style of, say, Raymond Chandler. He had a couple more shots at turning the modest Inspector into a cocksure, cockney wide boy and then gave up. Thames then offered the idea to two or three well-known film and TV writers in succession and they all failed. Sadly it was the end of that attempt to present Ghote to a wider audience. It will be ironic if he does finally make it as a series on the screen when it is too late for Harry to know, but it may still happen.

It was around this time, 1984, that Harry began writing another straight novel but it was not until 1987 that it was completed and he must have taken a conscious decision to put it into cold storage. At least it must be assumed it was a conscious decision because there is no record other than the two drafts of a novel called 'A Kind of Light', no indication of future intentions for the work which was found in the study cupboard after his death. It was typed on flimsy paper but manually corrected having been written on an electronic typewriter without any of the correcting facilities of today's computers.

Without a doubt it was written in homage to one of his idols, Conrad—the title is a quote from 'Heart of Darkness'—and the book aims to explore such major issues as the merits of marriage as opposed to free love; the benefits of civilisation set against savagery; atheism measured against religious belief. It also touches on the burgeoning disaster of AIDS. These issues as always lie beneath the surface of a fast-moving narrative.

It is set half in Victorian times with a gentlewoman, would-be botanist/explorer, in Africa as the protagonist, and half in the contemporary 1980s with a young couple, having heard about the resurfacing of some of the diaries the Victorian lady had kept, being determined to follow in her footsteps and make a documentary film about her audacious expedition.

Why was this manuscript there, in the cupboard, buried in among the other envelopes containing the typescripts of published novels? Was it intended to be found after Harry's death or had he completely forgotten about it? The second option seems highly unlikely but the first, as well as being in a way typical of his, at times, perverse sense of humour, presented several dilemmas. Was the second draft the final one? Would it be right to do a final edit, to impose someone else's corrections when he had not done these himself? Given his ability to destroy anything he felt was a failure he surely must have intended it to have a future. After reading it myself I passed it on to Camilla at PFD and with her concurrence then asked our eldest son, Simon, who had always had a great appreciation for fine writing and was also capable of being a stern critic, whether he would undertake the editing. He agreed and asked Jacob, his son, who had done a course in touch-typing, to transform it into electronic form. With Camilla's approval I contacted Audible, the on-line audio producers to see if they would like to do it as an original audio book. They were very enthusiastic and in 2016 I recorded it. Subsequently it became a paperback and an eBook but unfortunately very sloppily published and vanished when the company went into voluntary liquidation.

But back in the early 1980s and emerging from that time spent dreaming up possible follow-up TV scripts for the Ghote series as well as presumably working on 'A Kind of Light', there was still the question of the next Ghote novel to be written and a decision taken about what he would be up to this time back in India. Using the 'red-light' district of Bombay as a setting for a novel had been inevitable ever since the police, during the BBC visit to India in 1975, had arranged for Harry to be taken on a tour of inspection of 'the cages', as they were called. This would be the first time that sex would form an overt part of a Ghote book but there was more to it than that. He also wanted to write about a character who would mean different things to different people particularly on such a delicate, private aspect of life as prostitution together with general reactions to sexual acts. He analysed what he had set out to examine in the book when he wrote in the autobiography article, *'the subjectivity of our way of looking at things, particularly suitable for a detective novel, seeing, for instance, a sheriff either as a Wild West law-keeper or as an honorary officer of the Bombay High Court, seeing certain sexual activities either as rollickingly sportive or as utterly beastly.'* Here his approach to sex could be said to be diametrically opposed to the way he handled it in his Victorian novel 'The Underside'. No holds were barred in that case, with Godfrey Mann, the protagonist, plunging full tilt into the seamiest, darkest side of life. Now the reverse was true. The Times reviewer encapsulates the words of many of the other critics, *'Keating describes the seedy, the repulsive and the perverted with great sensitivity, evoking an atmosphere that is at once despairing and vividly alive.'*

Only three years had elapsed since Ghote's last appearance in print but it must have been very heartening to see the banner headline to one review: **'Ghote's Back'**. With the exception of one reviewer there was very little fault-finding. And that exception confessed he was not a fan of the series *'because so much of the "comedy" comes from Ghote's "goodness, gracious" speech patterns, not a long way from the racism of "It Ain't Half Hot Mum".* This was an astonishing comparison to have made considering the difference in approach between the TV series and Harry's books, both in philosophy and most certainly in the way humour is used, to say nothing of the wide disparity in the use of language. There are writers and performers who say that they never read reviews, Harry was not one of them. He was able, for the most part, to read them with objectivity and take on board valid criticism at the same time as ignoring what was plainly uninformed. After all for fifteen years he himself had been passing judgement on others.

Two pieces of paper nestling among the host of reviews would have pleased him enormously. One was a letter from an Indian, Meera Tamaya, an academic writing her PhD thesis in America, who had chosen Ghote as her subject. She had visited Harry in London and her letter is dated 1988, some four years after the publication of 'The Sheriff of Bombay' which she had just re-read prior to writing about it. *'I am really quite struck by the complexity of your vision of the prostitutes of Bombay—you portray a whole range of them without falling into the usual clichés of narrow moralism...did you actually visit Kamathipura or is everything in the book culled from your amazingly extensive knowledge of India? Again I am quite dumbstruck by your familiarity with the most arcane rituals etc.'.*

The other is an article from the Bombay Sunday Observer, in which the journalist, Vijay Sahni, while giving an overview of the way the series came to be written goes on to talk about 'The Sheriff of Bombay' in more detail. He is not without criticism, finding some of the speech patterns too repetitive for instance and castigating him for not realising that the Oberoi-Sheraton hotel had changed its name some six years earlier, but basically he approves. *'Keating has obviously done his homework and his characters ring true: a hijra gharwali, the virgin prostitute, the corrupt police inspector, the middle class call girl and the Pataud-like Sheriff.'* And adds, something very important to any author, that the novel is *'a page turner.'* Many times the reviews picked on points that Harry would always have been on the look-out for when writing his own critical columns.

In fact, although he had been writing his Times pieces for fifteen years, this had come to an end somewhat abruptly in 1982. The way this happened was, at the time, a bit of a jolt. One month, after he had made his choice of books to review, the literary editor contacted him to ask if he intended to review a title he had not so far included. When the answer was negative the book was offered to a couple of other reviewers who in turn said they would prefer not to do it. At this point the Editor of the Times, the big white chief, sent down a memo to the literary editor to say he would review the book himself as it was written by his secretary's husband and added, *'sack your columnist.'* There was no choice in the matter, it was an order. Harry was duly sacked but not before the literary editor had considered resigning, something that Harry assured him was the last thing he should do. Yet another sorry tale of life in the newspaper world, but in fact it had a positive result because the incredible three book marathon of 1982 could never have happened if there had still been piles of new books to read and time found for the regular column to be written.

Putting the year he stopped being the Times critic into perspective, it was probably comparatively calm on the home front. Two of the children had completely fled the nest, Simon making a fairly meagre living working in community theatre, and Bryony, better remunerated after getting her degree in Interior Design, working for the BBC in their visual effects department. Piers was only intermittently at home while struggling to build a career as an actor, leaving Hugo, shaking the dust of school from his feet and forging ahead with a career as an entrepreneur. He had installed himself in the basement which he had converted into a self-contained flat. I was with the RSC for their first season at London's Barbican but I was also house hunting. Not of course with a view to moving home in London but looking for somewhere that could be a weekend retreat.

There were three very separate things that had brought this about. The first of these was finance. I had received two smallish legacies after both my parents and my older sister had died and, our own circumstances being a bit easier, I thought I would like to spend the money on something concrete. Then, secondly, around this time Piers announced that he was getting married to someone he had met at college and that he and Hazel wanted to live in the country. There is no doubt that nothing should have been done to encourage him to live away from London because he was at the very beginning of his career and actors need to live within easy distance of any work that comes their way, but on the other hand they had absolutely no money, so a cottage in the country appeared to be a possible solution. The third reason was purely romantic. At the time, novelist Penelope Lively and her enchanting professor husband, Jack, were close friends and split their lives between a house in London and a beautiful old property in Oxfordshire. We had often visited them there and I thought that if we also had a house close by we would be able to see more of each other.

Knowing that Harry's reaction to owning a second home was likely to be unfavourable, I had begun looking before discussing the matter with him but after a while I had to come clean and tell him. After an initial negative response I have to say that he 'saw the other side of the picture' and became, if not enthusiastic, tolerant. There were quite a few places available around the Chipping Norton area but ones that we liked and would be big enough for the two separate families were outside my budget. It was Penelope who saw the advertisement for a property in the small hamlet of Heythrop, close to Chipping Norton. It had the advantage of actually being two cottages, one minute and the other slightly bigger, surely perfect for housing both the newly-weds and ourselves. The snag was that the original asking price was quite a bit beyond my means. We had to turn it down but found nothing to put in its place. Finally, however, the owners were desperate to sell—we did not know it at the time but they were having their lives made hell by a neighbour—and got in touch saying they were willing to let us have it at the price we had said we could afford. Actually, even then, it was more than the amount I had inherited, and Harry had to bite the bullet of needing a small mortgage.

By this time the date for the wedding was getting rather close and Harry nobly agreed. Apart from the neighbour it was a delightful pair of cottages. Piers and Hazel looked after the quite large garden and were the handymen/caretakers. We found a modus vivendi. Harry would spend the occasional weekend and one or two longer holiday weeks there but mostly remained in London, while I spent weekdays there if I was out of work, returning to spend the weekends with Harry in London. He had no actual objection to country living but he really hated living under two roofs and above all he hated being parted from his study. During the eight years we owned it, we all, including the rest of the family, enjoyed its peace and quiet and the opportunity it provided for country walks and the culinary advantages of pick-it-yourself fruit and vegetables. But it all came to an end when the young couple, now the parents of a one year old daughter, Charlotte, had had enough of rural isolation and wanted to move to Nottingham, where Piers, with a change of career, embarked on becoming a furniture restorer. Even I recognised that two-house living had its drawbacks and agreed that we should put the house on the market. Harry was glad to be shot of mortgage repayments and also, as it turned out, to sell at quite a reasonable profit.

Amusingly, some years later, when the person we had sold it to died and it was again up for sale, the Estate Agent decided Harry's name would be a good advertisement, saying in the details about the house that it was once owned and had indeed been re-named by the famous crime writer, H.R.F. Keating. The naming of the house had come about because the former owners had sentimentally called it 'Halcyon' which we felt had to be changed. We knew the history of the village, the whole of which had been built by Victorian

Squire Brassey to house his retainers. The houses were built in groups of three, each containing a large, medium and small residence and were apportioned according to the importance of their job. Our small property had been given to the lowly shepherd. Not too much creativity involved in renaming it 'The Shepherd's House'.

Back in 1983 mortgage companies were still resisting lending money to women, especially someone without a regular salary. Harry had to be the joint owner and so be part of the bureaucratic process of a house purchase, but finally all was successfully completed and early in 1984 Piers, at the tender age of 23 and still very much a struggling actor, got married to Hazel. They had met when he was doing his Drama and English degree at Loughborough and she was doing a fashion diploma at a nearby college. Hazel came from a Leicestershire family who were fairly strict Methodists so the wedding, if it was to be in a church, was always going to be a curious mixture even though Piers was no longer a practising Catholic. It was held in a charming C of E (Church of England) parish church, opposite the sprawling country property in Leicestershire where Hazel had lived most of her life. The service was conducted jointly by the incumbent of the C of E church and the Stevensons' usual Methodist minister, with a Roman Catholic priest in attendance. This last was very important to Harry's mother who was still going strong in her nineties and for whom no marriage would have been valid without the RC blessing. The reception, held at a nearby hall, could also have had problems. That it did not was due to the liberal-minded courtesy of Hazel's parents. Being Methodists they were teetotalers but agreed that the Keatings could provide some alcohol for those of us who were not. The consequent geographical divide in the hall of the drinking and non-drinking ends made no difference to everyone's enjoyment and this was the first of four very different but equally joyous family weddings.

However while family matters had been pleasantly occupying the hours spent outside the study Harry had, for some time, been getting increasingly restless about things on the publishing front.

Chapter 16

T he problem centred round the policy that Collins Crime Club was adopting. The imprint seemed to be concentrating less and less on the individuality of its titles and more and more on the importance of the collective Club itself. In many ways the problems had all started when George Hardinge moved to Macmillan and certainly Harry never had quite the same close relationship he had had with George with any of the succeeding editors at Collins. This is no reflection on their abilities, but, as with any co-operative venture, it is the chemistry between individuals which is important and that either happens or it does not. While Collins was doing a perfectly adequate job, the way the books were being handled seemed to be settling into a rut and Michael Sissons agreed that after 'The Sheriff of Bombay' a new publisher had to be found. Hutchinson—recently merged with Century Publishing—and managing director Anthony Cheetham were keen to have Harry as one of their authors.

The book they were offered was of crucial importance to Harry, as can be seen from his own words, *'There followed a book, 'Under a Monsoon Cloud' that might be looked on as my testament and Inspector Ghote's, I had now abandoned, perhaps for ever, the idea of writing a mainstream novel that would establish for me a reputation (fame is, as they say, the spur) and a wide readership (other minds filled with one's thoughts is the lure), but I hoped I could write a crime novel that did as much as the mainstream novel.'* He found in his new editor, Richard Cohen, someone with whom he had an instant rapport. It was unfortunate that the merging of Hutchinson with Century was in its infancy and it took a few years and much change of personnel for the merger to settle. Quite certainly Harry was unaware of the internal politics which made life for Richard difficult from the outset and would ultimately mean that he departed.

But initially there was good news because Richard persuaded 'The Book Seller' to advertise the book on its front cover. It is obvious from the deluge of reviews, many of which say it is not really a detective novel, that Harry had done just what he set out to do—write a major mainstream novel, using Ghote and thus keeping it within the realms of crime fiction. Indeed The Los Angeles Times had this to say: *'it is not really a mystery as such but a kind of moral suspense story, virtually a straight novel that happens to center on a familiar figure from another range of fiction.'* He had also managed, despite telling the story of the murder and who had done it in the first pages of the book, to sustain the tension to the very end, with The Eastern Daily Mail saying, *'This book had me sitting on the edge of my chair until it reached its brilliant and totally unforeseeable conclusion.'*

Among the reviews there was one that must have been enormously gratifying for Harry to read. Moving on from a comment on the book itself it says, *'Keating brings into this piece of crime fiction a feeling of coiled tension keeping the reader in a constant state of suspense,'* The Mid-Day, a Bombay newspaper, goes on, *'The author has been able to sniff out the essence of the place that is Bombay, which not many who have lived all their lives here would be able to do...he writes with a feel for the place and the people, as if he has always lived here.'* The reviewer has a worry that the novel is so Indian that those not living in the sub-continent may have difficulty understanding it fully.

He need not have worried because there was only one review which found both the premise and the solution improbable—and to be fair the solution is unquestionably very Indian and could have been quite difficult for a Westerner to accept. But no-one else had any problem and all the others, without exception, heaped on the praise using such phrases as, *' The best Ghote book for many years...;* *'orchestrates this excellent cliff-hanger with great sympathy, sweaty suspense and great guile'...;* *'is an absorbing triumph'...;* *'after twenty-two years the Inspector Ghote books are getting better and better'...;*

'First-class Keating is first-class anywhere.'

It surely should have been a time for the greatest celebration, reactions such as these must, this time, be enough to insure at least a tiny niche in history. But such are the vagaries of the Arts world that the book did not garner any of the possible awards and, even worse, Hutchinson apparently made little effort to make it into a bestseller. It is hard not to lay the blame for this at their door. Bestsellers are usually made by the publisher initially taking the risk of investing sufficient money in the book's promotion to ensure that sales will follow. The only charitable explanation is that problems within the publishing house itself distracted them from what needed doing.

There was a further interesting comment which came much later from the same Meera Tamaya who was writing her thesis on Ghote and had so much enjoyed 'The Sheriff of Bombay'. The thesis was published in 1993 and is entitled 'H.R.F. Keating Post-Colonial Detection—A critical study'. Meera had done her English MA degree at Madras University and received her PhD from the University of Massachusetts. She is perhaps uniquely placed to assess the work of a Westerner who had become almost an honorary Indian, given that her formative years and first degree were acquired in India and her subsequent post graduate years were spent in America. Her book, which begins with a biographical chapter, interestingly using the same article from the Contemporary Authors Autobiography series that has illuminated this biography so far, she then goes on to a critical analysis of the Ghote novels, with a third section devoted to his other fiction writing. The book concluded with the typescripts of two interviews she had had with Harry, the first in 1983 and the second in 1990.

The overall assessment is extremely positive, as is to be expected considering that she had chosen Harry's works as the subject for her thesis, although where she thinks one of the books is less good she says so, citing reasons. It is only when she comes to analyse 'Under a Monsoon Cloud' that she disagrees profoundly with the action that is the whole basis for the story. She maintains that a character as upright, as incorruptible as Ghote would never under any circumstances conceal a homicide. But even with that major difference of opinion she goes on to savour much of what the other reviewers praise. Tamaya, being aware of the article Harry contributed to the Contemporary Author's Autobiographical series, must have been aware of a couple of paragraphs on his hatred of violence and, even more appositely his own outbursts of temper.

'From where comes that hatred of violence and the timidity that goes with it? From, I suspect, my mother, infused through and through with a desire for things to go well to the point of being able to blot out the contradictory even when it was directly in front of her. It is from her, no doubt, I get, too, my inability to believe that anyone can be totally bad, which produced eventually a short story called, "Inspector Ghote and the All-bad Man". The trait, perhaps, is at its worst a desperate naivety. Its good side, I believe, is a generous allotment of author's empathy, the ability to see very quickly in the day-to-day world the other side of any case and, writing fiction, the gift of putting oneself on occasion into utterly alien shoes.

'It was from my father, also a person of remarkable niceness, however, that I got my occasional outbursts of violent temper, eventually the driving force behind my crime novel "Under a Monsoon Cloud". I was famous at school in my earlier days, I recall, for these rages, at one time getting private instruction when one master refused—I believe this must be right—to have me any longer in his classes.'

Some years later there was a further and totally appreciative, in-depth examination of the book. It was undertaken by an American lawyer, Peter Widulski, and he used his study as the basis for a paper he wrote, and which he delivered at a conference, on the religious content of the Ghote books and particularly 'Under a Monsoon Cloud'. Coincidentally that year, 2009, when he had ceased writing, Harry had agreed to my setting up an H.R.F. Keating web page which I was able to do with the professional help of Zoë, daughter of our good American friend and fellow crime-writer, Laurie R. King. It was by this means that Peter kindly made contact and sent his paper for Harry to read. Lest it should be thought that Harry had had a latter-day technological conversion it should be made clear that, although he meticulously answered all communications, this was all conducted second-hand through my computer and to his dying day Harry and the Internet maintained a strictly arms-length relationship. After Harry died I attempted to elicit opinions from people who might have read Widulski on the site, by posting a series of questions on the moral decisions taken in 'Under a Monsoon Cloud'. Perhaps I overestimated the average web user's desire to engage in serious debate through this means but there were disappointingly few responses. Actually—and this is straying from the biographer's brief—I have come to believe that there is very little serious debate generated online, it is essentially a frivolous and trivial means of communication which cannot begin to match the engrossing exchange of written correspondence of past centuries. However, like all websites, there are enthusiasts who enjoy keeping in touch and it has indeed been very cheering, since Harry died, to hear from people all over the world who have only recently found his books or are renewing a previous knowledge of them.

But back in 1986 when 'Under a Monsoon Cloud' was newly on the market and Harry's stock could not have been higher, he, rightly or wrongly, was still aiming higher, still hoping for the best-seller that would make its indelible mark in the literary world. Perhaps at this point he should have re-assessed the need to produce a book a year, given himself a breathing space.

Meanwhile another non-fiction book came out that year. 'Writing Crime Fiction' the slim volume published by A&C Black and a year later in the USA by St. Martin's Press, which then went into a revised second edition in 1994 and is still in print. It was also, as Harry himself says, a *'Spin off from what I see as my reason for being in the world.'* It is not only a short history of the genre but an analysis of what makes a book successful, as well as a study of the various types of story that come under that generic heading. There is then a chapter entitled 'How to Begin, Go on and Finish' and concludes with advice about how to approach publishers. The first edition was short at 84 pages and the second is only fractionally longer at 108 pages and although this is partly due to the bigger print used, there are a few additions to the text.

Harry's own preface to the second edition is in itself revealing. *'I haven't felt the need to alter anything except to take into account changes that have happened in the intervening years. So some of the nitty-gritty advice about publishers and publishing has needed updating, and here and there I have found newer and more accessible examples of the various kinds of crime writing I speak about, and once or twice I have put in new nuggets of the wisdom of others gathered in my reading over the last eight years.',* revealing because what he originally wrote, and still felt eight years later, was the distillation of what he felt passionately was achievable in crime literature and this remained for him unalterable until the day he died.

He re-enforces this in the preface when he says that his own evaluation of the book has changed over the years and been enhanced by its reception, firstly by the kind words of established colleagues such as Ruth Rendell who called it *'enormously entertaining'* and *'a private Godsend';* then by Margaret Yorke referring to it as, *'Magisterial';* by Joan Aiken who told him she still consulted it from time to time and P.D. James who, when they were fellow tutors at a literary course, gave it her imprimatur. And secondly by the letters he had received from would-be writers both here and in America, including one previously rejected writer who had been able to tell him that she had found a publisher after she had followed his advice.

Someone writing as 'Bloodhound' said of the first edition, *'This is not a How to Write manual. Brimful of Harry Keating's legendary enthusiasm, it is a celebration and good humoured analysis of crime fiction, a concise foundation course for aspiring authors.'* Inside the cover of the second edition copy, Harry has put a score of notes, written on scraps of paper, with nuggets he gleaned from others writing about crime fiction, showing that, even after thirty-five years of being successfully published, his mind was still open and that he felt the need to emphasise to himself the importance of the high standards required in reaching the peaks. These jostle for space with reviews, among them a page headed **SPOTLIGHT,** presumably a magazine, where the writer, James Gracie, gives anyone trying to market their book, this gem:*' Not only is it an overview of crime fiction…it is also a good read. Too good, because I found myself at three in the morning still pouring over its 115* (he included 7 pages of Index) *highly entertaining pages.'*

The year after, 1987, was to be another when three books were published, two fiction and one non-fiction. As already mentioned, it saw the third and last of the Evelyn Hervey books, 'Into the Valley of Death'. This offered Harry the opportunity lovingly to quote lines from Tennyson's sonorous poem which brought the Crimean War so vividly to light. But three Miss Unwin books proved to be enough and anyway the last Ghote title had been published in 1984 and ideas were queuing up from which he chose something a little different.

Somewhere along the line we are told, in the autobiographical article, he had picked up the message that America was keen on the old-fashioned British 'mystery' and he felt that he should write something that might pander a bit more to commercial pressures. Without too much difficulty he devised an Agatha Christie-style puzzle which he set in a famous hill station, Ootacamund, Ooty for short. In 'The Body in the Billiard Room', Ghote has been assigned, at the request of a former Indian Ambassador who has retired there, to solve the murder of the billiard marker who was found stabbed through the heart on the billiard table of Ooty's most historic club. The ex-Ambassador turns out to be a great reader of traditional crime fiction and sees Ghote as the embodiment of Poirot, Wimsey and Sherlock Holmes rolled into one and casts himself as Dr Watson, to the bemusement of the Inspector who knows nothing of these characters.

One reviewer suggested that Harry might have had his tongue firmly in his cheek and, while there is obviously an element of send-up, the success of the book lies not in this but in the down-to-earth story it tells, as well as the genuine mystification of Ghote as he steers his way through the mind of the ex-ambassador, Surinder Mehta—a mind so deeply rooted in fiction. Gerald Kaufman, himself a considerable buff of the earlier genre, suggests in the Listener, *'The charm of the book is that while sending up these conventions, it also scrupulously observes them.'* while The Liverpool Daily Post picks another aspect, *'the account of the decaying outpost of Empire is both humorous and in the last chapter, extremely moving.'* This is echoed by Margaret Hinkman in the Daily Mail, *'Keating captures more succinctly than much 'serious' fiction the sad reality of survivors clinging to the deluding pride of a bygone age of British rule.'* This *'sad reality'* is picked up in a letter from an ordinary reader which describes Ghote's encounter at the end of the book with one of those survivors, *'To take a stock 'pathetic' figure such as 'Ringer' Bell and his disgusting old dog, and then lift them from the two-dimensional and show the true depth of pathos is a stroke of great perception and depth of humanity.'*

When that manuscript was safely with the publishers, Harry, at 60, was very nearly cut off in his prime. Descending the outside steps to the basement of his home, he missed a step and crashed heavily to the ground. Fortunately both Hugo and I were there because he was unable to get up. Having been helped to a standing position it was obvious he had badly damaged a knee and an ambulance was called. After an immensely long wait in the A&E department of St. Mary's Hospital, Paddington, the X-rays showed that he had severed the tendon of his right knee and he was admitted to await surgery. There was some delay before they could operate because the anaesthetist said he would not contemplate giving him an anaesthetic until his fibrillating heart had been stabilized—Harry had omitted to tell them he had this condition for the simple reason that he had totally forgotten he had it.

This was typical of his attitude to bodily ills. It was all quite simple, if a medical expert has told you something is wrong, his diagnosis is bound to be right and you accept it, forget about it and get on with your life. Around the late 60s or early 70s, he had what he thought must be asthma while on holiday in Devon doing a lot of hilly walking through pine forests. As this did not entirely subside on his return to London he went to his GP, the same magnificent Stuart Carne who had at the eleventh hour delivered Piers and, once again, left no stone unturned and oversaw rigorous tests which were carried out at the Hammersmith hospital. These confirmed what Stuart expected, that the heart was fibrillating. However it was decided that things were benign enough not to need medication and having been told this, by undeniable experts, Harry accepted the verdict and promptly forgot about it.

Now, in 1986, in St. Mary's, the stabilisation took around forty-eight hours after which the repairing knee operation took place. He came home encased in a heavy plaster-cast from hip to ankle and found it very difficult to do what he had been instructed to do, wiggle his toes. The result was that after a couple of weeks he started to have chest pains and he was back at St. Mary's this time in the acute medical ward where they found a blood clot had formed in the leg and travelled to his lung. The NHS, as is usual in an emergency, showed themselves at their best and the clot was dispersed and with the comparatively minor annoyance of having to take Warfarin, he returned home. Not before he had had ample proof of how over-worked nurses can be in an acute medical ward and how cramped the conditions often are for patients. When Harry was still in quite a fragile state, an emergency case was rushed in and as a nurse flew by she called out to him, 'Keep an eye on old Mr. M...and call me if he tries to pull out his tubes.' Poor old M—who was plainly having a wretched time and whose life would depend on Harry's lung power if the tubes were once again yanked out—surely, he deserved more individual attention than that.

On a more personal level the time had come to read the proofs of 'A Body in the Billiard Room'. By now sitting up in his bed, with the patient in the next bed within stretched-out-arm touching distance, he tried to concentrate on the task. He recorded later that it must have put him in an irascible mood because he remembered jabbing down with a red biro in the margin some very direct not to say rude comments like, 'Fool' and 'Obviously not, see page so-and-so.'

Eventually he got home and when the plaster-cast came off he was assigned to a physiotherapy class at St. Mary's Hospital. His muscles had become so slack that he had to learn to walk again. He had fallen into the habit of moving the right leg with a sweeping circular motion which did not please the therapist and her full wrath was incurred on one occasion when he was leaving and, thinking himself out of her vision, had reverted to the circular sweep. 'Mr. Keating' a stentorian voice echoed down the length of the room, 'walk properly'. He was still using a stick by the end of the year.

This crowded year had him preparing yet another non-fiction book jointly published by Xanadu in the UK and Carroll & Graf in the States. Even in this next 21st century people are still extolling 'Crime and Mystery. The Hundred Best Books.' Patricia Highsmith, in her foreword, says, *'Keating modestly states in his introduction that he may have left out some fine writers,*

169

for which he anticipates reproach. But who in our time could have done it better?' Of course he knew that no-one would make exactly the same choices he made but over and over in the reviews, after the odd cavil, the critics admit that he made a remarkably sound selection. There is also praise for the two-page essays he wrote about each entry. Marvin Lachman wrote two separate articles, the one in the States saying, *'There isn't one which does not show evidence of wide reading, careful thought and graceful language.'* And the other, in the UK, which thinks they are *'masterpieces of succinct criticism and superb use of metaphor'.*

When the paper-back came out in America, Ed Gorman in Mystery Scene wrote a long eulogy. *'For me the best book ever published on the crime and mystery genre is H.R.F. Keating's The 100 Best Crime and Mystery Novels. This isn't to say I agree with every word Keating writes, but he is so good a stylist, so clever a critic, and so open-minded in his evaluations that he should not merely be knighted, he should be sainted.'*

Perhaps if he had spent more time going around both countries signing books and meeting his public or speaking at Literary festivals he would have attained bestseller status, but then he would not have had the time he did in the study and he would not have left such an amazing printed legacy behind. But that comes under the heading of speculation which, as he said is a sin in a biographer so it is better to stick to the hard facts of what turned out to be a hectic 1987.

Chapter 17

T he drama began on a Friday afternoon just before Christmas in 1988. The phone rang. It was the charismatic Indian film producer Ismail Merchant asking an extraordinary question. *'Do you still have the rights to "The Perfect Murder"?'* Answer: *'Yes, I think so.'* Ismail: *'Well, hang on to them over the weekend, would you?'* And after a few social pleasantries he rang off with no further explanation.

The next call came promptly on the Monday. Apparently there was an unexpected gap in his filming schedule and he hoped to fit in a six week shoot of 'The Perfect Murder' somewhere around the end of March. Then came the bombshell. There was an Indian director, Zafar Hai, already in place and would Harry please come out to Bombay and write the script with him? Although framed as a question it sounded more like a command. But Harry was quite determined to refuse after his recent lack of success with the TV series. He explained that he was a novelist not a scriptwriter and for five minutes managed to stand his ground saying, *'No, Ismail',* when he could get a word in edgeways. But the Merchant charm was too powerful and eventually he heard himself saying, *'Yes, Ismail, when would you like me to come?'* It was the secret of Ismail's success, his ability to charm the birds off the trees.

With filming due to begin at the end of March, it was urgent that the script be written without delay. By the end of January Harry was off and he and Zafar spent just over two weeks of dawn till dusk steady grind knocking the book into a workable film which included adding an extra strand of plot. Zafar said there needed to be an opportunity for an exciting chase which the existing plot did not provide so they dreamt up a sub-plot which involved diamond smugglers. Fortunately there was an instant rapport between them, although Zafar was constantly having to say, 'No, no the camera will do that for us there is no need for words.' An exhausted but quite exhilarated Harry got back to London knowing that in little more than four weeks he would be returning to Bombay for the actual film-shoot.

He had managed to persuade the doctors that he no longer needed to be on Warfarin—the treatment he had been on to disperse the clot and subsequently prevent further clots—so while in India he would not have to worry about regular visits to a doctor to get his dosage balanced—something that apparently was done differently in different countries—but he was still using a stick and still going one step at a time when going down stairs. Unfortunately before he had left London this one-leggedness had coincided with a much needed refurbishment of the triple-storied stairwell in Northumberland Place, including the purchase of new carpet. While the decorating was going on the stairs were bare boards which echoed to the 'ker-klomp' of Harry's laboured descent. The decorating was being done by Bryony's soon-to-be-husband, Rupert, who was an expert at specialist wall painting. This time it was 'sponging' in subtle greens and whites which has lasted until the present time, decades later—that also goes for other specialist decorating skills like the 'marbling', 'wood graining' and 'rag-rolling' with which Rupert adorned other parts of the house. Once Harry had gone on the writing trip the family decided that come what may, there had to be carpet on the stairs for his return. Just before he arrived back there was furious activity, resembling the gardeners' repainting of the roses in 'Alice in Wonderland', as we all tackled the banister painting prior to the carpet being laid, but the target was achieved and the noise abated.

All this excitement was punctuated by the delight of preparing for Bryony's marriage, which was planned for that summer. Of course for this second family wedding, as parents of the bride, the responsibility fell on Harry and myself. Most of the decisions were being made in between the two India visits because it was agreed that Bryony and I would go out for the filming as well.

Unbelievably Harry was also able to spare time and thought for the novel that would have to be ready for publication in 1988. Perhaps the present necessity to timetable his life contributed to the decision to write about a subject which had always fascinated him, time. His words about 'Dead on Time' are the final entry in the autobiographical article, which unfortunately for anyone wanting Harry's own thoughts on future books ends in 1987. Describing what the book is about, he says, '*it is a consideration of punctuality, being a slave to the clock or being too much freed from its trammels.*' Perhaps due to a certain tendency towards lateness in his mother which used to rile him as a boy, he was fanatic about punctuality all his life, which surely partly accounted for his acute anxiety whenever he was travelling, particularly by air with its rigid demands to be in a certain place by a certain time.

All in all the to-ing and fro-ing to India was achieved without too much mental strain, although returning after the filming was quite testing as Bombay airport was struggling under strike action. But before that there were to be some weeks of hard work for him—the 're-write' man'. Once again his journalistic training came in useful. He found it remarkably easy to think on his feet when instant script changes were required. It was a very tight schedule but was made much easier by Naseeruddin Shah and his wife Ratna Pathak who were cast as Inspector Ghote and his wife, Protima, as well as the experienced and talented cameraman, Walter Lassally. Because Zafar had previously directed documentary rather than feature films Walter was able to suggest ways in which the script, or the particular shots envisaged, could be tweaked to keep the story moving. His unerring eye for creating memorable pictures gave the finished product its visual success. The camera in Walter's hands depicted that same vivid picture of Indian life in all its simultaneous colour and squalor that readers found so compelling in the books.

In Naseer, Harry felt secure that Ghote was going to be the character that he had invented—Naseer, for his part, percipiently said, that when he looked into Harry's own eyes he at once had the clue to playing the character. The finished film was only a modest success and undoubtedly Ismail made an error in allowing it to be shown on the larger commercial circuit, instead of in Art cinemas, where the audience would have been more appreciative. But, all in all, it was a wonderful experience with Harry making a Hitchcockian appearance in a scene shot at the airport. In fact both Bryony and I were supposed, originally, to be in the same shot but ended up on the cutting room floor. We had all three taken suitcases out to the airport location to authenticate our appearance as travellers and, to give them a bit of weight, there was a pillow packed inside each case. When we got back to the hotel that night we were greeted by an irate proprietor who thought we had stolen his pillows. However when we explained the situation he was instantly transformed, he had not known that we were involved in making films and of course he was honoured that his pillows should be used for that purpose and anything else he could do he would be delighted.

I had been apprehensive about visiting Bombay because, unlike Harry, I had not previously come to terms, through writing about them, with the all-pervading poverty, the beggars, the smells and only too visible rats on the streets. I did, indeed, find it difficult to accept the deep divide between life for the impoverished majority and the opulence and lifestyle of the minority. On the other hand, we could not have met with more kindness and been welcomed more warmly by those who were part of that minority who entertained us lavishly. Bryony was much more level-headed and came to terms with what we encountered—apart from the rats which she really hated—so was enchanted by the whole India experience.

While Harry was fully occupied on the film set each day, she and I were able to sight-see in Bombay itself and spend a few days down in Goa, as well as, thanks to the generosity of Harry's old friends Partap and Sue Sharma, being driven up to spend a night in Mahabaleshwar, an old hill station. Obviously this was no longer the privileged white people's rest centre of colonial days but despite this it had not arrived in the twentieth century. We still seemed to be treated as privileged sahibs and somehow the tribulations of modern life had no place there and certainly, for a visitor, all was peace and tranquillity.

Bryony and I left a week before filming was complete because Bryony had to get back to her job in the Visual Effects department of the BBC. But we hit the worst of the airport strikes and could not get onto our flight which was overbooked. There was no hope even of getting onto any of the next day's flights but we spent the night sitting huddled together in a very draughty waiting room until the time came that we could reasonably disturb Harry back in the hotel. Very fortunately Zafar's wife Colleen was on the staff of Air India and she was able, after spending a great deal of time on the telephone, to arrange two seats on the next night's flight.

When the film was shown to lukewarm reviews it was tempting to wonder if things would have been very different if the original film, written by Jonathan Miller and directed by Anthony Shaffer, had actually been made. But, on balance, Harry felt that he had gained from the experience and was absolutely delighted to have had Naseer playing Ghote. There is a great deal of humour in the books but it arises subtly from the text and there is a danger that any actor will be tempted to 'play it for laughs' which would distort the character completely. Naseer's interpretation found a perfect balance. If, as Naseer said, he found that Harry himself illuminated Ghote, what a bonus it must have been to have him around at the time of the filming. On the other hand what an agonising experience it would have been for Harry if there had been an actor who had not been able to interpret the character as originally envisaged. There were a number of attempts over the years to make further films, as well as several options on TV series, both Indian and UK based, and it was very sad that none of them came to fruition when Naseer was still young enough to play the part.

Putting the glamour of the film world behind him, there was a certain amount of urgency, when back home, to finish revising 'Dead on Time' for its publication in 1988, and, more immediately in mid-April, there was Bryony's wedding only three months away. Her oldest brother Simon and his girl-friend Lee had set out on a nine-month round-the-world tour in October of 1986, a tour not without trauma, with Lee surviving severe illness in India as well as their itinerary coinciding with earthquakes in New Zealand, but they were due to arrive home in July, so the date was fixed for the 25th of that month. In the meantime Harry, with his basic dislike of travel, was able to get vicarious pleasure from their amazing photos of the world tour. Simon's skill with a camera could, should he have wished to do so, have offered him an alternative career.

Parents' genes are often a contributing factor to the careers pursued by their offspring, but so many other factors get mixed into the equation that the end result is not always predictable. Parental influence, over the years, has undoubtedly got less and less as teenage independence has grown. But perhaps the nurturing period does sometimes play a part. Simon, who undoubtedly inherited Harry's academically intellectual mind together with a tendency to be introverted, when asked about his memories of and reactions to Harry as a father, first of all said that he felt enormous pride in, and admiration for, the dedication that produced an amazing volume of work. He then went on to remember as did all the other children, the necessity for the house to be kept quiet adding that he felt this was, almost certainly, a contributory factor to his passion for making models and constructing intricate 'scenes' as backgrounds for his imaginary games, both being reasonably silent occupations. His obvious conceptual sense coupled with his definite ability to draw and paint led to parental suggestions that he should consider architecture as a career. Apparently this pressure only served to make him determined not to pursue that course and he decided to read French and Linguistics at University where he spent a large proportion of his time involved in theatre activities which resulted in him initially making a career for himself as a stage manager/director.

Bryony, on the other hand, who also showed real artistic ability, was determined from a very early age to make acting her career. That this did not happen was sheer chance. Although the Lycée did give them all a bi-cultural education and they all ended up bilingual, it had its disadvantages. The preferred choice for the English students, after ten years of French education, was to switch to 'O' Levels and 'A' Levels rather than following the French system through to the end with the Baccalaureate. At the time there seemed to be a reluctance for the separate English section to gear their teaching to the passing of English exams and this often meant that results overall were disappointing, which was the case with Bryony. She did not get her predicted grades and so was unable to take up her place to read English and Drama at University and she very sensibly chose to switch to a degree in Interior Design. This meant that, bizarrely, she ended up in the Art world whereas Simon, initially, went into the theatre.

Throughout, Harry remained a tower of strength and, although ready with advice, never sought to impose his ideas of what he felt would be best. Simon said wryly that he thought one of the reasons he got his place at Nottingham was because the Professor of French was a great Ghote fan.

The other three children while endorsing Simon's memory of the necessity not to make a noise, especially when going upstairs past the study, which was on the first floor, also joined him in recalling being driven mad by the way they were woken up each morning. An intercom system was in place between the ground floor and the top floor, where their bedrooms were, and Harry's voice would boom out, precisely at 7 a.m. the opening lines from the Rubaiyat of Omar Khayyam,

> *'Awake for morning in the bowl of night,*
> *Has cast the stone that puts the stars to flight.'*

But annoying though it might have been then, it remained as part of the legacy of Harry's love of words. Not, of course, just his ability to declaim them but also his love and understanding of the use of words. From his extensive reading he had accumulated an impressive vocabulary and he was never at a loss when asked to supply a word or its meaning. This extended to a ready explanation of facts, some of these, admittedly, being on the boundaries of credulity. That having been said, he did have a profound well of knowledge and a talent for retaining that knowledge. It was this ability with words which Bryony chose to recall when she spoke very eloquently about her memories of him at his funeral. She began by calling him a 'Wordsmith' and among other recollections was his ability to make up a story with a beginning, a middle and an end which he would manage to tailor to the exact time needed to cover the walk back after family excursions, bringing it to a conclusion as they reached the garden gate.

She also made mention of his speech-making skills. This was not confined to those he had prepared in advance but extended to those occasions when he was required to improvise. Her wedding was a case in point. This took place in the Roman Catholic Church in Soho Square which seemed fitting as both she and Rupert were cradle Catholics and had the intention of bringing up any children in the faith, to this was added the factor that Rupert's mother was a very devout Catholic. Francesca Sims, daughter of Rupert's older sister, was a beautiful, teenage bridesmaid and Harry's professional opera-singing cousin, Roderick Keating, performed an exquisite 'Ave Maria' during the signing of the register. The reception was held at the Groucho Club which was a short walk just round the corner. Fortunately the weather which had been unpredictable that July chose to stay fair which was just as well because it took some time for the rather large number of guests to progress down the welcoming line which was standing just inside the club entrance, resulting in a queue forming in Dean Street in the heart of Soho.

It was a convivial occasion with a splendid mix of bride and groom's friends as well as older colleagues and relations of both families all of whom mingled well. The formalities were observed and the speeches were well received. Harry as father of the bride seemed to have hit on the right mixture of anecdote and pride and had come to the point when glasses would be raised to toast the happy pair when he happened to notice that many of those glasses were empty. Nothing daunted he carried on seamlessly, while keeping an eye on the dilatory waiters, with the words, 'I haven't quite finished yet, I need to tell you about the time…' and continued improvising until the champagne was fully flowing. Perhaps after all he would have done well to make a career as an actor. The wedding photos were taken by Northumberland Place neighbour and well-known flautist, Richard Adeney. Among the best of these was one of Bryony's three brothers, who, acting as ushers, had all scrubbed up and dressed in appropriately formal gear.

In his sixty-first year he had been rescued from a life-threatening blood clot, published 'The Body in the Billiard Room' and the highly successful non-fiction 'Crime and Mystery', as well as visiting India twice and converted 'The Perfect Murder' into a film. To have the satisfaction of being a patriarchal father of the bride to add to all this epitomised not only the maturity he had attained as a person over four decades but should surely have left him in no doubt about his achievements as a writer.

Chapter 18

With the publication of 'Dead on Time' and all four children independent and myself back at work, it might have been thought that Harry would have been able to take life a little more easily. But that was not his way. Besides which the hoped-for new relationship with publisher Hutchinson was not turning out very well. Richard Cohen was no longer there and although his delightful successor, the soon-to-be-famous in her own right as an author, Kate Mosse, had taken over as his editor and the creative relationship continued to flourish, however there seemed to be little effort being made by the publishing house itself to build on Harry's reputation.

It was more a question of how the books themselves were being marketed. The newest Ghote, 'Dead on Time', had been, as usual, well received by many of the critics, with Marcel Berlins in the Times accurately deducing what Harry had wanted to convey: *'Keating's message that attitudes to time reflect attitudes to life.'*, There was one exception. Joan Smith, in the Evening Standard, baldly stated, *'I do not enjoy these books at all, stuck as they are in some kind of time warp in which all the characters talk like Peter Sellers's Indians.'* This perhaps did need saying because it did reflect the view of a section of the public. Not everyone had sympathy with Indians and the Indian way of life. But she is wrong in equating the reality of the Anglo-Indian speech in Harry's books with the caricatured Sellers's Indian speech, which was entirely done for its comic effect to enhance the 'comic' Indians he portrayed. Although even she grudgingly admits *'But Keating knows what he's doing, if you happen to like this sort of thing.'*

The other thing of note is that more than one reviewer draws attention to the longevity of the series, pointing out that this is the sixteenth outing. John Milne in the Daily Telegraph, while recording this fact, nevertheless means to praise when he says, '*Crime novels are generally not taken seriously as literature though occasional re-evaluations do occur (with P.D. James in England and Simenon in France), Keating will soon, too, be "discovered".* It was good that Mr. Milne thought Harry's books transcended their genre but surely sixteen outings were enough for that discovery to have already happened. Harry was not given to writing to reviewers, except occasionally to say thank you, but had he done so on this occasion he might well have said, 'How long, Oh Lord, how long?' Perhaps, not to put too fine a point on it, this was the moment that his publisher and, above all, his agent should have addressed this question.

Harry always kept faith with his ambitions not only for himself but for recognition, in some cases, of the superior merits of crime fiction over mainstream fiction but this did not mean that he automatically got his own way. There were difficulties when the next book he proposed to Hutchinson did not find a sympathetic ear in the editorial department. This was partly due to the nature of the book. It was a collection of Ghote short stories and these never at that time seemed to find favour with publishers. Although perhaps a book that was conceived as a silver jubilee celebration for the series, with the first Ghote being published in 1964, should have tickled the fancy of those who were marketing it. It had the added advantage of a longish introduction which talks the reader through Ghote's genesis and then goes on to chronicle not only his subsequent development but also Harry's own journey through those twenty-five years. He takes a look at each of the already published novels, up to 1988, and examines the themes underlying them. The thirteen short stories follow, the last two actually newly written in the publication year.

Finally publication was agreed and, once again, it was well received by reviewers who often included the non-fiction book that also appeared that year. 'The Bedside Companion to Crime' which was a joint publication between O'Mara books in the UK and Otto Penzler's Mysterious Press in the USA and it was intended as a 'fun' book. But in his introduction which, in deference to the title, he calls 'A Word Before You Drop Off', he manages to re-iterate his belief in the importance of the crime novel. Underneath the light 'book designed for bedside reading' there lies quite enough seriousness to make a reader feel that they've not been flipping through a glossy magazine.

Adopting the elimination theme of the Agatha Christie book whose original title was 'Ten Little Niggers', Harry numbers his contents table from ten down to one. In each section he addresses matters that are relevant to the crime novel in the broadest possible manner and gathers together facts and foibles from the world of crime writing, then deliberately presents them in an amusing fashion. To amuse had often been his aim from as far back as his desire to make witty speeches at college and although this was not his major preoccupation when writing the Ghote books, they would have been far less successful if the underlying humour had not been there. This was a book designed to be savoured at intervals, to be dipped into, although one reviewer did suggest that a crime buff might find it hard to put down.

But by the time these 1989 books were published, an extra dimension had been added to the Keatings' life. We became grandparents. Zoe was born to Bryony and Rupert on August 1, 1988. The vexed question arose of what we were going to be called. Granny, (Rupert's mother), and Gran and Grampy (my parents) were ruled out and I said I would go with whatever name Zoe called me when she began to talk. Who will ever know what put the sound of Ganga into the mind of a child not yet a year old but that is what was said and has remained in use ever since. For some reason Grumpy seemed to go with Ganga and however inappropriate that was, it is what Harry was called from then on. It certainly did not reflect his attitude because he delighted in his newfound status and thoroughly enjoyed being involved in the emergence of a new generation.

That same year Simon married Lee at the Registry Office in the Marylebone Road followed by lunch at home consisting of very superior fish and chips from a neighbouring shop and pink champagne. Bryony's beautifully crafted cake and the cutting ceremony was reserved for the very boozy evening party to which Simon and Lee's friends were invited. Northumberland Place echoed to the sound of loud music and revelry far into the night. That made the third family wedding to be celebrated, each of which was conducted to the full in three very different styles.

The following year in October 1989 Charlotte was born to Piers and Hazel and six months later in April of 1990 Simon and Lee produced Hannah. Then nine months after that in January 1991 Bryony and Rupert had their second daughter, Phoebe. Four grandchildren in around two and a half years and a beard getting whiter and whiter and more and more luxurious were indications that the slide into the role of beneficent patriarch had begun. An anecdote from the first days of Phoebe's life shows this. I would normally have been the one to offer help to Bryony on her return from the hospital birth but I was working in Edinburgh so Harry volunteered. His first day on duty he answered the front doorbell. The midwife introduced herself and her companion who added, 'Hello, I'm the trainee midwife.' Rapier-thrust fast came the reply, 'Hello, I'm the trainee grandfather.'

That he was capable of such easy repartee at that time is quite surprising. In the preceding week Michael Sissons, his agent, had sent him a bolt from the blue. The letter simply said that he felt Ghote had had a long enough innings and Harry should find an alternative for subsequent books. Of course Harry was devastated. I had only known Michael socially before but I decided that now I was justified in interfering. There had never been any question of my being involved in Harry's dealings with agents and publishers before, but knowing that I was going to be away, leaving Harry on his own at such a time, I was deeply worried, so I wrote a letter to Michael. I suggested that he had not perhaps realised what such a severance would mean to someone whose life had become completely intertwined with Ghote and India and I also suggested that he at once make an appointment to see Harry to talk over the matter, adding that it would be better if he did not know that it was I who had asked him to do this.

Mercifully Michael did arrange a meeting and Harry did not find out till many years later, when it seemed appropriate for me to tell him, that it had anything to do with me. A possible solution was found. It was agreed that

Harry would consider what sort of a series he could invent that he could write alternately with each new Ghote. But to this day I cannot understand how someone who had been Harry's agent for thirty years could have been so unaware of what made his author tick.

But prior to any of this in 1990 the normal one-book-a-year routine was continuing. The title of the book had been with Harry ever since he had worked in an editorial capacity with an author he much admired, Rebecca West. She had referred to blackmail as 'The iciest sin', and this became not only the title but also the meat of the book. Given the task of exposing an evil female blackmailer, Ghote finds himself inextricably caught up in a situation where he himself is vulnerable to blackmail, and as an added twist he himself uses it to bring pressure on someone involved in criminal practices. There is also an exploration of the many times blackmail in one form or another is employed in everyday life. An example close to home is when Ghote's young son, Ved, in those early IT days when costs were prohibitive, wants to purchase a smuggled 'home computer' at a bargain price. When Ghote refuses his permission on the moral grounds that the provenance of the computer was undoubtedly suspect, Ved himself resorts to blackmail and says that he will tell Protima, his mother, who was unaware of the fact that Ghote himself had perhaps once made a less than legal purchase of a TV. This is only one of the various side-issues that provide the background to the main story.

Computers must have been on Harry's mind because this is the first book he himself, very belatedly, wrote using a computer. Over the years he had had to abandon his beloved portable typewriter when parts for repair were no longer available. Until quite recently—when it was accidentally thrown away—it was actually still in existence and, as well as its journey to Japan, had been hired out to be used as a prop in a period TV series. But with its functional demise an electronic typewriter was substituted which more or less did the job but had none of the advantages of a proper computer. So reluctantly the decision was taken and Harry entered the world of modern technology but even he had to admit the benefits were enormous. There were some traumas ahead, especially when he managed to eradicate a whole book while doing the revision. He had not at that time learnt the elementary lesson that everything should be saved onto something outside the computer itself. Rather than pay a company their quoted £800 to retrieve it, he retyped the entire book from the first draft which, fortunately, he had printed out. He attacked the task with the ferocity and technique left over from the old days of the typewriter keyboard. He never mastered the lighter touch required by a computer and the thud, thud, thud continued to penetrate to the floor below.

Modern technology was, and to some extent remained, a mystery to him. He was far beyond the age of the generations who were growing up with it in their bloodstream. Coupled with the problems attached to finding an alternative to the Ghote books he must have felt fairly overwhelmed. However in the October of that year, 1991, he reached sixty-five and The Society of Authors pension fund, to which he had been contributing, matured. When the letter arrived telling him the lump sum he would receive and the monthly payments that would be made, he read it in disbelief, declaring that the company must have, by mistake, added an extra zero. Of course he had been aware that whenever there had been something to spare from sums being earned he had salted away a portion in the fund but he had not kept track of how much he had invested.

He had never been interested in making money as such and provided he could meet the bills he was happy to ignore the debits and credits. Many times he had said that he did not understand why it was necessary to take holidays although he did accept that not everyone was lucky enough to have a job that was as absorbing as his own. He was equally certain that no-one needed to earn the vast amounts which bankers, lawyers and captains of industry seemed to earn but then he had no desire to own yachts nor villas around the world.

But, of course, there was no mistake in the calculation of his pension and had he been so minded he could have taken the easy way out. He could have retired and lived very comfortably by his standards on the annual income. The idea never occurred to him. Life without writing was unthinkable and further, life without producing a book a year was still not an option. What those books would be was quite another matter but he never had any doubt that inspiration would come.

Another reason for remaining an author was that the same year he was very proud to be invited to become a Fellow of the Royal Society of Literature. As with his time as Chairman of The Society of Authors he regarded his five years on the Council of the Royal Society as a serious commitment and was a regular attendee of the meetings. He also enjoyed renewing friendships with writers he had known before, such as Michael Holroyd, the biographer, who later went on to become President of the Society and his wife, the distinguished novelist and literature expert, Margaret Drabble. When Michael became President he relinquished his link with a body looking into funding of public libraries and suggested that as Harry had previously been active in trying to secure Public Lending Right for authors he could take over from him. This task he did not enjoy as the committee he joined was bogged down in legalistic documentation and really seemed to have very little to do with maintaining Public Libraries as places for people to have access to books. But this was the only fly in the ointment and he was quite sad when his five years on the Council came to an end.

Nineteen ninety-one came to its crowded conclusion with the marriage of the youngest of the four children, Hugo, to Debra Overton. This happened on the shortest day of the year, four days before Christmas in the village of Mickleton in Gloucestershire where Deb's parents lived. It was a fairy-tale late afternoon wedding with the guests carrying flaming torches to light their short walk back from the church along a pitch-black lane to the house, on whose lawn a huge star-decorated marquee had been erected. As evening changed to night a feast was served and appropriate speeches were delivered before the dancing started and then around midnight the couple were driven away by a teetotaler friend in the classic Sunbeam coupé which was the bridegroom's present to his bride. Much to Harry's and my surprise, in the changing modern world, all four of the children were married.

Harry was not given to soul-searching—at least not to sharing any searching with others, but had he ever embarked on writing more than a sketch of an autobiography it would have had to ponder at this point on the journey he had made from callow youth-in-training at the BBC, deadening years as a soldier leading to the mind-changing revelations of academia, on via journalism to the many years of fairly impoverished life as a writer with a growing family, and finally, arriving at pensionable age with the realisation that his chosen career had made him financially secure and that he had become a patriarch. This last was emphasised over the next five years by the arrival of five more grandchildren.

April 1992 saw the arrival of Piers and Hazel's second daughter, Rosanna and Hugo and Deb's son Edward in October of the same year. Then in June 1995, it was Hugo and Deb's turn to produce Lydia, a sister for Edward and in January 1996 Simon and Lee produced a brother, Jacob, for Hannah, with Piers and Hazel completing their trio with daughter, Josephine, in August 1996. Between August 1989 and August 1996 the extended family increased by nine. All the families seemed to be keen photographers and after each birth Harry purchased an album to accommodate the plentiful pictorial records.

But back in 1991 the next Ghote, which had already been planned before the new system of writing alternate books had come into effect, had to be written.

Chapter 19

With part of his mind given over to the problem of what he could create as an alternative to Ghote it is not surprising that Harry found the task of moving from the planning to actually writing 'Cheating Death' more difficult than usual. In fact he was never entirely happy with it and thought of it as the weakest Ghote book. Strangely by no means all the critics seemed to endorse this although there were some who did. Christopher Wordsworth in The Observer could not bring himself to slate it but charmingly said, *'A qualified shabash this time.'* Susanna Yager in the Sunday Telegraph concluded that it was *'Enjoyable but less compelling than usual.'* and Matthew Coady in The Guardian echoed this with *'An agreeable comedic glow.'*, with The Evening Standard complicitly enjoying it. *'The Indianness of it all is conveyed with the utmost skill...A jolly good show I am thinking.'*

Part of the difficulty for Harry lay in the basic plot which concerned the theft of University exam papers which, with cheating being endemic in the Indian system, was for Ghote almost a routine and relatively unimportant crime. A statistic that Harry quotes says it all: *'In Delhi last year 3,400 cheats were reported. In Kanpur they had three rooms for their BSc exams, one for Rupees 1,000 where you could cheat on your own, one at Rupees 2,000 where you could take the help of the invigilators themselves and a Rupees 5,000 room where you could call for answers from outside.'* John Coleman in The Sunday Times had this to say, *'Teetering between farce and violence, Ghote tears about until his famous patience finally snaps...Keating hands over the protest marches and staff intrigue of Indian University life as confidently as if he held a chair in it.'* But another running theme of the book is wife beating which also seemed to be routinely practised in India, not least among Ghote's colleagues. Ghote had almost persuaded himself that Protima was exceeding her wifely duties and that he was in danger of being humiliated if he did not show her who was master of the house, creating another difficulty for Harry for this was something that would have sat as uneasily with him as it did with Ghote. Despite the Times in its review asserting that there was 'Not a sign of flagging invention or tiredness', it would seem that the book was written with Harry having, to some extent, put himself on autopilot.

It cannot have helped that a further change of publisher was in the pipeline. It was obvious that the hopes of a happy partnership that had begun with 'Under a Monsoon Cloud' had not been fulfilled and the severance was mutual.

Although George Hardinge was no longer at the helm, Macmillan held out a welcoming hand and Harry was ready with the first of the alternative new series. He had decided that he did not want to commit himself to a new series detective but would make the theme one that could be applicable to a range of different detectives. He would examine how certain characteristics could be a hindrance to them in their day-to-day policing lives. The first, 'The Rich Detective', centred round the dilemma faced by a policeman who was being ordered by his superiors to abandon the case he was building against an individual he was convinced was guilty. The possible flaw in Detective Inspector Bill Sylvester's character could be described as over-zealousness. Returning from a Spanish holiday where he had bought a ticket in the monthly national lottery, he promptly forgets all about it when he becomes involved in investigating suspicious deaths of old ladies in retirement homes. He becomes convinced he knows the killer but is warned off pursuing this line of inquiry by his superior. At this point he learns that his lottery ticket has made him a millionaire. Frustrated by the embargo on his investigations he decides to resign from the force and, having become the Rich Detective of the title, he is able to pursue the suspected criminal in a private capacity.

Perhaps because the filing of reviews was done in such an informal manner there is no explanation for there being virtually none from the

British press—there is one from Mike Ripley in the Daily Telegraph: *'Very professionally executed and with a genuinely fiendish villain'* but fortunately America was impressed, producing, among others, some comments from prestigious sources. This from The Kirkus Review: *'All the dry-eyed penetration of an English Simenon, coupled with* Keating's *usual sly humor: a treat not to be missed.'* and from Publishers Weekly, *'A sophisticated work: a slice of edgy crime fiction that hints at dark obsessions percolating beneath.'* And words warm enough to heat the cockles of any author's heart, from Time: *'In a season bringing the greatest abundance of high quality mysteries for some years, "The Rich Detective" is the richest.'*

It was an auspicious beginning, both for a new series and a change of publisher. But the next was to be a Ghote and if it was not in any way a new beginning, for the character at least, there was going to be a very different approach in this book. It had a very simple title, 'Doing Wrong', for something that was actually quite complex. There were many appreciative reviews, among them Jessica Mann's in the Western Morning News: *'Some fictional detectives take on a life of their own, becoming a part of a fictional reality. Up there, along with Hercule Poirot or even Sherlock Holmes, struts the endearing Inspector from Bombay, Ganesh Ghote...There is an undertone of seriousness to this entertaining story which adds a welcome depth to the portrayal of Ghote and his country.* But without doubt the lengthy piece in the Times Literary Supplement written by eminent crime writer and doyen of the critics, Julian Symons, in which he not only analyses the book itself but also assesses Harry's progress as a writer, is a pearl of its kind and it is certain that Harry himself would have liked nothing better than that it should be shared with those of you reading this book.

He begins by suggesting that at first glance Ghote may not have changed greatly over the thirty years of his existence, *'still likely to be awed by the new and strange, still wary of giving offence to superiors. He remains both fearful and courageous, and his thought processes, as shown to us, blend a simplicity that verges on the foolish with sudden bursts of understanding but the uses to which Ghote is now put by his creator are radically different from the fairly orthodox puzzles that confronted the detective in the early stories. Ghote has become primarily a medium through which H.R.F. Keating can express his interest in the philosophical and moral problems related to acts of violence. "Under a Monsoon Cloud" found Ghote complicit in concealing a crime committed by a superior whom he idolised, the morality of cheating at examinations was an underlying concern of "Cheating Death", the nature of time the subject of another novel.*

At this point Julian Symons begins his analysis of 'Doing Wrong' itself and for once a reviewer can speak openly about the plot because it is not strictly a whodunit, he will not be giving away any secrets by revealing the murderer's name because, as he says, *'From the second page of the book we know that the ambitious politician, H.K. Verma, has killed a woman because she was likely to reveal a damaging secret about his past.'* Because the victim is a national figure, a veteran freedom fighter and the crime is committed in Bombay, Crime Branch is involved, and when Ghote begins to suspect, from the evidence of a train ticket in the victim's flat, that the origin of the crime lies in Banares (Harry's recognition of the local spelling rather than the more usual Western one of Benares) he is allowed to go there to investigate. The review continues, *'Ghote soon suspects Verma, and there ensues what is less a cat-and-mouse than a guilt-and-innocence game, with passages alternating between the detective's investigation and Verma's state of mind. One of the book's principal achievements is in showing Verma as a figure moving constantly from sin to repentance, desperately immersing himself daily at his bathing place in the purifying Ganges, congratulating himself on his own integrity moments before telling lies to Ghote, whom he thinks of sometimes as a Bombay rat and at others as a little mongoose nosing out secrets. Contrasts between virtuous intentions and socially acceptable corruption provide a number of ironies. A businessman tells Ghote that he has found bribery works admirably in business and disconcerts him by saying that the dead freedom fighter did not hesitate to blackmail him on behalf of her good causes.'*

After discussing Verma's ambitions and his relationship with his son, Julian points to the subtlety and reality of the characterisations and then goes on, *'His interrogations by nipping mongoose Ghote are brilliantly done, culminating in two chapters where questions and answers are repeated, first from Ghote's viewpoint, then from Verma's.'* The review continues with a frank admission that the Indian speech and Ghote's circuitous approach in previous books had sometimes been a little irritating, perhaps making the character seem too nearly comic, he then continues, *'The final pages find the detective watching the ceremonial burning of Verma's body (the politician has been fatally injured in an accident after a final effort to destroy the evidence providing his motive for murder), Ghote meditates before the mound of smoking ash on his own death and possible reincarnation. The last line of what is certainly the finest and most serious Ghote novel is: "Have I done enough of the right in my life? Have I?"'*

This has an elegiac ring to it. It also raises the question of whether this is a cry from Ghote's heart alone. Could this also be the author's anguish? Whether it was or not, it would not have been in Harry's nature to admit, even to those closest to him, that that was the case. I would go further and say that it is unlikely that if you were a step removed from his inner circle but still thought you knew him pretty well, you would probably not be able to answer that question with certainty. The nearest you could get would be to read his books. Over the years he and Julian had formed a lasting friendship. He and his wife Kathleen probably knew us as well as anyone but I believe Julian would have acknowledged that he knew Harry best from his writing.

As well as playing life close to the chest he never reneged on a contract. The contract to be honoured this time was with Michael Sissons so he knew the next book had to be one of the new English detective series. Next up was a title that should perhaps have finished with a question mark, 'The Good Detective', because, in this instance, there was something from this detective's past that was definitely shady and could prevent him from functioning as the good detective he has certainly now become. John Coleman in The Sunday Times, having first called him the *'The redoubtable Keating'* for tackling, along with others in the genre, the integrity of the police force, follows this same thought, *'Keating presents a brilliantly shaking and unusual slant to the implicit leading question of his title: what does make a good detective in these troubled times.'*

Macmillan, in conjunction with Pan Books, now started to bring out the paperback of the previous hardback on the same date as the new hardback so that many of the reviewers addressed them both together. Alex Gordon of the Peterborough Evening Telegraph says the two books *'prove beyond all reasonable doubt that no-one shapes an investigative police story better than H.R.F. Keating.'* Whereas James Melville in that organ always known as 'The Ham and High', after nominating Harry to fill the shoes of the late doyen of crime fiction, Julian Symons, also manages to refer to the *'immortal Inspector Ghote'*, contrasting him with Inspector French from 'The Good Detective' who is, *'mean, hard and driven.'* The headline on his piece is **'The Not-So-Good Detective who isn't Very PC'** and it finishes, *'he is forced to take stock of himself as unsentimentally as he views others and accepts there can be no happy ending for him. The conclusion of this fine novel is a bitter mixture of triumph and personal defeat.'* There is one personal letter, from old friend and fellow writer Josephine Pullein-Thompson, among the reviews where, having said that she had found the book engrossing, adds, *'You must have an arrogant, sadistic streak that I have never glimpsed. But it must be miniscule.'*

Whether that was true or not Harry threw himself whole-heartedly into the new series and proved that diversifying was not a problem. Of course his earliest books and his forays into the world of the straight novel had had him writing in many different styles so this new venture merely corroborated that he was truly a man of words quite capable of adapting his skills to the necessities required of him. But he still had tasks to perform away from his desk. The year before 'Doing Wrong' was published, 1993, as President of the Detection Club, he was invited to attend the conference being held in Madison, Wisconsin, to celebrate the centenary of the birth of Dorothy L. Sayers. As she was one of the founders of the club they wanted to include something about it on the agenda.

It turned out that going to the conference led to rather more than he had envisaged. Among the proposed attendees was an American academic, Catherine Kenny, who had written a Sayers biography. More recently she had completed a one woman play with Dorothy as the protagonist and asked if it could be given a reading in Madison. Knowing that I was an actress and would be accompanying Harry, the organisers passed on the suggestion to us. Having read it I agreed to do it and we flew to Chicago to stay overnight with our friends Alzina and Chuck Dale. The next day the Dales drove us to Madison and I, slightly suffering from jet lag, found I had been allocated the evening of the first day for the performance. It was given a rapturous reception and the decision was taken to go for a full theatre presentation, first in England and then in America. So, in the January of 1995 it ran for a week in a small theatre in Oxford but not without many contributions from Harry. First of all he made an admirable recording of a short but vital narrative piece that Catherine had written to be played towards the end of the drama. The lights were temporarily dimmed on the setting of the play, a gallery in Piccadilly in the middle of London, where Dorothy had come to view a recently finished portrait of herself after a day's Christmas shopping. Out of the darkness Harry's disembodied voice tells of her return home to an empty house after the day in London and then the discovery, the next morning, of her body slumped at the bottom of the stairs having suffered a massive and fatal heart attack. The lights are then brought up again and the play picks up where it left off, allowing Dorothy to tie up the remaining loose ends and bring her reminiscences to a conclusion.

But apart from this very moving recorded contribution by Harry as an actor he also helped me in my capacity of producer by undertaking the rather more onerous tasks of press officer and general administrator. His efforts were richly rewarded because publicity had brought us splendid audiences so that after paying the designer and stage-manager the weekly Equity minimum and footing the bills for things like printing costs and hiring the theatre, the production broke even—quite an achievement for a fringe show. Mind you it must be admitted that without friends and family the balance sheet would have looked very different. For instance Hugo's scene-making company provided the set, Debra, his wife, herself a set-designer, found or made the props and Bryony designed posters and publicity cards, while my favourite director, Ian Wooldridge, devoted many hours to pulling the show together in the fortnight before we opened. We were deeply grateful that all of them gave their services, free of charge. The Dorothy L. Sayers Society and its Chairman, Christopher Dean, recommended good and not expensive printers as well as giving enormous moral support and drumming up a substantial audience from among the Society's members. Further help came from P.D. James who offered accommodation in her then Oxford house as well as hosting the party after the first night.

When in 1997 the play finally went on tour in America, Harry's duties extended to unofficial prompter—sometimes needed—occasional operator of sound and lighting equipment when the venue failed to produce anyone to do it and on one occasion reading the death announcement live because there was no available socket for the tape recorder. Added to this, at several venues, after the play was over, he gave a talk about Sayers and the Detection Club. But probably his greatest contribution was the moral support he gave to me, especially when the first venue for the USA tour was unable to provide space for a final rehearsal. Not having performed the play since 1995, this was an essential exercise which eventually happened in our hotel room with Harry at close quarters as an audience of one.

The tour was a revelation to us both and was a lesson in how to extemporise and make do with what was on offer. But there were other demands on Harry's time which involved being interviewed for local TV and radio, not only about Sayers and the Detection Club but about his own writing. This was something that he had learnt to do very well over the years and he was always very relaxed, resulting in easy viewing or listening in programmes often mounted by locals in their spare time.

During our visit to Scottsdale in Arizona we were made to feel like royalty by Barbara Peters and her husband Rob Rosenwald. Barbara is a tower of strength in the American crime-writing world and runs both the Poisoned Pen bookshop and Press, she had taken over organising the tour of the play after the author, who had said she would do it, seemed to run out of steam. The play became part of that year's annual Scottsdale crime convention. She also knew people living in adjoining—well only a hundred miles away—areas which led on one occasion to Harry and me being driven miles across the desert and back in order to be part of a TV Arts programme run as a spare time activity by the local dentist, who was also our driver and the interviewer for the programme.

Throughout the tour there were many specialist crime bookstores to be visited and Harry, when speaking, was always given a fantastic welcome. His essential Englishness coupled with the warmth of his personality seemed to endear him to his audiences and fans of Inspector Ghote were to be found in great numbers. The Dales had continued to offer hospitality whenever the tour brought us anywhere near Chicago so that their house became a second home for us. Nevertheless we both heaved a sigh of relief when it was time to return to England especially as granddaughter Phoebe—aged four—had been diagnosed with a hole-in-the heart which was going to require surgery. It is good to record that a miracle occurred and against all medical prediction the hole closed itself before surgery took place.

But of course between the first reading of the play in 1993, the UK showing in 1995 and the American tour in 1997 there was the routine for Harry of bringing out a book a year to say nothing of the march of time which brought with it the celebration of Harry's 70th birthday in 1996.

Chapter 20

I t was to be a year of celebrations because a few months before the birthday, the Crime Writers' Association gave Harry their award for excellence, the Cartier Diamond Dagger. As its name suggests this was a dagger richly studded with diamonds and was not retained by the recipient but kept in the Cartier vaults in between the annual ceremonies. But a lasting tangible proof of the award was offered, either a pair of cuff-links bearing the image of the dagger or a small replica dagger brooch. Harry generously chose the brooch which he gave to me. The grand presentation was held in one of the riverside rooms belonging to the House of Lords and Monsieur Bamberger, London managing director of Cartier, made the speech. He had lived for many years in London but his English accent remained—almost certainly by choice—Parisian. Each year he made sure he used the word sleuth which he pronounced *slute*. Harry in his speech of acceptance wittily drew attention to this with the result that, in subsequent years, the use of the word always produced laughter not only from those assembled but from M. Bamberger himself. Jokes aside Harry was, of course, genuinely delighted at being honoured with the Dagger.

Three of the children were able to be there to see him receive the award and we took advantage of the occasion, when Harry was occupied elsewhere, to discuss what sort of celebration there should be for the 70th birthday which was only five months away. Everyone favoured having a grand dinner and realised that it might be difficult to persuade Harry that it was right to spend so much money just to honour him, so it would have to be kept secret. Organising a secret celebration can be a nightmare but on this occasion the family between them managed it. Sending out the invitations with the RSVP to be sent to Bryony was the first step and worked splendidly with two exceptions. In one case this was understandable because our friends Nina Bawden and Austen Kark were in Greece and wanting to express their regret at not being able to be present, telephoned us at home. Fortunately I answered the phone and, realising that the conversation would be bound to give the game away, made an excuse of having to find information that was in another room, so replacing the receiver I made my way to the other phone. Disaster was averted. But the gaff was nearly blown on the day of the party itself when his agent's secretary rang to say that Michael was unable to be present due to illness but was sending round a case of wine. Fortunately there was still time to divert it to another address and Harry never knew of the call. A further slight hiccup presented itself when it was time to get ready for what Harry thought was going to be a restaurant meal with the immediate family. He was never one to wear a tie if it could be avoided and he could see no reason to dress up on this occasion and it was only by saying that the boys had decided to wear suits that he could be persuaded that a small gesture to formality in the form of a suit and tie would be appropriate.

Arriving at the restaurant, Harry was astonished to see a fellow author and long-time friend, Francis King, standing there with glass in hand. 'How extraordinary that Francis should choose to dine here tonight as well,' was Harry's comment. Fairly easily gulled he might be but it did not take long for the penny to drop as more and more familiar faces appeared, and I was anxious in case he decided to turn tail at the thought of a party in his honour—which he was quite capable of doing. But all was well and the evening went ahead as planned. Everyone having consumed a splendid feast provided by the canal-side restaurant, it was time for the birthday cake. A reluctant Harry was faced with the desecrating act of having to cut into a remarkable piece of edible sculpture. Bryony had baked a cake designed as an open-paged book pierced by a replica of the diamond dagger with a message from the family and a list of past winners of the Dagger written on the pages. Making edible sculptures was something that Bryony had learnt to do when she worked for the visual effects department of the BBC and on many occasions later she was in great demand when a special cake was required. This was not the first nor would it be the last family occasion to benefit from her skill.

The invitation had rather stupidly omitted to say 'No presents' and a side table groaned with some very imaginative gifts from family and friends, among them another sculpture—non-edible. Bryony had been working on a bust of Harry for some while and she had it ready for the birthday. It is an exceptionally good likeness and, unlike the cake, remains as a lasting memorial.

Crowded into this year of celebrations there were two new books, the third in the Detective series, 'The Bad Detective' and another Ghote, 'Asking Questions'. 'The Bad Detective' was first out at the beginning of the year. The review from the Yorkshire Post deliberately copies the style of Harry's own efforts when he was the Times crime fiction reviewer where, after the longer reviews of one or two books there would be a column of shorts, each around thirty words long and pithily summing up the merits of the book. Here in twenty-nine words is the Yorkshire Post's contribution: *'Detective Sergeant Jack Stallworthy takes backhanders and is a thoroughly bad cop. Harry Keating takes a thoroughly plausible villain and is a thoroughly good writer. The combination is brilliant.'* In a rather longer piece 'S.E.' of The Times Literary Supplement reiterates what the actual Superintendent Kulkarni, of the Bombay Crime Branch, gave as one of the reasons why he would have liked to have had Ghote on his police force—his ability to get inside the head of the criminal he was investigating. Here is the beginning and end of the final paragraph: *'Keating, the elder statesman of crime fiction, understands how deviants think. He takes us inside Stallworthy's head…He is weak-willed, cunning and stupid, and yet Keating manages to evoke sympathy for this rotten apple.'*

What gave Harry the ability to understand how deviants think or for that matter to get inside a villain's mind? The answer to those questions is the answer to how he managed to write about India before he had visited the sub-continent or indeed how he managed to describe life in Victorian times so convincingly. He had within him a chameleon-like quality which enabled him to immerse himself in the particular personality of the character, or the time and place that he had researched, and then let his imagination take over so that the transformation became reality. He could not have achieved this without an amazing ability to concentrate. Those undisturbed hours in the study were vital. An anecdote that shows this concentration has often been told as a joke—one summer's day while he was in the study, which overlooks the small back garden of our house, he emerged from India, where he had been writing a vivid description of the monsoon, to hear me saying to some guests, 'I think we'll have lunch in the garden.' Still thousands of miles away he apparently said to himself, 'Stupid woman how can they sit out in all this rain.' But there can be no doubt that the intensity of his concentration played a vital part in the truth of his writing.

But then he applied the same concentration to whatever he was doing. If he was interrupted while reading a book he would first place his finger on the word he had reached and then turn with a slightly injured look to find out the reason for the interruption. Unquestionably this sent an off-putting signal to the person who had interrupted but there had been no intention of issuing a rebuff, it was simply that he needed to concentrate fully on one thing at a time. Whether creating his own books or reading what others had created he would lose himself entirely in that world. Taken to its extreme it resulted in the incident already narrated when he drove on the wrong side of the road in fog. In this instance his job was being a driver and as such he needed to keep track of the road. The verge would enable him to do that as he needed to be able to see it. From his place at the right of the vehicle he would be able to do that so he would drive on the right. Did the imaginative gene, there from birth, dominate his life? The answer must be yes and no. Yes, because there is no gainsaying that he functioned best when he was deep inside his own created worlds. No, because he was capable of rising to the occasion when it was necessary for him to be part of events going on around him. But he was no multi-tasker, he needed to keep all occupations separate.

The problems of wayward policemen having been dealt with, it was back to his beloved India for 'Asking Questions' where he tackles the skullduggery of someone connected with the Mira Behn Institute of Medical Research who has been illicitly smuggling out a dangerous drug made from the venom of highly poisonous snakes. One American reviewer is particularly struck by the style of the book where in the first four pages, four very different questions are posed by four of the leading characters in the story and the remaining two hundred and seventy-one pages are spent providing the answers. Alma Joyce Hahn in the Benton Courier goes on to say, *'Ghote knows that if he asks the right questions, he will be successful. Keating knows that questions can be used effectively to tell a story.'* As this is the twentieth Ghote novel it is quite surprising that anyone writing a review had not encountered him before, but this is the case with David Ross of the Bournemouth Evening News and it is good that he says that he was, *'enchanted to share his company as he doggedly continues "asking and asking his questions".'* He also contradicts those few, like Joan Smith in her review of 'Dead on Time' who have suggested that Ghote is not a real character, that he does not ring true, with his concluding sentence *'Keating makes the character thoroughly and believably Indian—without being patronising or presenting us with a Peter Sellers parody.'*

That he was able to make the setting for 'Asking Questions' believable was partly due to a fortuitous meeting with one Rosemary Tootle who worked in a medical laboratory in London. She not only provided him with details he could use about the smuggled ACE inhibitors—the pills used to control high blood pressure among other things—but also gave him a tour of the hospital laboratory where she worked. Of course the Behn Institute bore no resemblance to her laboratory but it supplied enough solid fact for Harry to present a convincing establishment. Quite remarkable how authors have over the years made many a background seem totally authentic when they originally had no first-hand knowledge of the subject. But the advice to new authors in the 1987 Writing Crime Fiction to write about what you know might seem strange in view of the fact that Harry hardly knew one end of a test-tube from the other. Perhaps he should have added, 'and if you don't know anything about it, make sure you do your research thoroughly.' The scientific medical world was no more difficult to investigate than India had been earlier on.

That year also saw an off-spin publication when Pan Books decided to bring out an omnibus of the first three Ghote titles. On the face of it a great idea to keep back titles in print but how anyone who was fond of books can have imagined that a massive tome of some seven or eight hundred paperback pages could ever be a comfortable read, beggars belief. Having said that, all those equally over-sized, popular blockbusters must be selling or they would not keep on being published. To be fair an occasional copy of the triple volume still sells more than two decades after it first appeared, perhaps justifying the sad fact that in publishing, as in everything else in the modern world, it is money not cultural values that matter. But putting three volumes together virtually for the price of one is no different from the marketing ploy of selling three books for the price of two and simply equates books with groceries.

Harry, at the time, did not allow himself to dwell on the niceties of the publishing world but just got on with supplying the product. 1997 saw the publication of another in the Detective series, this time his detective is 'soft' or in the plain-speaking, derogatory words of his female sergeant, *'Soft as a duck's arse.'* Inspector Benholme acknowledges that his approach to crime solving could be called soft but believes that this stems from his ability to see the other side, to view things from the other person's point of view which allows him to get inside the head of the criminal. The reviews for this book were unanimous in their praise for the portrayal of the central character. The Birmingham Post went so far as to suggest that 'The Soft Detective' and indeed the whole detective series could be better than the Ghote novels. Whatever the comparative merits, this comment is really only stating what has emerged time and time again, that what is fundamental not only to Ghote and Benholme but to Harry himself, is that they all bend over backwards to see both sides of a question. A quality which undoubtedly was helpful when writing about his policemen but possibly meant that he neglected to pursue commercial matters that affected his professional life with the single-minded vigour needed to achieve the success he deserved. The Birmingham Post review concluded with a final plaudit: *'It is a small masterpiece of story-telling, well worthy of the man who is certainly among the best three or four male crime writers we have.'*

Tucked into Alex Auswaks' splendid review in the Jerusalem Post is a sentence which must have delighted Harry: *'The picture of multi-lingual and ethnically-diverse England is spot-on!'* That delight would have stemmed from the importance he attached to the background truth of his stories, whether that was the vast canvas of life in India or the seamy underside of the Victorians. He was apparently succeeding in one of his ambitions, to emulate the truth that Simenon achieved in his books. But reviewing was expanding—the internet was providing a platform. On a website called 'Tangled Web UK', fellow crime writer, Martin Edwards, pointed out that choosing to write about detectives whose weaknesses affected their work was an intriguing idea, adding that Harry *'has come up with an impressive number of intriguing ideas over the years...one of the most original crime writers of the post-war era...finest novel since the splendid Inspector Ghote novel "Dead on Time".'*

Later, in 2005, at the annual American crime convention Malice Domestic who gave Harry a Lifetime Achievement Award, Martin was asked to write an article about him for Mystery Scene magazine. The research required must certainly have taken many hours and remains as good and perceptive a run-down of Harry's life and work as could be desired, no less than a mini biography, which deserves to be read in full and is attached as an appendix at the end of this book. Martin's appreciation was in fact just one of several that appeared at intervals during Harry's life which showed the esteem, admiration and fondness that fellow crime writers felt for him—most notably one written by Mike Ripley in the form of a lavish interview online, again a mini biography and there were several written by Simon Brett both before and after Harry's death. They, all three, wrote amazing obituaries, as did crime writers Ruth Dudley Edwards and Peter Guttridge. Posthumous tributes are wonderfully heart-warming for those left behind; how splendid it would be if they could also be read by the subject.

Prior to all this and to add to the publication of 'The Soft Detective' in 1997, there was another collection of short stories. Once again mainstream publishers were not interested but saviours both here and in America were found. In the UK it was Flambard, a small press who mostly published poetry, owned by Peter Lewis, an academic, and his wife, Margaret Lewis, a biographer. In America it was Douglas Greene of Crippen & Landru who came to the rescue.

The stories had accumulated over the years that Harry had taken his early morning walks in Kensington Gardens and were based around the park's landmarks, the young Queen Victoria's statue; the memorial to the explorer, Speke; the Albert Memorial and the sculpture 'Physical Endurance' among others. Both editions of 'In Kensington Gardens Once' were produced in the superior glossy, semi-paperback style that is not only a delight to handle but also long-lasting. The book was illustrated by artist and fellow Lycée parent, Gwen Mandley. Both editions were beautifully presented and Harry was enormously grateful as well as being extremely proud of the result.

Surprisingly for a collection of short stories published by a small firm with no cash to spare for publicity there were a fair number of reviews which remarked on the accuracy of the detail in their ten very different settings as well as praising Harry's skill in telling a good story in this shortened form with Alex Auswaks comment that it *'Beats a guidebook any day',* and praise indeed from PC Stan Fisk a Royal parks policeman who was asked by The Friends of Kensington Gardens to write a piece for their magazine. *'One cannot but admire the sensitivity of the writing. Nothing too slushy, nor gratuitous violence so often seen on today's screens...portrays, in my opinion, the many faces of the gardens as seen on a normal day to day basis.'* The Tangled Web once again noticed the book and this time it was another fellow crime writer, Andrew Taylor, who reiterates this observation about the day to day nature of the stories, adding, *'Keating has the knack of showing us the familiar from an unfamiliar perspective. Several of these stories smudge still further the constantly disputed borderline between crime fiction and mainstream fiction. Wry and sometimes surreal, they are shot through with delicate humour.'* It is quite clear that whatever he was writing, underlying social comment was second nature to him. He would never consciously 'thump a tub' but nor did he shy away from low-lighting the downside if it was pertinent to the story he was telling.

Short stories were a recurrent feature of Harry's life from the truncated 'Jim's Adventure' through his student days and indeed throughout the whole of his writing life. He kept a list of all the ones that were published, all one hundred and seventeen of them. Many of these were commissioned by the editors of anthologies such as the series Winter's Crimes, whose first editor was George Hardinge, but his markets were diverse. At one time BBC radio bought quite a lot from him, some of which he read himself. And in the seventies and early eighties he was regularly published by Puffin Post. This was Penguin's nod towards their younger readers and was the magazine you received if you signed up as a member of the Puffin Club. Edited by the exuberant Kay Webb, it was a news round–up about authors and their recent publications but each edition contained a short story as well. Those of Harry's stories that appeared here were mostly about children or written through a child's eye, something that seemed to come naturally to him. Many probably had their genesis in the stories he would tell our children. Because we had no car, our share of taking and fetching from school had to be done on foot and he was told by one parent that when he was the one doing it no-one objected to the walk because they had the compensation of being told an absorbing new story. It is tempting to think that this skill stemmed from all those solitary boyhood hours living in his imagination.

It was much easier to get a short story published then than it is nowadays, particularly in America where Ellery Queen's Mystery Magazine appeared every month. A good two thirds of Harry's stories are to be found there, either as originals, or reprints of those that had appeared previously in British magazines or on the BBC. A welcome addition to the market came with a rebirth of the famed Strand Magazine that, in its first incarnation, had given the world Conan Doyle's Sherlock Holmes' stories. In the millennium year Andrew Gulli in the States was responsible for the re-launch. One of Harry's stories was in the first number and thereafter they kept appearing quite regularly. He was very lucky to have so many outlets, authors today do not have so much choice.

From time to time he would also be commissioned to write articles, mostly relating to books and writing but on one occasion he was delighted to be asked to write a profile of Bombay for National Geographic Magazine, to be one of a series on major cities. Nothing could have pleased him more and he came up with an enthusiastic and detailed description of all the highs and lows that could be found there but not told in the strictly factual manner of a guidebook. His aim was to make the city live for the reader so the piece was very atmospheric, even romantic. The magazine had also commissioned one of the best Indian photographers to take the pictures. Alas either the magazine had not briefed him fully or it could be that his own research into previous examples in the series was inadequate because it was rejected on the grounds that it did not fit the house style. Infuriatingly Harry must have decided that as it had been rejected it had no further life because I could find no trace of it in the crammed study cupboard, but I vividly remember reading it at the time and thinking that it did indeed bring the place alive, making me feel I was actually seeing what he described.

But any gaps between books and any years which did not see an actual publication, and there were very few of them, would have found him writing short stories, articles and the occasional foreword to a classic reprint such as the one Dent did for the Chesterton Father Brown stories in 1987. But 1998 was different. This was largely devoted to the preparation of a bold and thoroughly new departure, even for Harry.

Chapter 21

Ever since Vikram Seth had published his novel in verse 'The Golden Gate', a book Harry greatly admired, he had been fired with the notion of writing a crime novel in verse. He decided he would make the setting an outpost of the Empire in the days of the British Raj, and he wrote in the preface, *'seeing life through (Ghote's) eyes has enabled me, by contrasting Indian ways with Western, to bring to the fore the common aspects of our humanity and perhaps to look at them a little more deeply. Much the same things occur, I feel, in contrasting not Indian and Western ways but the habits of thought in India in the 1930s and our habits of thought today.* There was the added advantage of having already done a great deal of research into the period when he was writing 'The Murder of the Maharajah'.

The stored envelope for this venture, with the typescript, notebooks and many of the actual stanzas written in longhand, weighs a ton. The ambition simmered on the back boiler with the first entry in the first notebook being dated 27th Dec/94 in which he stated that he had managed to write an opening stanza which reassured him that he was capable of writing in this style. The pages are filled with questions that he asks himself about the characters he will create, the feasibility of possible strands in the plot, period phrases like *'Up Guards and at 'em',* jotted down at random, as well as the on-going story he was going to tell. At one point he abjures himself, *'At all costs keep the people real, don't let them become cardboard figures.'* At another he gives himself a warning to make the story a simple traditional one to offset the difficulty of it being in verse which could *'try a reader's patience'.*

He was realist enough to know that no mainstream publisher would touch it with a barge pole and, sadly, after he had completed it, he was proved right. He kept a copy of a letter from his editor at Macmillan to his agent. She explains that although she enjoyed it very much her marketing team were not behind her and she had been unable to find other publishers willing to share the costs of a limited collector's edition so although they valued having Harry as an author she was going to have to *'pass on this one'.* But, despite foreseeing the outcome, he had been so fired with the need to write it, that he worked on it intermittently for three years before making the final push in 1998.

The preface contains the following lines from the start of Vikram Seth's own book,

An editor—at a posh party
... seized my arm: 'Dear fellow,
What's your next work?' 'A novel...' 'Great!
We hope that you dear Mr. Seth –'
'In verse,' I added. He turned yellow.
'How marvellously quaint,' he said,
And subsequently cut me dead.

There had never been any doubt in his mind that he would employ the verse form used by Seth who had, in his turn, borrowed it, via Charles Johnston's translation, of Pushkin's great narrative poem 'Eugene Onegin'. The rhyme scheme and the rhythm propelled the lines with urgency and with a page-turning quality ideal for telling a story. Harry knew he had a talent for versification, although he never called himself a poet. But, in this instance, he challenged himself to abandon prose and write within the strict discipline imposed by this particular verse form.

In the preface he admits he was not skilled enough to emulate entirely the alternating masculine and feminine rhymes, but, interestingly, adds, *'Nevertheless, I discovered, as I guess he (Seth) too did, that paradoxically the difficulty of expressing one's thoughts in the apparently restrictive rhyme-form we have both adopted allows one to say extra things which might never have arisen from the subconscious if one was writing straightforward prose.'* Just before this he acknowledges another debt to Vikram Seth by quoting three lines from

'The Golden Gate':

'The old folks settle down with books:
He with *Tom Jones*, she with a thriller
Entitled *Jack the Lady-Killer*.'

The Prologue begins:

'*Jack the lady Killer;* there's
my title, chosen for this tale.'

And then, before the actual start of the story proper, there is a page devoted to what Harry calls **The People of the Poem.** This run down of the characters posits each of them as a candidate for the role of hero at the same time as helping to set the tone of the poem. Take the first half dozen,

Little brown gramophone. A small Indian boy, a *chokra*, with a curious gift. Could he be our hero?

Jack Steele. A rather bigger English lad, a new recruit to the Imperial Police Service in India. Could *he* be our hero?

F.H.R. Guthrie. District Superintendent of Police. He would, if he knew he was in the story, be certain he was its hero.

Edward Carter. A planter. Flashy enough to be a hero, only he hides his light under a bushel.

Dr. Prosser. Civil Surgeon at the station. Fat, fussy and, to tell the truth, usually drunk. No sort of a hero.

Bulaki Ram. A police sergeant or *havildar*. If, in the days of the British Raj, an Indian could be in any way a hero, he would qualify.

In the manner of, say, Coleridge's 'The Ancient Mariner', from time to time, there are marginal lower font notes to tell you that 'Jack Steele
an innocent
abroad, arrives
in the India of
the British Raj.

or later,

> 'Finding his
> Feet, he does
> Well in the
> Club tennis
> tournament.

And much further on in Part Nine of the story,

> 'Failing to gain
> Feminine
> consolation, he
> sinks into gloom.'

These elements of almost poking fun all add to the enjoyment generated by the forward-rushing style in which it is told. Then there are what the publisher describes as 'decorative tailpieces' which appear occasionally at the conclusion of a 'Part'. These are credited as Captain Mundy's *'Pen and Pencil Sketches, Being the Journal of a Tour of India.'* For these the book is indebted to Peter and Margaret Lewis of Flambard Press who had, once again, come to the rescue and dared to tread where grander publishers had been more cowardly, producing a beautiful, glossy paperback.

They had been introduced to the book when Harry was up in Cumbria at a convention contributing to celebrations of Wordsworth and where the curators of Wordsworth's Dove Cottage had kindly allowed him time to read from his own work in progress. Being written in verse it was closer to the books the Lewis' usually published than Harry's book 'In Kensington Gardens Once' which they had previously done. Nevertheless, it was more a labour of love than a money-spinner. They are publishers of the old tradition, doing it from a genuine love of books, and certainly Harry always said that he owed them an enormous debt of gratitude for allowing him to see it in print, and equally to Barbara Peters and Rob Rosenwald of the Poisoned Pen Press in America, for co-publishing it. From the reports that came back, those who read it enjoyed it greatly. The trouble was to persuade people to take the plunge and actually begin reading anything written in verse. But the title still comes up from time to time in magazines looking at some of the more unusual forms that crime literature has taken, mostly expressing amazement that such a task was ever so successfully undertaken.

But knowing that 'Jack' was never going to provide much bread and butter there was also a new Ghote title in 1999. This time the Inspector, together with his wife, Protima, visit Calcutta, where she was born, to investigate the property she has inherited there. Those who are put off by Anglo-Indian speech will probably never get past the cover of this novel because of the title, 'Bribery, Corruption Also', but those who have got used to it and indeed find it an integral part of the whole will be interested to find a Ghote very ill at ease in the alien Calcutta environment. Harry himself had by this time visited Calcutta during a whistle-stop tour of India for the British Council when he was, to some extent, waving the flag for British culture. In each city he would give a talk about crime writing in general and of course about his own books. Quite a lot of time was devoted to giving interviews to the media. The beauty of the mostly female journalists in their exquisite saris rather outdid the accuracy of their reporting but Harry did not raise too many objections. He did feel slightly overwhelmed at his reception and was so struck by a headline on one of those articles, **Noted British Author**, that, as has already been told he subsequently used it as the title for a short story. But of course being treated as a celebrity as he criss-crossed the sub-continent massaged his ego very satisfactorily and even if Calcutta was to be the only Indian city he chose for the setting of a book away from Bombay, he brought back a wealth of Indian experience from Delhi—managed to view the Taj Mahal at dawn—as well as visiting the south of the sub-continent.

Ghote's reaction to the city of his wife's birth and the truth that lay behind the book's title, 'Bribery, Corruption Also', were very much a product of the Siamese twin nature of the Harry/Ghote relationship. It seems that Harry did not feel at home in Calcutta in the way he did in Bombay and he created a situation for Ghote which was intolerable. Protima is convinced that her inheritance has opened up a whole new way of life for them and that they will be able to leave Bombay and live in luxury in her new property. For Ghote this is nothing short of disaster. He will have to give up the career he has spent so long nurturing, give up the work that means so much to him. To add to his woes, from the moment they arrive their troubles begin, nothing is straight-forward, there is corruption all around them. Protima has never been a docile wife and faced with what now looks like a total collapse of her aspirations she becomes a tiger. However, despite his aversion to the idea of living in Calcutta, Ghote sets out to protect his wife's rights. It is a book that reveals the ups and downs of their married life which from time to time has a leavening of humour as well as giving the book an ending that is an endearing picture of Ghote family life.

Harry's own family life was shortly to become upheaved. After much deliberation I had decided to accept a job that would take me out of England for six months and in January I set out for Angers, in France, where I would be performing in a new French play, 'Hudson River, un désir d'exile'. Although playing an American in this intellectual play, my character would be speaking, for the most part, in idiomatic French, so it was a challenge. I decided to immerse myself in as much of the language as possible and chose to read Harry's novel 'Dead on Time' in the excellent translation, 'Temps Mort', which had been done by Denise Meunier. Probably because I had to concentrate much harder when reading in French, I found it even more enjoyable than I had done in English, discovering hidden depths which I had missed when reading at greater speed.

The job took me on an extensive tour of France and in each town I would visit the book shop and generally found rows of Keating titles on the shelves. Should they not be there I would chat with the manager who invariably expressed dismay at the absence but said I was not to worry, there were more copies in the storeroom. They would immediately be fetched up. I was bowled over by the esteem the French felt for Harry and Inspector Ghote. There had, of course, been many foreign translations, not only the Japanese but, among others German, Italian, and Spanish but undoubtedly the enthusiasm of Fayard, the French publisher, together with Denise Meunier's sensitive translations, accounted for the really excellent sales in France.

Meanwhile back in London Harry was on his own having to come to terms with elements of domesticity that he had hitherto eschewed, like doing the ironing. He even managed that, in the same way that he had had to learn how to darn his socks in the dark days of his National Service. Family and friends did not desert him and to begin with he enjoyed the freedom of being able to spend even longer hours in the study. He also agreed to read the Audio Book of 'Bribery, Corruption Also' himself. Having seen the time that I spent preparing before I recorded, and remembering things I would do to make the task easier, he was able to arrive at the studios reasonably confident that he would do a good job. But he had to confess that after the two full days he was there he was absolutely exhausted. It was to be an unabridged recording and, however well it is prepared, completing 279 pages in two days can be very taxing. A professional reader would probably have been offered three days for a book of that length but presumably the audio company, Isis, felt that the actual author should be able to manage in two. He thought that, on the whole, he would leave it to an actor in the future and concentrate on what he did best—the writing.

The whole question of Audio Books was quite important in the Keating family because I, from my early days reading for BBC Radio, Book at Bedtime, the Woman's Hour serial, short stories etc, had now moved on to recording unabridged books commercially and both of us knew how important it was for them to be read as well as possible and for it to be produced by a company who cared about the quality of the end result. More than a decade earlier, Anthony Cheetham, when about to publish 'Under a Monsoon Cloud', told a meeting of writers that they should have nothing to do with this new development, where 'honey-voiced actors' attempted to make audio versions of an author's writing. To be fair he must have changed his mind since that time because, subsequent firms he managed had their own audio book departments where abridged versions were read by star actors. All the Ghote books, however, have been issued as unabridged titles, most of them superbly read by Sam Dastor. They have become very popular particularly in America where they are often listened to on the immensely long car journeys that are much more necessary over there. Some authors do read their own books because they enjoy doing it, but it is not a skill that they all possess. Anyway Harry did not repeat the experiment.

Eventually he and Bryony made the journey to Angers for my first night. The French take the Arts very seriously and apparently realise far more than we do, over here, how important culture is to a quality of life. The result is that theatre is much better subsidised than in Britain so the first night was a gala occasion with a reception and full sit-down dinner to follow the performance, for at least a hundred people. It was not just that much more public money was available for productions but the audience attitude was also completely different. They were quite prepared to sit for two and a half hours without an interval and concentrate on what was a serious play, well-written, but not for a low-brow public. Fortunately, the family's French being better than average, they, too, lasted out this marathon and even said that it was enjoyable and had not seemed anything like that long. I also had visits from Piers and Hazel and Hugo and Deb which must have been an endurance test for the wives, not being bi-lingual, but in no way fazed the men were able to air their French during supper with the company after the show.

It was early summer before the tour was over and by then both Harry and I felt we had had long enough leading separate lives and both of us were delighted to resume normal living. When the day came for the homecoming, Bryony came to meet me off the Euro Star train at Waterloo while Harry helped the granddaughters, Zoe and Phoebe put the finishing touches to the beautifully lettered banner that was fixed to the front door, saying, **Soyez le Bienvenue.** Not a dry eye in the house, as they say.

Chapter 22

During the time that I had been away Harry was planning the fifth in the Detective series. It seemed logical having done the 'Good' and the 'Bad' to do another opposite, so having done the 'Soft' he needed to find someone whose hard-nosed approach to the job might prove an obstacle to total success. For some unexplained reason he found that no imagined character came to mind. Perhaps being on his own was preventing his creative juices from flowing in their normal manner, but, look at it how he would, the problem went unsolved until, for whatever reason, it occurred to him that if he made this particular detective a woman everything would fall into place. At the time he did not realise that his choice of Detective Chief Inspector Harriet Martens would have such far reaching repercussions. In this book, 'The Hard Detective', she is introduced as a woman in a man's world knowing that to succeed she has not only to be as good as her male colleagues but a percentage or two better. She has been running a 'stop the rot' campaign in her division which is slowly dealing with the criminals who had been getting out of hand. Then not one but two of her officers are murdered in quick succession. It transpires that a serial killer is out there seemingly using the biblical 'Eye for an eye, Tooth for a tooth' to mark each crime. The race was on to find the perpetrator before 'Hand for a hand' and the other four revenge cries from the Book of Exodus quotation were committed.

Once having established the hard personality, Harriet remains totally unbending as the tense story agonisingly unwinds. Unlike most of the novels up to this time, the suspense, which is very tense indeed, is deliberately more important than character development. Perhaps at the time it was enough that his protagonist was a woman and that she was personifying that hard quality for which he had been unable to find a man. Frustratingly among the rows of other large envelopes that contain planning notebooks and a hardcopy of the first draft, there is not one labelled 'The Hard Detective'. The thought processes during the planning and the writing stages are not chronicled and, with conjecture on my part forbidden, the book itself has to be its own explanation.

What is undoubtedly true is that Harriet had fired Harry's imagination, later on he said that it was what I made of the character, when I read the audio book, that made him feel he could develop Harriet into a series detective, but it is more likely that it was just the notion of writing about this feisty woman that inspired him.

But before deciding whether to use Harriet as a series character or not, there was another Ghote to be written. At what exact point Harry made up his mind that 'Breaking and Entering' was to be the final Ghote has never been made clear, but by the time the reviews were written the secret was out. Many of those who wrote about the book chose to make some sort of farewell comment. Mike Stotter in Shots Magazine says, 'We have watched Ghote evolve into a very engaging Inspector with his "questioning-pestioning". If "Breaking and Entering" is to be Ghote's farewell then it is a fine novel from which to say adieu.' While Vic Buckner in Crime Time, after praising the ingenious plotting, goes on, 'there is no sign that Keating has lost the freshness and inspiration that characterised his very first book.' While Peter Guttridge in the Observer added 'another much loved police inspector bites the dust...there is nothing elegiac about the novel. Indeed, it is as fresh, lively and entertaining as the first—a delight.'

Harry, perhaps, intended to give us a small clue that Ghote's life might have come full circle when he decided to give another airing to the Swedish policeman, Axel Svensson, who had helped—or hindered—Ghote in 'The Perfect Murder'. But there is absolutely nothing in 'Breaking and Entering' to indicate that the Inspector himself is saying farewell. There is no dramatic termination, Ghote does not perish or resign or get sacked at the end of the book. On the contrary he is obviously well regarded by the Deputy Commissioner who says to him, *'Yes, Inspector. Yes, report to me tomorrow, will you? There's a rather tricky case that's just come up to me. I think you're the chap to handle it.'* And in inimitable Keating fashion the last lines give absolutely nothing away, leaving us inside Ghote's head with plenty of room for speculation. *'Ghote stood by the big desk, watching the cabin doors swing to and fro in the wake of the departing Deputy Commissioner and a hurrying Inspector Alik. Soon his head became filled with pleasantly vague thoughts.'*

Because Harry had made the parting gradual he seems to have been able to survive the loss. But a grievous loss it undoubtedly was and there was something akin to funeral rites in the ceremonial carrying round to the communal black rubbish bin of the vast concertina file, containing his initial India research. After a time he told the story against himself of his fear that I might discover what he had done before the Council had had a chance to carry it away, and that, in some way, I might manage to retrieve it. I do hope I would not have had the presumption to do that. But to make absolutely sure that this did not happen he did not dump it in the nearby bin, where I could have spotted it, but staggered on to one a little distance away.

His besetting sin may have been a tendency to prevaricate or, as he would say, to see both sides to any question, but in this instance it was nowhere in sight, his determination was rock solid. If he was no longer to write about his alter ego then this strong link with the past must be removed. That having been accomplished, he turned his attention back to Harriet Martens.

In 'The Hard Detective' her character had shown very little development. Realising that he had left no chinks in the armour of hardness that had enclosed her in that first book, in this next book he makes sure she is a human being at the mercy of temptation. While still telling a convincing, onward moving story he writes what the Nottingham Evening Post describes as *'more of a meditation on the nature of sexual love and its all-pervasive power than it is a whodunit.'* This is a trifle misleading because 'A Detective in Love', is concerned with a murder and requires detailed investigation which, because the victim is a well-known young tennis star, has the added complication that it will attract a great deal of media attention. The, at times, explicit examination of passionate sexuality is a parallel storyline. It is interesting that, although Harry had written about the physical side of love in his straight Victorian novel, 'The Underside', it is a departure from the norm in his detective fiction.

In 'The Hard Detective' we had learned that she is married and has adult twin sons, but her husband does not actually appear. We are told that he is away on one of his usual high-powered visits on behalf of the global insurance company which employs him. But in this second book he is back home and, with his endearing—or perhaps some might feel irritating—habit of having a quotation handy for any situation, also turns out to be both understanding and forbearing. Theirs is a relatively open marriage which perhaps excuses Harriet and explains, a little, the relationship that develops between her and the Detective Inspector she is working with.

By far the most interesting review, as usual tucked away in the first edition for me to find, is from quite a well-known figure, a nun with a liking for detective fiction, including the Ghote books, who writes about the genre in her spare time. Sister Wendy Beckett is perhaps the last person who would be expected to take a tolerant enough view of Harriet's transgressions to be able to describe the book thus: *'What gives this novel its lunatic charm—a charm unique to Keating, delightful and engrossing—is the interplay of the nouns in the title: "detective" and "love"...Love and detection enter into a breath-taking match, with the winner undecided until the final pages. We may see early on who the murderer must be, but Keating keeps us in genuine suspense as to whether love or duty will emerge victorious.'* She concludes with a simple sentence that is a golden seal of approval: *'This is an engaging and exemplary book.'* Harry succeeded in establishing that Harriet was no longer just a cypher, just 'The Hard Detective', although the label would be used in many later books, much to the lady's fury. Her reputation for toughness remained but in this and subsequent books she became a complete human being.

However, it was that essential toughness that was the reason that in the third book she was seconded from her Midlands fastness of the apocryphal Greater Birchester to London with the task of investigating corruption in the country's most prestigious crime-fighting team. But the manner in which the colleagues she encounters treated her made the assignment almost too much for her and she had to call on all her inner reserves to stay the course.

At this time Harry, himself, was almost as unhappy as Harriet, feeling very frustrated with the modern world of publishing. Whether publisher Macmillan was miffed that having bought Keating and Ghote, they now had to make do with Keating and Harriet Martens, it is hard to say. What was certain was that publishing was rapidly changing. Authors no longer had that one-to-one relationship with their editor who, in the past, would have overseen every stage of the book from initial acceptance of the manuscript through copy-editing and writing the blurb on the dust jacket, to its arrival in the bookshops. There had been a sea-change, each operation was now handed over to a separate department and editors had far less power. Budgets for publicity were almost entirely reserved for a bestselling title or to promote a promising newcomer. With the consequence that if sales had previously been no more than on the high side of average they were, now very likely to plummet. If, sales-wise, you were a 'middle-of-the-road' author you were slowly being squeezed out.

Instead of discussions over any difficulties, there were battles. In the case of this third Harriet Martens book which took her to London, there was not even a battle, just an outright refusal over the title that Harry wanted. Very much as a joke, young Hugo had once referred to a sister-in-law as a 'dozy Northern tart', a phrase that had been remembered by his father who had stored it away for future use as the title of a book. This storyline provided the ideal opportunity with 'provincial' Harriet Martens being the butt of snooty London colleagues—not that she was in fact provincial, her origins being an upper-middle class Southern family—but it was obvious the new colleagues did not know this. It was enough for them that Greater Birchester, somewhere 'up there' in the back of beyond, was where she worked. But back at Macmillan there was a blinkered response and the decree was issued, no mention of dozy tarts, Northern or not. Something had to be found more acceptable that would not offend the ears of what they conceived as their genteel readership. The prosaic and, to Harry's mind, boring, alternative was found, 'A Detective Under Fire.'

But that was minor compared with the much greater all-enveloping problem which was worldwide—profit-chasing. This manifested itself in the publishing world by the obliterating emphasis that was now put on sales figures. It is hard for someone already seventy-six years old, still very much able to do the job he has done so successfully for the last half century, to be made to feel that quality is no longer important, that the sole thing that mattered now was to be commercially viable. He could have stopped writing but the problem has always been that, on the whole, if your job is in the Arts world you do not retire, you just carry on until you drop.

There were, however, some things that Harry felt he could no longer do as well as he could formerly. For instance, in 2001 he decided that he was no longer capable of fulfilling the duties required of him as President of the Detection Club and he resigned, passing the baton to the younger, ideally suited, Simon Brett. The letters he received from members regretting that he felt it necessary to retire were deeply appreciated and are still preserved.

Ultimately he did retire from writing as well, but not until 2008, and he was by then eighty-two. He came to this momentous decision for two completely separate reasons. One of these concerned his health but the other was an extension of the inescapable fact that the books, although still being of an exceptionally high calibre, were being published with absolutely no marketing and moreover that little effort was being made to make them available in the bookshops, consequently the sales were diminishing. The actual amount of money he was earning was irrelevant because the pension enabled us to live very comfortably. What was not acceptable was that a very small percentage of readers even knew he had written any more books. He had stayed with Macmillan for a further two Harriet Martens titles and then moved to a smaller publisher, Allison & Busby, who, under the guidance of a young live wire, David Shelley, seemed to be flourishing. Unfortunately before Harry's first book with them went into production, David left, having been head hunted.

A&B is owned by a Spanish family and once the dynamic managing director had gone, the new and very pleasant all female team appeared to have little autonomy. However much they may have wanted to give their authors a better deal they had to do as they were told and worse still on a very tight budget. There was more and more reliance on internet sales, virtually leaving shop sales to take care of themselves and, even worse, they found it too expensive to produce proof copies so reviewers hardly ever got a copy in time for inclusion in the forward planning of their columns. It also seemed that sending out review copies once the book was printed became rarer and rarer. Harry knew that he was not the only one suffering this treatment but that did not make it any easier to tolerate.

But before the retirement eventually came there were to be not only six more books but also some memorable celebrations. The first of these coincided with the publication of the fourth Harriet Martens title, 'The Dreaming Detective', still with Macmillan as publisher. Here she is tasked with investigating, with the aid of the comparatively new DNA testing, a murder committed thirty years previously. Had Harry been someone who set great store by anniversaries it would be tempting to suggest that this exploration of the past was prompted by pondering on his own approaching Golden Wedding Anniversary. However once again that would be conjecture and in this instance probably unlikely. But whether one thing influenced the other or not, the anniversary was a truly unforgettable occasion and the entire family was involved. The evening of the day itself, Friday, October 3, 2003, Harry and I marked the occasion by having dinner in Basil Street at the hotel where the wedding reception in 1953 had been held (now, alas, demolished), and then the next day when all the family could be together there was a banquet at Hugo's home in Chertsey. They were in the throes of converting a rather ugly extension, which had been added by the former owners of the old cottage where they lived, into a large living room more in keeping with the original architecture. It was at the time undecorated and unfurnished but large enough for an improvised table to accommodate the nineteen Keatings for a wonderful feast.

The room under Debra's expert designer guidance became a golden paradise with contributions to the separate decorative details done by all the family. The catering was also done by the family and the entertainment

221

drew on the many skills of the grandchildren and ranged through music and acting to conjuring tricks. As if this would not have been as ample a demonstration of their affection as anyone could wish, there was more to come. We were presented with two tickets on the Orient Express travelling to Venice where we were to spend three nights before flying back to the UK.

The English part of the express took us to Dover where we transferred to a coach which took us through the Euro tunnel to Calais. Staying on the coach we were driven to where the train we would take for the major part of the journey awaited us. There is only one word to describe the Orient Express experience, 'affluence'. The carriages, while retaining all the period detail, are equipped with everything needed for modern comfort; the service is oilily smooth, we were looked after by a Venetian who at the point of disembarkation, having received a suitable tip, blew us a kiss and said, 'I luf you'; the portions at dinner were obviously designed for American appetites. As the majority of the passengers were American that is not surprising, and most had followed the suggestion that a dinner jacket would be appropriate for the occasion—Harry, needless to say, did not conform.

The train chugged on through the night with intermittent stops and it would have been surprising if we had had much sleep in a carriage which had been converted into bunk beds while we ate our dinner. Lest this reaction should seem a trifle curmudgeonly, mention should be made of an enormous bonus. We woke at dawn to the sight of the snow-capped Alps. This magnificent sight was literally just outside our carriage window, a romantic start to what was, in fact Harry's 77th birthday and which had an equally romantic conclusion as we completed the journey to the hotel in a motorised dinghy.

The next morning we woke to a very different outlook—torrential rain which, as it accelerated, became the renowned Aqua Alta. Fortunately we had packed rain-wear and we set out to explore. Before long the duckboards were laid down and we viewed a water-logged St. Mark's Square. Following instructions, we found the place to buy books of tickets for the vaporetto and, determined not to be put off by the wet, we explored the hinterland of small canals and bridges, getting lost of course. Harry was wearing a splendid leather Rastafarian cap, which I had bought for him in the Portobello Road, and which normally offered very adequate rain protection, now it became so sodden that black dye ran in rivulets down his face and neck. Wet we may have been, but damp in spirits we were not. Eventually, having had a meal and bought some suitable snacks and a bottle of wine we returned to our opulent rooms—the bedroom was a gallery which overhung the living room, bathroom and kitchenette below and having showered, and in Harry's case got rid of the rivulets of black dye, we changed into the luxurious bathrobes provided by the hotel and spent a warm and dry evening in our suite.

Before leaving London I had sent a letter to a crime writer, Gregory Dowling, whose books Harry and I had greatly enjoyed and who was now living and working as an academic in Venice, suggesting that we should meet up for a drink. There was a fax message waiting for us on our arrival at the hotel inviting us to supper on the Saturday evening at their flat. It is extraordinary how spending time in the home of people who actually live in the place in which you are just a visitor adds so much more colour to one's appreciation than sightseeing alone can achieve. Gregory is married to an Italian, Patrizia, and the evening was spent in delightful company, with appetising food. The occasional snatches of Italian conversation with their two young sons made it even more atmospheric and it all contributed to our celebration of fifty years of marriage.

In the Harriet Martens book that came out that year, 'The Dreaming Detective', she is plagued by a new and hostile Chief Constable. The assignment this time is a 'cold case', the murder of a boy preacher, famous nationwide but done to death, some thirty years ago in his native town, Birchester, in the grandiose ballroom of the Imperial Hotel. The young Mr. Newcomen, already nicknamed Newbroom by Harriet, is the youngest Chief Constable in the UK, and wants to make his mark. How better to do it than by finding the killer in this unsolved case? But there is no time to lose because the hotel is about to be demolished and what evidence was there to be found was about to be lost forever. Harriet knows that, despite being able to use the comparatively new DNA techniques, her task is going to be uphill all the way and she also knows that, perversely, Newcomen has chosen her to lead the investigation because he knows the task is almost impossible and, having, for some reason, taken a dislike to her, she will be the one to be blamed.

It is obvious from the ninety-five tightly hand-written pages torn from a notebook that is enclosed in the envelope containing the typed manuscript, that Harry's planning for this book was meticulous. Before even working out the intricacies of the plot, there was a necessity to go back thirty years and search his memory for what life was like in the 1970s; to examine the attitudes that people would have had to such fundamentals as sex; to study the effect that preaching had on both preacher and the preached to. In the early pages he reminds himself of the books he has read over the years by other writers like Julian Symons, Peter Lovesey and Patricia Highsmith which touch on topics that will be relevant to the story he is planning. He also records, with pasted in newspaper cuttings, details of some of the recent examples of re-investigations of old crimes and the subsequent overturning of verdicts. Having decided on his seven suspects and given himself thumbnail sketches of each one he had then spent a considerable time working out how he would reach the solution. It is a record of someone still at the height of his powers revelling in the process of producing an on-going story with an authentic factual background, peopled with genuinely original and rounded characters.

Publication was, as usual, a damp squib, it trickled out together with the paperback of the one before. The latter, at least, could be found in bookshops but the hardback priced at £16.99 (this was 2003) was unlikely to attract the average reader who would be much more likely either to borrow it from the public library or go on the internet to find it more cheaply. There was no launch party and nothing from the publisher that marked publication day. Presumably they had also stopped subscribing to a cutting agency because they no longer sent photocopies of reviews to the author. In fact there were fewer and fewer newspapers filling their column inches with book reviews. Bookshops, too, had their problems, particularly the small independent ones who were having to battle not only against the internet but also the American conglomerates invading our shores. It seems that it was felt that

224

books were no longer being regarded as cherished possessions, instead they were expendable commodities purchased in bundles of three for two in order to grab a bargain.

It says a lot for Harry's belief in himself that, outwardly at least, he showed no sign of being crushed by the doldrums of the publishing world. There were disturbing reports of hitherto well-regarded authors being dropped by their mainstream publisher and in many cases this was done with no warning, just a letter of rejection when the latest book was delivered. If the quality of the rejected manuscript had gone downhill this might have been justified but the reason given was always that the last book had sold insufficiently. Loyalty to an author who had been with them for years simply did not enter into the equation.

There can be absolutely no doubt that for authors caught in this soulless downward spiral the mental effort to keep on writing must, at times, have been almost impossible to muster. The only slight change in Harry himself was that there were some signs his physical energy was diminishing, but really no more than could be attributed to his age and, by the time the Golden Wedding celebrations were over, he was already preparing the next dramatic episode in Harriet Martens' life.

There is not a lot of evidence that Macmillan sent Harry any reviews of 'A Detective at Death's Door' and of course he had no idea how many copies were sent out to reviewers. Those he did see however demonstrated that he was still writing to a very high standard. Take a couple of extracts, from the American publication Booklist: *'Keating is known for character-based, intricately plotted mysteries. The latest is a marvellous example of his craft. First Rate.'* and from Publishers weekly, *'Harriet is a very attractive character...a first-class reading experience.'*

But perhaps the long review in The Guardian from Maxim Jakubowski put the situation in a nutshell. Maxim, himself a crime writer, as well as an editor of crime short story collections and an owner of a crime bookstore at the time, was known to be an admirer of the tougher, noir type of story which had originated in America, so his appreciation of a title which was not of that sort was all the more to be welcomed. It begins by acknowledging

Harry as one of the uncontested doyens of British mystery fiction and a highly regarded crime book reviewer for the Times at a time when none of the broadsheets took crime writing seriously. The elegiac review then goes on, *'After nearly four decades of witty entertainment in the footsteps of his Bombay detective, the endearing Inspector Ghote, his latest series featuring female sleuth Harriet Martens has made few ripples, and it's a pity. Go no further if you want to read classic British crime plots that update the Golden Age with a clever dose of modernity. Elegant, urbane and clever.'*

A fellow crime writer, Sarah J. Mason, wrote him a letter which is preserved with the book, thanking him for a most tense and thrilling read. But even more than that she praised him for the accuracy with which he describes Harriet's alarming journey back to life from the poisoning which very nearly finishes her off. The words in the title 'Death's Door' were strictly accurate. Almost certainly drawing on personal experience, she instances other well-observed details: *'the up-and-down nature of her recovery'* which included *'the exhausted collapses'* leaving her with a *'fuzzy brain.'* And the unsettling description of Harriet's car journey when she is travelling back home from hospital where, and she finds a splendidly evocative word, *'the whole world is stroboscopically wired for both light and sound.'*

As Harriet fights her way, agonisingly slowly, back to normality, the poisoner strikes again and then again. In time she is able to take on tasks to help her colleague who has been assigned to the case, a delightfully three-dimensional character, Detective Superintendent Murphy, whose words tumble off the page in unmistakable genuine Irish brogue. The narrative races forward, creating almost unbearable suspense, with Murphy's investigation desperately trying to identify the serial killer before he can murder anyone else and Harriet's yo-yo recovery, sometimes showing progress only for her to be overwhelmed once again. Right up to page 257 of the 261 page book the outcome is unsure and, after all has been revealed, the last four pages are no laborious unwinding of a plot, it is done in one paragraph under the witty heading, **A Few Words of Explanation, If You Need Them** which, in turn, is followed by an **Envoi,** a word usually associated with a poem, and in this case, although not in verse, as a joyous finale. How could such expertise lead to anything but triumph?

Chapter 23

Health issues now began to be a bit of a problem and around this time some routine blood tests revealed that Harry had developed type 2 diabetes. His GP made light of it and having prescribed metformin sent him on his way. The surgery had decided that running a diabetes clinic was unnecessary and did not even provide advice about anything such as diet. Harry, possibly not realising that not all doctors were of the excellence of our long-term GP, Stuart Carne, assumed that his present doctor knew best and apart from searching out some suitable low-sugar products and avoiding eating things like cream cakes, took the pills and carried on as normal. Actually low sugar jams and marmalades are rather revolting as well as turning out not to be necessary. It was quite some time later when the family had finally persuaded him to change to another doctor in the practice who put him in touch with another surgery that did have a diabetes clinic that he got the attention and advice he should have had from the start.

None of this affected his writing routine but the next book, 'One Man and His Bomb', brought about the move of publisher, already mentioned, from Macmillan to Allison & Busby. The theme, a subject which six years into the new millennium was all too often grabbing the newspaper headlines, was terrorism. The first pages plunge Harriet and her husband into personal tragedy. They receive a phone call telling them that their twin sons, two young policemen, have been the victims of a bomb attack in Notting Hill Gate. One of the twins is killed outright and the other is appallingly injured, lying in a coma in a London hospital. Returning to Birchester from visiting him there, she is persuaded to do a television interview where it is expected her grief will be all too apparent and this will rouse the public to rage at the perpetrators of terrorist acts. Facing the camera and a brash interviewer, her emotions are frozen and she sees herself as something akin to a hologram Harriet. It is only when the interviewer asks one crass question too many that something snaps and she finds the words are flowing. But instead of doing what is expected, showing her grief and denouncing the criminals, she finds she is instead passionately denouncing the world for allowing so many communities to live under conditions so intolerable that they resort to acts of terrorism in order to show the rest of the world their plight.

It is interesting that Harry, although writing what would probably be categorised as a police procedural novel, is still able to write about not only world problems but also about his own fundamental beliefs. But even now, in his late seventies, he is still stating these beliefs at a remove. They may be his own criteria, but they emerge through Harriet, this fictional character.

In this book, Harriet's boss is a sympathetic Scotsman and although she has not managed to stir up quite the public sympathy he had hoped for from the television interview, he understands her point of view. Now he believes it would help her if she had work to do. He tasks her with an urgent investigation into the theft from an experimental laboratory of a mega-poisonous substance that could potentially threaten the world's vegetation. The rest of his team is at full stretch on other cases and so she has to work on her own and moreover in total secrecy so that the thieves will not be alerted before she can discover and arrest them. Her days are now divided between dashes up and down the motorway with John to visit the injured Malcolm in hospital and setting up a series of interviews, with as varied and colourful a collection of characters as Harry has ever imagined, in her search to identify the thieves.

From the very beginning the time-bomb-ticking investigation into the theft of the poisonous chemical is conducted with clinical efficiency but always with an underlying pulse of personal emotion, which she struggles to keep tightly in check. When recording the Audio Book I was aware that I needed to match that control so that my own emotions did not cloud the discipline of the writing—a challenging experience. Emotion, although occasionally surfacing, is reserved for the end when the funeral of Graham, the son who was killed, takes place. It is as nicely a judged final chapter as Harry has ever written with his characteristic barbs of wit punctuating the genuinely moving occasion.

Unfortunately most of the bookshop buying public will have been totally unaware of the book's existence and very little, if any, effort was made to publicise it. Here was a highly topical crime novel written by one of the past-masters of the art and moreover an author who was a new acquisition to their list but the publisher pulled out no stops. Would it have been so difficult to send out advance copies and garner some comments like this later one from the Good Book guide, 'A gentle but rigorous exploration of duty, devotion, love of family and love of country—and riveting from beginning to end.' which they could have printed on the cover?

Shortly after it was published however there were more celebrations to distract him. The year is 2006 and Harry turned eighty. That year his birthday fell on a Tuesday so the actual day's celebration was a visit to the theatre. I was delighted to have procured two good seats in the stalls for Tom Stoppard's new play 'Rock 'n' Roll'. The delight was because Stoppard, together with Harold Pinter were considered by Harry to be the best of our modern playwrights, but the title of the play should have been a warning. The serious story of Czechoslovakian politics was inextricably bound up with the Rock and Roll musicians who were at the heart of that country's troubled times. With the result that at frequent intervals their recorded music would be played. It was, apparently thought that, to get the authentic atmosphere, each time this happened the sound should be turned up to at least triple fortissimo. Loud noises of all sorts were a complete anathema to Harry who, as a result, spent most of the evening with his fingers in his ears. A sad occasion on the whole.

But never mind, more celebrations were to come. At the weekend it was to be a family gathering and this time we took over an entire small hotel in Pangbourne, a small town on the Thames. We assembled in the afternoon for cake, made of course by Bryony, and presents. The hotel did not serve dinner so the eighty-year-old couple, our four children and their spouses and the nine grandchildren went to the nearby railway station where we took a train for just a couple of stops further along the Thames, to visit a highly recommended restaurant. Thankfully the music that was playing there remained gently in the background and the food was absolutely delicious so a great evening was had by all.

But there was more to come. During the visit to the Malice Domestic Convention the year before, Doug Greene of Crippen & Landru publishers had talked with me about Harry's approaching 80th birthday and together we had formed a surprise plan. He would contact Simon Brett, President of the Detection Club, with the suggestion that they should emulate what Harry had done as a tribute to Julian Symons on *his* 80th birthday, which the club had published and he had edited, a collection of short stories written by fellow members, each with the title 'The Man Who...', echoing the title of one of Julian' own books. This time Doug would be the publisher and the club would find an editor to organise it. Simon was in agreement and Peter Lovesey, fellow crime writer and dear friend of many years, agreed to act as editor. Ultimately Allison & Busby joined in to publish the book simultaneously in England. Despite emails flying between Doug and Peter with most of them being copied to my address, there was never any danger of Harry getting to know because he maintained his complete oblivion of anything that was to do with the Internet. Even if he was in the same room when a message had just been received, he never asked who it was from.

Seventeen Detection Club members, all long-standing friends, contributed a newly written story to which was added an old one of Harry's written in 1992. It was called 'Arkady Nikolaivich' and the first part has a very young Ghote, still a police cadet, sent as a representative of the Indian police to a conference in Moscow where, after getting rather over-involved with the interpreter, he falls foul of the secret police. The second part is set some years on when Gorbachev visits India after glasnost has been declared and Ghote re-meets and has a revealing talk with one of the entourage, the same policeman who had had the task off evicting him from Russia. It has always been a favourite of mine among the short stories and I am pleased to say that Harry, when he saw the collection, approved the choice. As the icing on the cake, Dick Francis, who shared the same Halloween birth date although six years Harry's senior, wrote a warmly-worded foreword to the collection that ended, *'Happy 80th birthday, Harry. Still a youngster.'*

Before each story there is a short personal reminiscence from the writer, all of them so filled with love and affection that if Harry had had doubts what his colleagues thought about him before, they vanished once he had read them. Choosing the title did cause some divisions but in the end they settled for 'The Verdict of Us All'. This enabled Doug to have a judge, in full robes and wig, on the cover of a beautifully presented glossy paper back, while the gold lettering on the red leather of A&B's presentation copy to Harry made it very impressive.

The formal dinner of the Club was held that year at the Ritz in early November. With more devious planning, Doug, apparently by coincidence, would be in London at the time and was invited to be the guest speaker. The usual delicious dinner having been eaten, Simon Brett rose to make the announcements that always precede the honoured guest's speech. Then, the secret still intact, Doug embarked on a light-hearted history of the club, ending with listing the past Presidents. As he came to Harry's name he paused dramatically and the moment had come. With few, but appropriate, words he handed over a copy of the American edition. The managing director of Allison & Busby, Susie Dunlop, came forward with their special edition. Harry's astonishment was absolutely genuine, the book was a total surprise and he was, for once, at a loss for words to express his gratitude. Later he managed to write individually, on the Bryony-designed headed notepaper, to everyone concerned, one of his famous hand-written letters which had become his trade mark.

Of course the book that appeared the following year, 'Rules, Regs and Rotten Eggs', had been completed before Harry had had the opportunity of finding out how revered he was by his colleagues, and, also, perhaps, the degree of enthusiasm there was for Inspector Ghote, otherwise the constant references within it to a possible retirement for Harriet Martens, could have been interpreted as the first indications of a change to come. As it is they must only be taken as an indication of the frustrations she had been experiencing. Unfortunately the kindly Scotsman who was Harriet's boss in 'One Man and His Bomb' has been replaced by a man who, as she tells husband, John, *'has risen up the ranks by sticking firmly to the regulations and rules, as if he's climbing some sort of rope ladder. And in the end he's simply got to a place that's too high for him.'* He has had no opportunity to get to know her and she is convinced that he thinks of her, as a result of her son, Graham, having been so recently killed, as a useless detective and only fit for the simplest routine jobs. This has led her to have serious thoughts of resigning. However she gets wholly caught up in the investigation of an attempted murder which becomes an actual murder and leaves no room for anything other than putting the murderer behind bars. Jessica Moyer in the American publication, Booklist, has this to say about her: *'Harriet is less of the hard detective than she used to be, but she's not ready to retire either, although the 'assistance' of Detective Constable "Bolshy" Bill might push her over the edge. With crossword clues, a shady private clinic and a secret public-school-alumni club, this is a top-notch English police-procedural mystery, and the exciting ending in downtown London will keep readers glued to their seats.'* Once the case is over she is again ready to terminate her career and it is only at her husband's insistence that she finally agrees to give the matter more thought.

Harry had once again done exactly the same thing as he had done back in the millennium year with Ghote, he had left the question of any continuation of Harriet's career hanging in the air, what he would write next was anybody's guess. But the decision he arrived at, seemingly a bolt out of the blue, could really have been foreseen by anyone who knew him at all well, although others may have found it quite astonishing.

233

Chapter 24

Harry never discussed with me whether he should abandon Harriet, nor for that matter did he talk to Michael at PFD or Susie Dunlop at A&B and after all what was there to discuss? It was nothing to do with Harriet getting fed up with policing as the final book suggests, but much more to do with Harry getting fed up with her. He had maintained the high quality in style and content that readers expected of him through all seven books but writing about her no longer inspired him. On the positive side it had a great deal more to do with a yearning for a return to India and Inspector Ghote. Certainly the emotions and memories that were provoked by being given 'The Verdict of Us All' had stirred up a past which he thought he had put behind him. There were obviously a lot of pros and cons to be considered before coming to any decision but there was really only ever to be one outcome, Ghote was going to be reborn. Not only was Harry going to return to writing about his alter ego but there were going to be a new series of twelve, a book for each year of the Hindu calendar.

No dramatic resurrection was needed, no explanation, Ghote was waiting. If he was not quite where he had been left at the end of 'Breaking and Entering', he was certainly still very much alive and waiting for his puppet-master to set him going again. There was stage management to be done as well as some minor problems to be overcome. The series, begun in 1964, had more or less managed to ignore the passage of time, but would it be acceptable, starting again, to ignore the fact that the Bombay of old had modernised itself into Mumbai? What about all the advances in technology? The almost instant contact achievable by mobile phone although no problem for Harry when he had been writing about up-to-date Harriet Martens, would make a nonsense of the slower, gentler plots that had given the previous Ghote books their charm. The solution was ingenious. The new story would go back to the beginning, Bombay would still be Bombay and Ghote would be back in the pre-IT 1960s, at the start of his career in Crime Branch.

There was something else that might also have proved a stumbling block. Would the necessity that Harry had felt to make a clean break, not to mention his obsession with throwing out what he no longer needed, be his undoing? Would that trek to the black bin with the vast India files mean that too much research would have to be done all over again to make the project feasible? But common sense came to the rescue. The facts revealed by the research had after all already been converted into novels. All he needed to do was to take them down from the shelves and re-read them one by one. He more or less achieved this at the rate of one a day so the process was not overlong and, fortunately, for the most part, he found the experience enjoyable. He had no difficulty in being objective in his assessment and readily admitted that there were inequalities in the writing but at the end he knew he could get himself firmly back on track, the fascination was still there and he could see the way ahead quite clearly. He began to plan 'Inspector Ghote's First Case'.

He subtly introduced the connection with the Hindu calendar early on in the first chapter. Ghote, a humble Assistant Inspector in a backwater area of Bombay called Dadar, is about to read an official letter headed, *From the Commissioner of Police, Bombay March 15th, 1960 1 Chaitra, 2017'*.

Chaitra being the first Hindu calendar month the scene is set and the letter tells him that he has been promoted to the rank of Inspector and been posted to the Detection of Crime Branch, Bombay Police. It is the realisation of the dreams he has had since he was a boy, to be one of this dedicated, elite band of policemen, The words that come into Ghote's head when he has read the letter do not just express the young policeman's enthusiasm and idealism but are equally Harry's own response to what was, for him, if not the beginning of a life, most certainly a re-birth. *'Yes, now, he found himself thinking, my dream has burst into the light of day. And, yes, yes, look at the Hindi version of the date on this letter. The first of Chaitra, Gudi Padva day, the very start of the Hindu calendar. What a fine moment for my life to begin.'*

Ghote has been given a short period of leave before reporting to the Crime Branch and this too is cause for joy because his wife, Protima, is heavily pregnant with their first child and he will be able to spend time with her. Sadly this, because things never seem quite to work out for poor Ghote, does not happen. The Commissioner of the Bombay police, Sir Rustrom Engineer—with Independence the first Indian to hold the post—asks him to carry out an investigation in Mahabaleshwar, an old hill-station from the days of the Raj. He has to try and find out the reason for the suicide of the wife of a 'staying on' sahib who is an old friend of the Commissioner and Ghote is being asked to do the job unofficially, as a personal favour. Of course he cannot refuse but the unfolding narrative in faraway Mahabaleshwar, of what turns out to be a murder investigation, is punctuated by his anxiety for Protima's welfare. As in the books that had already been written, much is demanded of Ghote.

Could it be that Harry, already eighty-one, would be able to sustain the zest for life and energy that his so much younger alter-ego—age unspecified—would have to show in this story and, even more, would he be able to sustain that energy for more than a decade if there was to be a new book for every month of the Hindu calendar?

Unfortunately it was not only the reserves needed for the writing that would be required because it soon emerged that A&B had no plans for a celebration of Ghote's return. When Harry inquired what was being done to publicise the event there was no specific answer, nothing more than hopeful generalities. If there was to be any sort of effort to let readers know about the forthcoming publication it would have to be made by himself. He was, of course, being treated in the same way as most other authors, self-publicising was expected, particularly since the introduction of websites. Had he been born a decade or two later he might perhaps have felt capable of all this entailed, of sharing his life with the potential masses, but even that is doubtful. Although he was always prepared to play his part at literary events and share his knowledge, and love, of the written word, as well as in printed articles and books, the idea of writing a diary in public, of letting the world into his personal life through social networking, was abhorrent to him.

In 2007 public libraries still gave more importance to books than to Internet affairs, so I agreed to try and contact some of the larger ones that could be visited easily on public transport, as we no longer had a car, and ask them to mount an event at which Harry could talk about crime fiction in general and the return of Ghote in particular. There was quite a reasonable response and a small campaign began. Being Harry, there were always doubts before we set out but once there and finding a lot of enthusiasm for his writing and in particular for Ghote, he enjoyed doing it. The first date was at Erith where the head librarian, Will Cooban, was a delight. He was a keen reader of crime fiction as well as wanting to promote books in general. One of the ways he did this was through giving library users the opportunity to form readers' and writers' groups. They formed the nucleus of an audience which was augmented by individuals who were fans of Ghote and Harry. They listened appreciatively to what he had to tell them before having the opportunity to ask questions. So often this part of an event is marred by an individual who has no question to ask but takes the floor to give their own lecture. Under Will's chairmanship this did not happen and the questions were intelligent and gave Harry the chance to talk about aspects of crime writing he had not covered in his speech.

Will had also set up the library's own website which, as well as disseminating information, ran features about authors, particularly those who had given talks. The event was covered extensively—even Harry had to admit that there could be some use for modern technology. On that first occasion Harry had agreed to talk on his own but on two other occasions the format was to be different.

The first of these was at Swiss Cottage and Simon Brett very generously agreed to give his time to do an interview. Simon has a natural ability both with an interviewee and with an audience. He is always knowledgeable about the book under discussion but also does his homework about past works.

He is infinitely courteous and, almost as important, he is witty, inducing laughter which, in turn, makes for a wonderfully relaxed atmosphere.

The second occasion nearly failed to happen. It was down in Bath, not exactly local to Notting Hill, but in this instance business could be combined with pleasure. Over the years a mutually beneficial arrangement had been arrived at between the Keatings and Gay and her actor husband, Jonathan Newth, who live close to Bath. Whenever Jonathan had a part in a West End play he would stay with us in London and whenever I was recording a book in Bath I was able to make my home with them. The Public Library had originally been going to host the event but then seemed unable to get organised. Actually a good thing, as it turned out, because a local independent bookshop, Toppings, was able to step in. They could not have been more welcoming and more efficient. It was astonishing, given the competition from the chain bookstores, with their three for two offers, and other cost-cutting policies, that they were able to survive but survive they have while still maintaining the very highest standards of book retailing. They not only stocked huge numbers of books but did everything in their power to promote authors. A large part of their success was due to the importance they put on customer relations.

At this event another old friend and fellow crime writer, Andrew Taylor, was the interviewer. Andrew, being much younger than Harry, had grown up with an admiration for the Keating novels and he was able to ask some genially phrased but penetrating questions. Andrew, too, is an experienced critic and had been very generous when reviewing the newest Keating. They had always found it easy to talk to one another and as Andrew had recently published his gripping historical crime book, 'Bleeding Heart Square', which Harry had enormously enjoyed, the questioning was able to go both ways to the advantage of both. The evening was a great success not only for the audience but for the two of them as well.

The short library tour was the only publicity Ghote's return was given but there had been sufficient enthusiasm from the audiences to encourage Harry to continue with the resurrection. The second book, as usual, was already planned by the time the first came out and although the period when 'A Small Case for Inspector Ghote?' was being written coincided with the decline in Harry's health, he was determined to complete the task. It certainly took longer than previous books to write and he was exhausted at the end of each day but I doubt that any reader would know that from the finished product.

There is absolutely no indication that this is going to be the final story that Harry would tell about the character who had begun life with no thought of existing beyond one book, but had gone on for forty-four years, years during which he had found a place in the hearts of readers on both sides of the Atlantic and diverse other foreign countries. On the contrary, the Inspector tackles his first case since officially joining the ranks of the prestigious Crime Branch with the same dogged determination that is such a hallmark of the later cases that Harry had written about in the earlier books. Nor is Ghote's life any less complicated than usual. He has discovered evidence in his very own office of a brutal murder but when he takes the evidence to the Assistant Commissioner he has been ordered to drop any investigation because it concerns the murder of a lowly paean and so is not worth being investigated by the prestigious Crime Branch. But Ghote's conscience will not let him abandon any crime on those grounds and determines to continue unofficially at the same time that he is pursuing the official case with which he has been tasked. The book has an intricate plot with a great deal of fast-moving action, a lot of which is set in Bombay's underworld and graphically describes those areas of 1960's squalor. The unexpectedly triumphant finish, however, has an almost valedictory feel to it that could, with hindsight, be construed as a faint clue that Harry might be writing the final full stop, but there was no pronouncement to that effect at the end.

It has often been said that the NHS is wonderful in an emergency but not so good when a condition is on-going. This to a large extent is true in Harry's case. Regular check-up visits, supposedly to see the chief consultant cardiologist he had seen originally, were never in fact that, it was someone different each time. They would be extremely courteous but being merely a junior member of a team they had no power to initiate anything unless there were positive signs that there was deterioration. If tests showed little change from the previous time it was no good the patient saying, 'then why am I feeling progressively worse?', which is what happened in Harry's case. Once again he was undoubtedly his own worst enemy believing, as he did, that if an expert told you there was no more to be done that must be true.

Normal life became just that bit harder to lead, particularly when his publisher proudly told him that she was sure he would be very pleased that he was to be the subject of a series in the Independent called 'Forgotten Authors'. Pleased was not his reaction to what the well-meaning journalist, Christopher Fowler, had to say. The article was a reasonably adulatory run-down of his life and achievements over fifty years but quite plainly implying here's this wonderful old codger still going strong in his eighties but actually there aren't too many of his books to be found in the shops.

This, together with lack of publicity for the new book, began to have a depressing effect and it became increasingly difficult to persuade him that, whatever was happening in the present, there was still the past with its fantastic legacy and that he was by no means forgotten. His response was always the same, 'I'm a "has-been".' In some ways he was justified because there were many examples among his author friends of rejection after a lifetime of writing critically acclaimed books. Of course it was a vicious circle, if there was no publicity for a book no-one could know it existed and therefore sales would diminish and if sales fell below a certain level you were no longer viable as a commodity to the publisher. It could be argued that there was publicity on the Internet and while that is undoubtedly true there was no consideration given to the demographic of who would be using the Internet. A mass of our increasingly aging population, while using new technology, do not embrace it fully and certainly do not spend the hours browsing to the extent younger people do. And, naturally, fans of those writers who started out in the sixties were themselves getting older. It could be argued that Harry was among the fortunate ones, he was still being published, but the trouble was that not many of his staunch following of readers were aware that there were new books available.

It had been decided to keep a five-year diary some years ago. It sat by the telephone and was used only to record appointments and other facts that might otherwise get forgotten. Leafing through these to check some facts, I found that, from around 2008, there are the occasional rather scribbled notes about lows and highs in health. These were presumably a small attempt to have some sort of reference to back up assertions to doctors at his next hospital check-up that he was in fact getting worse rather than staying static. However in 2009, among these health bulletins, there was a rather different note, 'Even if sales for "A Small Case" are minimal I will write another book.'

One of the earlier factual notes that year had been the reminder, 'Burns book due back'. The idea had been simmering for quite a while before he finally decided to write about a traditional event in Bombay which was obviously a relic of the days of the Raj, the celebration of Burns Night. Sadly no-one will ever know how Ghote was to get involved with the Scottish revels because the book never got beyond the planning stage although the detailed notes in existence are evidence that he was nearly ready to start writing.

But not everything was downbeat. An actual celebration did take place. For some years Harry had had it in mind to throw a 'house' party to celebrate fifty years of the Keatings living in Northumberland Place. Although we had actually bought the house in April 1959 it was not till the July of 2009 that the party happened. As luck would have it, at the very last moment, a date for a long-awaited cataract operation was offered and it was just two days before the party. Arrangements for the party were so far advanced that the decision was taken to go ahead. In those days the eye-pad put in place after the operation stayed on for slightly longer than the twenty-four hours that happens now, so feeling rather like a wounded soldier Harry was installed in the very majestic peacock cane chair that held pride of place in the study and rather as if he were royalty the guests came in turn to pay homage.

An account of the final years of anyone's life is likely to be a trifle low key. Mobility was something of a problem and daily exercise was restricted to going round the block instead of going to Kensington Gardens or the earlier alternative of a walk along the canal. In fact the rather deserted early morning canal had had to be abandoned after he had been mugged. In retrospect it made an entertaining story but at the time it was quite upsetting.

Nearing the end of his walk on the deserted canal a figure suddenly barred his way with his hand behind his back. As he advanced the individual thrust out his hand and Harry saw he had a knife in it as he uttered the words 'Gimme your wallet or I'll stick this up your livver (sic).' Wisely thinking discretion the better part of valour he got out his wallet and was about to extract some money when it was snatched out of his hand. The man pulled out the cash that was in it and pushed that into his pocket and then, still holding the wallet, turned to go away. At which point Harry said, perhaps somewhat naively, 'At least give me back the wallet.' Amazingly the man threw it on the ground and ran off. Shaken and a few pounds the poorer Harry shakily made his way home vowing to take his walks in more populated places in the future.

He did pursue the idea of writing the Burns book for a time but eventually had to acknowledge that he did not have the sustainable energy that would be required, and made up his mind that his writing days were over. However his life as an author did not come to an end because the PFD agency had decided to employ someone to look after their author's backlists and the person appointed, Camilla Shestopal, was determined to keep the Keating name alive.

Chapter 25

C amilla had plans which were far-reaching, some of which are still very much on-going as well as others which came to pass. Harry was no longer alive when she succeeded in bringing Keating into the digital age. Bloomsbury Reader, the eBook branch of the main publishing house Bloomsbury, was launched and they bought fourteen of the backlist to publish as eBooks. These did not include any of the Ghote titles for which she had different plans. Now that these were once again in 'print' they became attractive to Audio book publishers. As already mentioned 'The Long Walk to Wimbledon' has been recorded and I have been able to do the three Victorian governess books for AudioGo, now the property of Audible, as well as the Victorian crime story 'A Remarkable Case of Burglary' and the much earlier 'Death of a Fat God' with Mrs. Craggs as sleuth. Recording Harry's books posthumously was a pleasure but also a bit frustrating because I could not discuss any points that were not completely clear with the man who wrote them. On the other hand it was also an opportunity to go back into the past to 1963, 1975 and the 1980s and re-establish contact with the much younger writer. Naturally questions arose in my mind of the 'what-if' variety and if these inevitably could not provide answers, they could at least help in the writing of this book designed as an exploration of how his life is reflected in the books he chose to write.

With his own writing days over by 2010, Harry was principally occupied re-reading all Trollope, all Dickens as well as many much more recent titles. These included Julian Barnes factual novel 'Arthur and George' and Vikram Seth's 'An Equal Music', both of which he returned to more than once, together with many of our dear friend Nina Bawden's titles. Then there were crime books to be re-read, those by Simenon, Wilkie Collins, Edgar Allan Poe and among a host of old friends, some living and some dead: Eric Ambler, Patricia Highsmith, Julian Symons, Peter Dickinson, Andrew Taylor, Dick Francis, Phyllis James, Liza Cody, Michael Z Lewin, Simon Brett, Peter Lovesey, Reg Hill and of course Len Deighton who was for him the outstanding master of the spy story. Len was not only an inspiring writer he was a lifelong friend and also very generous with his time. On one occasion he spent some hours with one of Bryony's boyfriends who had thought up a new crime board game, advising not only about the content but the best way to market it.

The following year, 2011, revived memories of times when film crews would arrive to conduct interviews to be used in programmes relating to diverse literary matters. These would be recorded in the drawing room, almost all involving the use of the imposing wicker-work peacock chair. In fact it was used so frequently that it eventually fell apart and had to be replaced by another from Hugo's stored supply of film and TV props. It made an impressive background, particularly in later years when Harry's Tolstoyan white beard completed the picture. But on this much later occasion in 2011 the chair was not used because what was required was something less formal. The subject of the film was the crime writer Ngaio Marsh and it was a company from her home country, New Zealand, who was making a film of her life and work and had come over to record interviews with anyone who had any connection with her. Harry's personal contact was a fairly tenuous one—sharing a car on the way to some distant conference at which they were both to speak—but he could talk about her books and her place in the history of the crime novel.

By chance the actor Belinda Lang, who had played Troy, the wife of Ngaio Marsh's detective Inspector Alleyn, in a TV series, was a long standing friend and colleague of mine and happened also to live just down the street, so she too was able to be interviewed the same day. Although Harry found it very exhausting it was an enjoyable occasion for everyone involved in the filming which took place on either side of an informal but convivial lunch.

One thing that both Harry and I dreaded was ending our days in an old people's home and Bryony and Rupert had allowed us to build a retirement apartment onto the back of their house in Shepherds Bush where there would be no flights of stairs to battle with. It was very fortunate that their house, which was quite small, had an extensive garden with two tumbledown, but quite large, outhouses so that planning permission was comparatively easy to obtain. Bryony and Rupert used their interior design qualifications to have an apartment built which was capable of being either self-contained or by opening an interior door become part of the main house. We decided that we were still capable of living in Northumberland Place but we 'weekended' in the 'West Wing', as the grandchildren christened it, many times in Harry's final years.

Essentially the year that followed the cessation in writing was quite fallow, being taken up mostly with visits to doctors and consultants, but there were some brighter moments such as when Harry and I met Susan and Charles Ward. Susan was just setting up the first literary festival to be held in the Devon town of Budleigh Salterton and she was hoping to make Trollope, who had a connection with the place, the central theme. Richard Perkins, the Keating's best of neighbours, and an old friend of the Wards, idly mentioned the festival, with its Trollope connection and Harry, without too much persuasion, admitted that he would love to make a contribution. By the time the meeting with the Wards took place plans had changed and, although there was one talk about the Trollope connection, the festival widened out to cover a range of literary topics so Harry never got to talk about the great man but he was still invited to attend and be interviewed by none other than Simon Brett.

Simon, who has always been a brilliant raconteur, had been booked primarily to do one of his personal memoir/crime writing talks but undertook the interview as well. Later in the programme he also helped me when I was performing a varied programme of verse and prose connected to the sea. Together we performed a high comedy scene from Noel Coward's play 'Blithe Spirit' because, appropriately, it contains a scathing attack on Budleigh Salterton as a venue for a honeymoon.

245

Harry was always grateful for the tact with which, on this occasion, Simon steered him through some moments of elusive memory thus making it an enjoyable half hour for the audience. But the writing was on the wall. Recognising that speaking in public would entail him having to rely too heavily on others, he resolved that it would be his last appearance.

During that year, whenever I had tried to argue that what he had achieved was quite sufficient for the names Keating and Ghote to have carved out a small niche in literary history, he repeated that he was a 'has-been'. He acknowledged that there was a time when it might have been true but was convinced it was no longer so. There is absolutely no doubt that the increasing lack of physical energy was pulling him down and this certainly affected his ability to summon up the mental energy to remain positive. But each time he went to the cardiology clinic and told yet another member of consultant Dr Malik's team that things were getting worse he would get the same reply that the tests were not showing a deterioration. Perhaps he, or at any rate I, should have insisted on a second opinion.

Three days before the last visit he paid to the clinic he had an echo cardiogram which showed that the already diagnosed leaking heart valve had ruptured and three days later, attending the routine clinic the doctor he was seeing became worried and asked Dr Malik for advice and it was only then that a procedure was mentioned and we learned that it was possible for a clip to be inserted to seal the valve. This operation was done by going through the groin which was, of course, much less invasive than open-heart surgery. Having told us about it, Dr Malik immediately dismissed any possibility of considering it because the NHS were no longer providing funds and an unspecified and very large sum would have to be found which, without private health care it was assumed we would be unable to afford. I found out later that there had been twenty-five procedures performed, classed as experimental, starting in 2009, mostly at the Hammersmith hospital which is part of the same health trust as the one Harry had been attending in Paddington so why were we not told about it until there was a crisis. It is unlikely that Harry would have been chosen as one of the twenty-five original guinea-pigs because of his age but he was never at any stage asked if we would be able to find the £30,000 needed to have it done privately.

That day Harry was sent home to await further tests. The following day I had an appointment and not wanting to leave Harry on his own we went over to the apartment in Shepherd's Bush where Bryony would be on hand painting with her friend Louise. When she had finished her main task Louise then did a sketch of Harry sitting absorbed in a book which, together with one done later by Bryony when he was in hospital, are a wonderful memory of the last days of his life.

The end of all this was dramatic. The following day, Saturday, having complained of a progressive all-body coldness, he collapsed. Everything that is said about the NHS in an emergency is absolutely accurate. Within minutes of being summoned the ambulance arrived and with enormous expertise the paramedics assessed the severity of the situation and having deftly transferred him to a stretcher, rushed him to the resuscitation unit of the nearby Hammersmith hospital. There a team of doctors took over and were shortly joined by a consultant cardiologist, Dr Bellamy. It is hardly surprising that Harry had been cold because he had a total collapse of lungs, liver and kidneys. For around four hours Dr Bellamy and the emergency team worked to stabilise him. Hugo and Deb had driven over from Chertsey and Bryony had joined me in the long vigil. Despite having been called out on a Saturday evening and then spending hours fighting to save Harry's life, Dr Bellamy, at 2 a.m., sat down with us and patiently explained exactly what it had been necessary to do and how long he would probably be in deep sedation.

There followed four weeks of anxiety, during which the family spent each afternoon at his bedside in the intensive care ward—Bryony and Hugo managed their work schedules so that one or other of them could be with me each day except for those weekends that Simon was able to get down from Nottingham and Piers up from Somerset. Nobody could fault the dedication of the nurses who were quite obviously at full stretch due to under-staffing. Progress was slow and not always steady. From time to time one of the many nurses would get worried about hygiene and would suggest that it would help if they shaved off Harry's beard. We were horrified at the suggestion, knowing that when Harry realised this had been done he would be desolate. He would feel he was no longer himself. Fortunately they accepted what we said.

The unexpected bonus was that Dr Bellamy turned out to be the cardiologist who had been doing the experimental heart-clip procedures and he said that as soon as there were signs that Harry was strong enough they would assess whether it would be appropriate for him. He warned us that the NHS was withholding funding until the procedure had been written up in the medical papers and so become officially accepted, but that if he decided to do it, recognising that there was no private insurance, he would press to get some financial help.

The other warning was that if the procedure was not performed Harry would never leave hospital because there was no way he would survive open heart surgery and his heart, with the ruptured valve, would not be strong enough to sustain a normal life. In fact, Dr Bellamy said, we would be faced with deciding what would be in Harry's best interests, to continue palliative life-saving treatment or switch everything off. Fortunately we never had to make that decision. Harry was in no condition to be consulted about spending the money required for the operation but the family unanimously agreed that whatever the cost this chance must be taken. Dr Bellamy's team decided there was every sign that the procedure could be performed successfully and set the date for the morning of Friday the 25th of March. The NHS decided late on the evening of Thursday the 24th of March that they would not fund. The money had to be deposited, upfront by eight o'clock on the morning of the 25th before the procedure could go ahead. There was no way that such a large sum can be found without a banker's order and the banks were not open during the time available to us. Had it not been for entrepreneurial Hugo we would have been lost. He managed to produce £20,000 in cash as a loan and the extra £10,000 could be done on a card.

The procedure was a triumphant success and on Saturday Harry was so improved that arrangements were being made to transfer him out of Intensive Care into a Cardiology Ward. And then in the early hours of

Sunday morning things deteriorated, his pulse dropped dramatically. When the family visited in the afternoon he was able to communicate but said he was feeling wretched. As we left at the end of visiting hours I turned and blew him a kiss, which he returned. Half an hour after reaching home the telephone rang with an urgent summons from the hospital. He had stopped breathing during the minutes when the daytime staff were handing over to the night nurses so no-one actually saw it happening. He did not respond to prolonged efforts at resuscitation.

There was a post-mortem and they also asked permission to retain the heart for more tests. It was confirmed that the clip procedure had been a 100% successful and no-one could find any reason to explain his death. Perhaps the euphoria of Saturday so quickly eclipsed by the return of weakness was the final straw and Harry himself made his own decision to die. That will, of course, remain a mystery. Had he been able to read the obituaries in all the major British papers as well as in New York and India he might have died a happier man, perhaps even being convinced that he was more than a has-been. There is, of course, no telling.

However what he *had* known about was one of the first things Camilla Shestopal had achieved and it was a real coup. She approached Adam Freudenheim, who was the publishing editor of the Penguin Modern Classics series, about doing some Ghote titles in their collection and in the summer of 2010 an agreement was signed. They ultimately published four of them simultaneously. Harry and I had chosen 'Under a Monsoon Cloud' and 'Inspector Ghote Trusts the Heart', Camilla chose 'Inspector Ghote Breaks an Egg' and Adam felt that they should do 'The Perfect Murder' as it was the first in the series. A short while before all this the author of 'The First Lady's Detective Agency', Alexander McCall Smith, in an article in the Times, had included Harry among a list of prestigious authors, such as John Buchan and Robert Louis Stevenson, in a list of those he thought it was imperative to include in a crime library, and Adam agreed to ask him if he would write a foreword to the collection. As if being published as a modern classic was not enough, what McCall Smith wrote should have convinced Harry that he was not a has-been. Although the actual books were not in the shops until a week after Harry died in 2011, he had had the opportunity to read the introduction and he had seen the designs of the striking covers. Penguin did what the publishers of the few last books had never achieved, they had displays of Keating titles on the eye-catching tables of all the major bookstores.

The family hoped that the civil funeral at Mortlake Crematorium that they planned was what Harry would have wanted, although, strangely he and I had never discussed it. The children all agreed to talk about their recollections and feelings about their father, each managing to emphasise something different. His dear friend Phyllis, Baroness James, spoke first, talking warmly about him as a person and as a writer, after which the four children spoke of their own personal recollections and feelings.

Simon started with a broad overview, drawing attention to the number of times in the obituaries and in the private messages, people spoke of Harry as a gentle man and then more personally went on to talk about his own pride in all his father's achievements and his admiration for the fierce determination and discipline he showed in pursuing his chosen career of writing.

I read Elizabeth Barrett Browning's poem 'How Do I Love Thee?'

After that Bryony chose to concentrate on his skills as a wordsmith, calling him the king of the spoken as well as of the written word and recalling that he would create stories for them all when they were children with the proper beginning, middle and end, always managing, when they had been out for a walk to bring them neatly to a conclusion as they reached the garden gate, and she illustrated through anecdotes her depth of feeling for the witty, humorous man who had been her father.

Piers, who would later describe him as a hard-working dreamer, decided to read a poem he had written one night when he was up from Somerset during Harry's last few weeks in hospital. The poem is a kaleidoscope of childhood memory moving on to his changed relationship with Harry, when Piers himself became a father, ending with his thoughts as the weeks in intensive care drew to a close. It is a poem that can be better appreciated by studying the words and can be found as an appendix to this book.

Hugo, who said of himself that he was more a man of numbers than words nevertheless spoke eloquently, outlining Harry's qualities and above all what he had meant to colleagues: '*a fair critic and a relentless ambassador for their genre of writing, great company and a lifelong friend, if perhaps slightly eccentric. To his friends he was humble, gentle, a good listener, quiet when required but always the good entertainer.*' About his own feelings Hugo said quite simply that he felt that as a dad he was 'always there quietly in the background supporting me.' He then announced that we would be singing 'Good King Wenceslas' to conclude the celebration of Harry's life, explaining that although this might be considered eccentric it had a particular significance for the family, who recalled Harry's unique rendering of the King when carols were sung at Christmas gatherings, recalling the gusto of the characterisation but also '*the strange range of notes that Dad managed to introduce every time he sang it*'.

Singing 'Good King Wenceslas' had been meant to end the proceedings on a note of celebration but in the event, for several members of the family, it broke the barriers of stoicism we had so far been able to maintain and probably means none of us will be able to sing it ever again.

It was left to Peter McNulty, the civil funeral celebrant, to conclude the occasion and this he did in a remarkable manner by reading his own choice of a traditional Indian prayer. Certainly Harry would have approved.

'*When I am dead,*
Cry for me a little,
Think of me sometimes,
But not too much.

Think of me now and again
As I was in life,
At some moment it's pleasant to recall,
But not for too long.

Leave me in peace
And I shall leave you in peace,
And while you live
Let your thoughts be with the living.'

251

Appendix 1: Article Written by Martin Edwards

Along with two legendary figures of a previous generation, Julian Symons and Michael Gilbert, Harry Keating was undoubtedly one of the towering male writers of British crime fiction in the second half of the 20th Century and, now that we are in the 21st Century, he is heading serenely towards the 50th anniversary in 2009 of the publication of his very first crime novel. Keating is, and perhaps will remain, best known as the creator of Indian detective Inspector Ganesh Ghote, but his achievements have been remarkably diverse. He is a Fellow of the Royal Society of Literature, has served as Chairman of the Crime Writers' Association and the Society of Authors and as President of the legendary Detection Club. He has written many short stories as well as "straight" novels and much non-fiction. For fifteen years, he reviewed crime for The Times and, in addition to editing and introducing books, he has written countless articles. Symons, in an essay written for The Oxford Companion to Crime & Mystery, writing not long before his death said: "The tone and manner of Keating's crime stories are wholly original in modern crime fiction. They spring from a mind attracted by philosophical and metaphysical speculation, with a liking for fantasy held in check by the crime story's requirement of plot. Early books like Zen There Was Murder (1960) and A Rush on the Ultimate (1961) gave readers the pleasure of seeing a writer kick up his heels in defiance of any critical perception of what a crime story ought to be like." Henry Reymond Fitzwalter Keating (no wonder he is universally known as Harry!) was born in 1926. He says: "I always wanted to be a writer, a novelist." Like many before him, he spent a number of years working in the newspaper business and came round to the view that "it would be easier to get a crime story published" than a mainstream work of fiction. He wrote a couple of mysteries "which got nowhere" and a third did not meet with the approval of his original literary agent, because it was "a bit odd". Undaunted, Keating sent the manuscript to Gollancz, whose yellow-jacketed crime novels were at the time synonymous with quality in the genre and one morning Victor Gollancz himself telephoned Keating to say that he wanted to publish Death And The Visiting Firemen. At that point, Keating had not thought of writing a follow-up, but he found another and more sympathetic agent who made it clear to the young writer that he ought to have the manuscript of his second book with the agency at the moment when the first was published.

Keating acknowledges that his aim in writing Death And The Visiting Firemen was "pure entertainment" but adds: "When my copy came, I turned it over in my hand and it occurred to me that I could use this simple whodunit form to become the novelist I had vaguely always wanted to be." He conceived the notion of writing about Zen Buddhism and behind the whodunit plot asked the question: "What is truth?" It was Keating's yearning to break into the American market that prompted the creation of Inspector Ghote. His first five books were published in the UK but not in the States, evidently because they were perceived at the time as being "too British". Keating therefore asked himself how he could be "less British" in his writing. Although, at the time, he had never travelled to India, the thought of writing about the sub-continent appealed to him and he thought it might well appeal to American readers too. Keating offers a fascinating insight into his work in the introduction to his short story collection Inspector Ghote, His Life And Crimes (1989):

"I had it in mind to write a crime story called The Perfect Murder that would be somewhat of a commentary upon the problem of perfectionism, and one of the few notions I had about India was that things there were apt to be rather imperfect. Good symbolic stuff. Then, out of nowhere, into my head there came this man, or some parts of him... A certain naivety, which should enable him to ask the questions about the everyday life around him to which my potential readers might want answers ... At this point, however,

I saw Ghote's life as being a short one, a single book's span. My specialty in 1963 was detective novels without a running hero, but within each a different, more or less exotic background … I saw India as just one more in that series. But the book unexpectedly won the Gold Dagger Award for 1964, and an Edgar Allan Poe award in America … Ghote was granted an indefinite extension of life." The lightness of touch and generosity of spirit that, to my mind, are the key characteristics of Keating's crime fiction also inform his writing about the genre. He has written a number of books and edited, introduced or contributed to a great many more. If Julian Symons is the pre-eminent British crime fiction critic, then Keating (whose judgements tend to be rather gentler) is not too far behind. Much of his writing about the genre has sprung from his experience of reviewing and publishers have regularly beaten a path to his door with commissions for non-fiction projects. An early example was an approach by an old college friend, which led to Keating's writing a brief and affectionate account of British detective fiction in the Golden Age, Murder Must Appetize (1975). Four years later, he came up with Sherlock Holmes, The Man And His World (1979), which he regards as one of his most successful studies. Crime & Mystery: The 100 Best Books (1987), boasts an admiring foreword by the legendary Patricia Highsmith. Although their books were very different, Highsmith and Keating got on famously after they met through Keating's neighbour, who happened to be Highsmith's editor in the UK. Highsmith even agreed to read through a book that Keating set in the US, to see whether he had effectively captured the American idiom—and Keating recalls that she kindly pointed out to him that "to knock up" in the sense of an early house-call had a rather different meaning in America than in the UK. He included in his selection of 100 classics of the genre Highsmith's The Talented Mr Ripley and The Tremor of Forgery. Any exercise in selecting "the best" from a large field is bound to be highly subjective, but Keating makes an appealing case for his choices, which include amongst the classics a number of relatively unfamiliar titles, such as The Sands Of Windee by Arthur W Upfield, The Last Best Friend by George Sims and All On A Summer's Day by John Wainwright. Keating joined the list of those who have sought to pass on their professional expertise when he published Writing Crime Fiction (1986; second edition 1994). This is one of the shorter guides of its kind, but in my opinion (and I confess that I have read most of the others) it is one of the best. Especially illuminating is that Keating points out that a crime writer may also seek to slip the reader "a Mickey Finn by way of telling you something about this world you live in". As he says: "The crime story can, to a small extent or to quite a large extent, do what the pure novel does. It can make a temporary map for its readers out of the chaos of their surroundings—only it should never let them know". The book offers a good deal of wisdom, not least in Keating's words of caution about writing short stories: "The crime short story is perhaps the most difficult branch of crime fiction to write, except in the mere matter of the number of times it is necessary to put finger to word-processor key. Yet it is there. It holds out a challenge. Few crime writers can resist it forever." One can only be grateful that Keating has so often yielded to the temptation to write short stories himself. They include a collection featuring the cleaning lady Mrs Craggs and also In Kensington Gardens Once ... (1997). I had first-hand experience of his sheer professionalism when I invited a number of luminaries to contribute to Mysterious Pleasures (2003), an anthology celebrating the Golden Jubilee of the formation of the Crime Writers' Association. Harry Keating was the first to respond to my overtures, and the first to write a story for the book: even more importantly, "The Hound Of The Hanging Gardens", a brand new Ghote story, was typically enjoyable. Keating's literary style is by nature quirky and interesting. The very way in which he tends to form sentences is slightly off-key, yet arresting and appropriate. The same is true of his approach to writing novels and non-fiction. The Bedside Companion To Crime (1989) opens with an introduction entitled: "A Word Before You Nod Off". He explains that his aim was to "have garnered as many of these fun facts as I could find or remember and arrange them in neat piles, with little flags on top like the ones on sandwiches at big tea parties to give a hint of what's inside." For good measure, he addresses the often-asked question of why people read crime stories and provides answers both sociological and psychological, yet in his usual pithy and readable style. He acts as a persuasive advocate for crime fiction "as a powerful and beneficial factor in life"—and it is impossible not to warm to a commentator who includes in his amiable assessment of the genre's byways a section on the part played in classic detection novels by "breakfast, lunch and tea".

As long ago as 1972, Keating edited on behalf of the Crime Writers' Association an anthology called Blood on My Mind which brought together new pieces by CWA members "about real crimes, some notable and some obscure". He contributed a chapter himself, about the Eugene Aram case, but this was a rare venture into true crime. As Keating told me recently, he prefers the ingenuity associated with fictional murder to the horrors of the real thing. Keating's popularity amongst crime writers has contributed to his success as an editor. For Agatha Christie: First Lady Of Crime (1977), for example, he was able to persuade the duo who wrote under the name of Emma Lathen to contribute a chapter which remains one of the most incisive analyses of Christie's technique. Crime Writers: Reflections on Crime Fiction (1978) sprang from a BBC television series. Contributors included Symons, P D James, Reginald Hill and Troy Kennedy Martin, whose credits include the original screenplay for the classic film The Italian Job. Keating's own contribution to the book, New Patents Pending, looks into the crystal ball. Of the young writers whom he picks out, Jacqueline Wilson soon abandoned the genre for children's fiction and went on to achieve enormous fame, but what is striking is how many of Keating's predictions have been borne out over the last quarter of a century. As he said, "this exploitation of our moral uncertainties is ... a trend I would expect to see running ahead for a good many years to come." He also forecast more "books where a woman takes a clearly leading role, and more violence." Above all, I suggest that he was right in his conclusion that: "One major movement can be detected. It is that the crime story is steering itself back into the general current of fiction. It has been slowly doing so for a long time, and I think that the process is accelerating." Few television tie-in books are as illuminating as Crime Writers. Whodunit?: A Guide To Crime, Suspense And Spy Fiction (1982) again contained much of interest from a glittering array of contributors and amongst those explaining how they wrote their books, Keating said: "What starts me off writing a crime novel is, almost paradoxically, a philosophical idea. Flying a bit high? Well, like it or not, it is ideas of this sort—can the world ever do without violence? How many lies should we tell?—that give my imaginative faculty the necessary fire." The book also contains a fascinating, if highly idiosyncratic "consumer's guide to writers and their books", which serves the invaluable purpose of highlighting for the fan a number of intriguing novels which they might otherwise never be likely to encounter. Keating has also edited a CWA collection of fiction, Crime Waves 1 (1991) and an 80th birthday tribute to Julian Symons by fellow members of the Detection Club The Man Who...(1992). (One hopes that his fellow Club members will produce something similar to celebrate Harry's own 80th next year). When a writer, over the course of many years, has done so much and so well, it must be difficult to decide what to tackle next. Keating's solution to the problem was to embark on a sequence of pairs of books. Thus we had novels about a "good" detective and a "bad" detective. A novel about a "soft" detective was to be succeeded by another about a "hard" detective—but Keating had trouble with this concept until he realised that he could write about a "hard" detective if she was a woman. Thus was born Harriet Martens, and a new series. Harriet's latest case is recorded in A Detective at Death's Door (2004), which is prefaced by a short note paying tribute to Agatha Christie "whose sure hand with her narratives taught me more than perhaps I even now recognise." Over the years, Harry Keating has collected many accolades. A splendid book, The Murder of the Maharajah (1980) earned his second CWA Gold Dagger and he received the UK's premier award for crime fiction, the CWA Cartier Diamond Dagger, in 1996. He has been the subject of a full-length critical study, H.R.F. Keating: Post-Colonial Detection by Meera Tamaya (1993). And, throughout, he has succeeded whilst refusing to play safe. I am not sure whether it is more astonishing that he has written a lengthy crime novel in verse, Jack The Lady Killer (1999), or that the bizarre experiment is a great deal of fun. Soon after publication, he inscribed a copy to me with a twinkle in his eye and I found that he had written: "I dare you to have a go." So far, I am sorry to say, I have not managed to take up the challenge! In Writing Crime Fiction, Keating said of the crime writer's special contract with their readers that the key pledge is to put the reader first. No one can doubt that, in this worthy aim, he has succeeded with a rare and admirable consistency.